GUIDE TO INVESTMENT STRATEGY

OTHER ECONOMIST BOOKS

Guide to Analysing Companies
Guide to Business Modelling
Guide to Business Planning
Guide to Cash Management
Guide to Commodities
Guide to Decision Making
Guide to Economic Indicators
Guide to Emerging Markets
Guide to the European Union
Guide to Financial Management
Guide to Financial Markets
Guide to Hedge Funds
Guide to Management Ideas and Gurus
Guide to Managing Growth
Guide to Organisation Design
Guide to Project Management
Guide to Supply Chain Management
Numbers Guide
Style Guide

Book of Business Quotations
Book of Isms
Book of Obituaries
Brands and Branding
Business Consulting
Business Strategy
Buying Professional Services
Doing Business in China
Economics
Managing Talent
Managing Uncertainty
Marketing
Marketing for Growth
Megachange – the world in 2050
Modern Warfare, Intelligence and Deterrence
Organisation Culture
Successful Strategy Execution
The World of Business

Directors: an A–Z Guide
Economics: an A–Z Guide
Investment: an A–Z Guide
Negotiation: an A–Z Guide

Pocket World in Figures

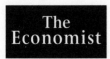

THE ECONOMIST GUIDE TO INVESTMENT STRATEGY

How to understand markets, risk, rewards and behaviour

Third edition

Peter Stanyer

PUBLICAFFAIRS
New York

Typeset in EcoType by MacGuru Ltd
info@macguru.org.uk

Library of Congress Control Number: 2013955896

ISBN 978-1-61039-391-1 (PB orig.)
ISBN 978-1-61039-392-8 (EB)

First Edition

10 9 8 7 6 5 4 3 2

To Alex

Contents

Appendices

List of figures

List of tables

Acknowledgements

I OWE A DEBT OF GRATITUDE to many individuals who helped me with this book. First and foremost to my wife, Alex, for her continued support and patience through this edition's labour. Elroy Dimson and Steve Satchell provided invaluable advice and suggestions (as for the previous editions). Stephen Collins provided important advice, suggestions and introductions. Colleagues at Delmore Asset Management and the Financial Planning Corporation have been particularly patient as I have been preoccupied with the book. Many former colleagues have also been generous with their suggestions. I also owe a substantial debt to the trustees and principals of the funds that I have been privileged to work with over the years.

I have been privileged to attend a number of seminars organised by Norway's Government Pension Fund (Global) in the past few years. This book has benefited considerably from the insights gained at these world-class meetings, which debate the interface between academic research and practical investment issues.

Generous and insightful contributions on particular issues or chapters were provided by Victoria Barbary, Paul Barrett, Jörg Behrens, Nick Bucknell, Jeff Bryan, Ewen Cameron-Watt, Forrest Capie, Norman Deitrich, Robin Duthy, Hugh Ferry, Geoffrey Fiszel, Charlie Goldring, Howard Goldring, Dietrich Hatlapa, Arzu Huseynov, Tim Lund, Yoram Lustig, Cesar Murillo, Arlen Oransky, Steve Piercy, Mark Ralphs, John Pullar-Strecker, Max Rayner, Christof Schmidhuber, Paul Stanyer and James Wyatt. I am most grateful to each of them, but any mistakes are my own.

I am also indebted to those firms whose data I have used in the numerous tables and charts. Without their support the book could not be published in this form. I would also like to thank Stephen Brough at Profile Books for his encouragement, suggestions and support. My thanks are also due to Penny Williams, who skilfully and patiently edited the book.

This book aims to help inform the process of seeking and giving professional advice, but it cannot be a substitute for that advice. It draws on and summarises research and investor perspectives on a wide range of issues, but it is not punctuated with footnotes citing sources for facts or opinions. Although important areas of debate are flagged with references to leading researchers, in other areas ideas which are more commonly expressed are presented but not attributed. Sources which were particularly important for each chapter are listed in Appendix 4.

Please note that the views expressed in this book are my own and may not coincide with the views of the investment funds on whose boards or committees I am honoured to serve.

In conclusion, let me say how privileged I am that Elroy Dimson, Emeritus Professor of Finance at London Business School, has agreed to write a foreword for this third edition of the book. Although my appreciation of markets owes a great deal to the economics that I learnt at Cambridge University, particularly from the late Michael Posner and from Michael Kuczynski at Pembroke College, the London Business School's Investment Management Programme gave me an invaluable bridge from economics to modern finance.

Foreword

INTEREST RATES HAVE COLLAPSED. Savers who put aside money now, to spend in the future, will earn little by way of interest. To accumulate a target lump sum, they need to save more than they once planned. Retirees, who wish to live on their savings, can now expect to receive a smaller income from their investments. They must adjust to having less to spend than they expected.

Of course, low interest rates and low bond yields were for some time clear for all to see. It was less obvious that low interest rates imply low prospective returns on all assets, including equities. Because investors require some compensation for the higher risk of the stockmarket, equity returns must be equal to the interest rate plus a "risk premium". It follows that, other things being equal, a world with low interest rates must also be a world in which stockmarket investors receive lower returns.

What are the implications of this dramatic change in the financial environment? Peter Stanyer's response is that every saver needs a coherent investment strategy. Strategy must be underpinned by an understanding of how markets move, how risk should be judged, how markets reward investors and how investors behave. In this third edition of his outstanding book, Peter Stanyer addresses these issues and elegantly surveys the entire field of investment.

He helps us to formulate an investment strategy that is realistic. The projections made by many asset managers, retail financial product providers, pension funds, endowments, regulators and governments are optimistic. Overly optimistic estimates of future returns are dangerous, not only because they mislead, but also because they can mask the need for action.

Investors vary in their need for liquidity, their tolerance for risk, and their capacity to follow a disciplined investment strategy. They therefore need to devise a strategy that reflects their salient characteristics. The strategy should be founded on three pillars. The first pillar is financial theory – how financial markets can be expected to behave; the second is empirical evidence – how markets actually do behave; and the third is the investment environment – the current condition of financial markets.

Peter Stanyer reviews the relevant aspects of financial theory in a highly accessible way. He extends our knowledge without resorting to complicated mathematics, explaining the central concepts of modern finance in a clear exposition of the arguments for and against different approaches. To better understand markets, he turns to the evidence of financial history, often interrogating the long-term, global dataset that my colleagues and I have compiled. He allows the record of securities markets to enlighten us about events in the past and to underpin informed judgments about the future.

To interpret the current investment environment, Peter Stanyer presents us with a wealth of data. Drawing together theory, evidence and information on the financial environment, he does not flinch from expressing a firm opinion. He presents valuable advice on how to construct a fixed-income portfolio, how to think about liquidity, what quantum of risk is acceptable for different investors, what factors influence investment performance, whether investments of passion are a store of value, and what behavioural biases investors should guard against.

There is something for everyone in this book. It is comprehensive, but never forbidding or opaque. The surveys of each of the main asset classes – equities and risky debt, alternative assets like hedge funds and private equity, and tangible assets like real estate and artworks – are highly informative and the complexities of modern investing are explained with great clarity. This book will help you meet the challenge of investing for your future.

Elroy Dimson
December 2013

Introduction: lessons from the global financial crisis

THE YEARS SINCE THE CREDIT CRISIS of 2007–9 have seen a number of refreshingly simple investment messages gain traction that should enable investors to weather future storms in better shape. These messages are as relevant to individuals managing their own retirement savings as to the managers of the largest investment funds.

One, emphasised by Antti Ilmanen, is that the timing of investment volatility matters as much as its magnitude. Andrew Ang stresses this by asserting that the two most important words in investing are "bad times". This is a theme running through this edition and it has several aspects. One is that past performance patterns can easily give a falsely reassuring impression of the likelihood of "bad times". Another is that investors should initiate discussions about how an investment proposal might perform in bad times. If the investment will help mitigate losses of income or capital and give flexibility in bad times, it will be an attractive investment; if it might amplify them, and impose inflexibility, investors will need to be rewarded amply for that and to understand why the reward is expected to be sufficient, given their circumstances. This applies with particular force to the costs imposed by illiquid investments.

Almost all investment products offer an alluring combination of risk and return. When these offer a better prospect than normally offered by the market, investors should always ask, how? Better than market performance must reflect some combination of rare skill; exploiting a market anomaly (but see Chapter 6); or a reward for risk-taking (see Chapter 7). The victims of the Madoff fraud suffered because they or their advisers accepted the description of past apparent good performance with low volatility of his fraudulent funds as descriptions of how they did, and so would, perform. The victims' suffering was all the worse because their trust was betrayed by Madoff (see Chapter 1).

All investors need to ask for explanations of attractive performance. Low volatility strategies in equities and credit are always popular, and Chapters 7 and 8 encourage investors to suspect that obscure risk-taking may be the explanation. If it is, investors are forewarned that the attractive risk-return trade-off, which is a characteristic of normal times, might provide little protection in "bad times". This was a message of John Campbell and Tuomo Vuolteenaho's (2004) article "Bad Beta, Good Beta" (see Chapter 7). It is also the message that hedge funds and private equity are risk assets, and a usually reliable short cut is to see them as types of equity investing. They will probably not provide much help in "bad times", but might nevertheless provide interesting opportunities (Chapters 9 and 10).

After 2008, some complained that the poor diversification offered by strategies of risk assets could not reasonably have been anticipated. These investors had often been encouraged by the prospect of superior returns to abandon the safety of high-quality government bonds. In the event they provided the security of income and, largely, the diversification of capital values that would be expected of a safe harbour in a time of crisis. As André Perold wrote in 2009: "Risk is a choice rather than a fate."

Among those investors who emerged least scathed from the financial crisis were many whose strategy comprised an allocation to cash or government bonds (whose size was dictated by the investor's risk aversion), offset with an allocation to diversified equities. This approach echoes the portfolio separation theorem of the late James Tobin (see Chapter 5), and many financial advisers (and some institutional investors) served their clients well by adhering to this simple approach. However, the era of ultra-low interest rates in the years after 2008, and the purchase of one-third of the US national debt (and also large quantities of high-quality mortgages) by the Federal Reserve and of one-quarter of the UK's national debt by the Bank of England, forced cautious investors to take more risk and to scale back holdings of increasingly expensive government bonds. The dilemma of choosing between credit risk and interest-rate risk has hung over income-seeking investors of all types in the years since 2009. This dilemma underlies the debates about whether investors can hope to "time" markets and the role of fixed asset allocation models in Chapters 4 and 5.

Negligible interest rates have had an all-pervading impact. In Chapter 4, survey evidence is reported of substantial holdings of liquidity by high net worth individuals across different wealth bands. The loss of interest income by these wealthy families will have significantly lowered the opportunity cost of indulging in investments of passion. This almost certainly helps to explain the buoyancy of markets ranging from classic cars, stamps and vintage wine to fine art (see Chapter 12). The far-reaching influence on these markets of the Federal Reserve's response to the global financial crisis was reflected in an article in the *New York Times* in early 2013: "Whether he intended it or not, or even realises it, Ben S. Bernanke has become a patron of the arts."

I would welcome any feedback and can be contacted at the following email address: peter@peterstanyer.com.

Peter Stanyer
December 2013

PART 1

The big picture

1   Setting the scene

Think about risk before it hits you

Risk is about bad outcomes, and a bad outcome that is expected to arrive at a bad time is especially damaging and requires particularly attractive rewards. Investors and their advisers have typically judged the riskiness of an investment by its volatility, but in the words of Antti Ilmanen, author of *Expected Returns: An Investor's Guide to Harvesting Market Rewards*, not all volatilities are equal, and the timing of bad outcomes matters for risk as much as the scale of those bad outcomes. A theme throughout this book is that investors should think about how investments might perform in bad times as the key to understanding how much risk they are taking. There is little discussion of what constitutes a bad time, which will vary from investor to investor, but it is best captured by Ilmanen, who defines it as a time when an extra dollar of ready cash feels especially valuable.

What constitutes a bad outcome is far from simple. It is determined by each investor (and not by the textbooks). It varies from one investor to another and from investment to investment. If an investor is saving for a pension, or to pay off a mortgage, or to fund a child's education, the bad outcome that matters is the risk of a shortfall from the investment objective. This is different from the risk of a negative return. In Chapter 5, the distinction is drawn between threats to future income (which is of concern to a pensioner) and threats to the value of investments (which matter to a cautious short-term investor). This shows that the short-term risk of losing money is inadequate as a general measure of risk.

Risk is about failing to meet particular objectives. But it is also about the chance of anything happening before then which undermines an investor's confidence in that future objective being met. Since those working in the investment business are uncertain about market relationships, it is reasonable for investors to be at least as uncertain. It is also reasonable for their confidence to be shaken by disappointing developments along the way, even if those developments are not surprising to a quantitative analyst. Investors' expectations are naturally updated as time evolves and as their own experience (and everyone else's) grows. So far as the investor is concerned, the perceived risk of a bad outcome will be increased by disappointments before the target date is reached, undermining confidence in the investment strategy.

The pattern of investment returns along the way matters to investors, not just the final return at some target date in the future. This focus on the risk of suffering unacceptable losses at any stage before an investor's target date has highlighted the dangers of mismeasuring risk. An investor might accept some low probability of a particular bad outcome occurring after, say, three years. However, the likelihood of that poor threshold being breached at some stage before the end of the three years will be much higher than the investor might expect. The danger is that the investor's attention and judgment are initially drawn only to the complete three-year period. As the period is extended, the risk of experiencing particularly poor interim results, at some time, can increase dramatically.

The insights from behavioural finance (see Chapter 2) on investor loss aversion are particularly important here. Disappointing performance disproportionately undermines investor confidence. The risk of this, and its repercussions for the likelihood of achieving longer-term objectives, represents issues that investors need to discuss regularly with their advisers, especially when they are considering moving to a higher-risk strategy.

Research findings from behavioural finance emphasise that investors often attach different importance to achieving different goals. The risk of bad outcomes should be reduced, as far as possible, for objectives that the investor regards as most critical to achieve, and, ideally, any high risk of missing objectives should be focused on the nice-to-have but dispensable targets. Investors may then be less likely to react adversely to the disappointments that inevitably accompany risk-based strategies. They will know that such targets are less critical objectives.

Risk is about the chance of disappointing outcomes. Risk can be managed but disappointing outcomes cannot, and surprising things sometimes happen. However, measuring the volatility of performance, as a check on what the statistical models say is likely, can be helpful in coming to an independent assessment of risk. But it will always be based on a small sample of data. Thus we can attempt to measure risks we perceive. Risks that exist but that we do not have the imagination or the data to measure will always escape our metrics. There is no solution to this problem of measuring risk, which led Glynn Holton to write in *Financial Analysts Journal* in 2004: "It is meaningless to ask if a risk metric captures risk. Instead, ask if it is useful."

More often than not, the real problem is that unusual risk-taking is rewarded rather than penalised. We need to avoid drawing the wrong conclusions about the good times as well as the bad times. This theme is captured by a photograph at the front of Frank Sortino and Stephen Satchell's book *Managing Downside Risk in Financial Markets*. It shows Karen Sortino on safari in Africa, petting an intimidating rhino. The caption underneath reads: "Just because you got away with it, doesn't mean you didn't take any risk."

The Madoff fraud

If risk is about bad outcomes, to be a victim of fraud is a particularly bad outcome. But when we look after our own savings and investments we are often our own worst enemies. Many people expect savings and investments, in which they have no particular fascination, to be a difficult subject that they do not expect to understand. Any opportunity that presents itself to take a short cut and, in the words of Daniel Kahneman, a Nobel laureate in economics and Eugene Higgins emeritus professor of psychology at Princeton University, to "think fast", which easily leads to avoidable mistakes, rather than "thinking slow", which requires some concentration and effort, will be tempting. Our lazy inclination to "think fast" (see Chapter 2) is readily exploited by fraudsters who are attracted to our money and our behavioural weaknesses like bees to a honey pot. The enormous Madoff fraud that unravelled in December 2008 provides salutary lessons for us all.

At the end of November 2008, the accounts of the clients of Bernard L. Madoff Investment Securities LLC, an investment adviser registered by the US Securities and Exchange Commission (SEC), had a supposed aggregate value of $64.8 billion invested in the supposedly sophisticated investment strategy run by Bernie Madoff. His firm had been in operation since the 1960s and it is thought that his fraud started sometime in the 1970s. It lasted until 11th December 2008 when he was arrested and his business was exposed as a huge scam, probably the largest securities fraud the world has ever known.

The amounts that Madoff's investors thought they owned had been inflated by fictitious investment performance ever since they had first invested, and the amount that Madoff actually controlled was further reduced because early investors, who then withdrew money, were paid their inflated investment values with billions of dollars provided by later investors. The court-appointed liquidator has estimated the actual losses to investors of money they originally invested to be around $17.5 billion. Nevertheless, at one stage investors believed that they had assets – which, unknown to them, were mostly fictitious – worth $65 billion invested with Madoff. By September 2013, the liquidators had recovered or entered into agreements to recover, often from early beneficiaries of the fraud, $9.5 billion or 54% of the estimated losses of amounts invested with the firm, and actual distributions to investors totalled $5.6 billion. It is likely that the trustee for the liquidation, Irving S. Picard, will succeed in recovering much more than was initially feared of the amounts originally invested. Nevertheless, investors have been left nursing huge losses from what they believed was their wealth. Unless they remain alert, others are in danger of repeating the mistakes that led so many to lose so much. So how can investors protect themselves?

Madoff's investment strategy seemingly offered the attractive combination of a long-run performance comparable to the

FIG 1.1 **If it looks too good to be true, it probably is**
Madoff's fictitious cumulative performance compared with market indices,
Dec 1990–Nov 2007, Dec 1990=100

Sources: Barclays, Fairfield Sentry client reports; MSCI

stockmarket but, supposedly thanks to clever use of derivatives, with
little volatility.

Marketing material from fund distributors presented the track
record of Madoff's fraud in the way shown in Figure 1.1 for Fairfield
Sentry, a so-called feeder fund which was entirely invested in Madoff's
scam. It showed the seductive combination of apparently low risk
and high, but perhaps not outrageous, returns. But an experienced
adviser or investor should immediately recognise that the track record
shown for Fairfield Sentry looks odd. It is always safe to assume that
no investment strategy can deliver such smooth returns well in excess
of the guaranteed rate on Treasury bills and that there are no low-risk
routes to returns well above the return on cash.

Madoff's strategy was a simple Ponzi scheme, whereby a
fraudulent rate of return is promised, seemingly verified in this case
by the experience of those early investors who had been able to
withdraw inflated amounts. So long as only a few investors demand
their money back, they can be paid what they have been told their

investment is now worth. But what they had been told was a lie, and the inflated returns were delivered to a few by redirecting cash from the most recent investors. As with any Ponzi scheme, Madoff relied on robbing Peter to pay Paul.

Ponzi schemes are named after an American fraudster of the 1920s, and they are usually built around a plausible-sounding investment story. However, these scams always collapse as soon as the demands of investors who want to sell their investments outweigh the cash provided by new investors. The Madoff fraud grew so large because it survived many years. Its undoing was the credit squeeze of 2008 when too many investors, who were presumably happy with Madoff's reported investment performance, had to withdraw funds to meet losses elsewhere. This caused the Madoff house of cards to collapse.

The victims were mostly based in the United States, but there were also many from around the world. They included wealthy individuals, charities and a number of wealth managers, but relatively few institutional investors. Many were introduced to Madoff through personal recommendations, which would have stressed his respectable community and business pedigree as a former chairman of the NASDAQ stock exchange and philanthropist.

A large part of the problem is that so many people can be seduced by the belief that they have found a low-risk way of performing surprisingly well. And yet, surprisingly good investment performance always involves risk.

Madoff is not the only instance of large-scale fraud or suspected fraud of the past few years and these episodes provide important lessons for investors and for their advisers. Some of Madoff's investors were following the recommendations of investment advisers, who appeared to take pride in their professional diligence in identifying good managers. The advisers could often point to the name of one of the leading accountancy firms as the auditor of the third-party so-called feeder fund that was the conduit to Madoff Investment Securities, but this provided no protection for investors.

How was someone who had followed the recommendation of an adviser or a friend supposed to identify the risks? Ten old lessons re-emerge:

1   The old and seemingly trivial saying that "if it looks too good to be true, it probably is" remains one of the most valuable pieces of investment advice anyone can give.

2   Returns in excess of the return offered by the government can be achieved only by taking risk.

3   Risk is most obvious when an investment is volatile and is least obvious when a risky investment has not yet shown much volatility. This is rarely mentioned in books on investment.

4   Investors should be particularly questioning when an adviser recommends a low volatility investment that offers superior returns.

5   Do not invest in something you do not understand simply because a group of your peers is doing so. A desire to conform can explain many decisions that we would otherwise not take.

6   Whatever your adviser says, make sure that your investments are well diversified. But keep in mind that diversification is most difficult to assess when risky investments are not obviously volatile.

7   Pay particular attention if an adviser gives you inconvenient cautious advice (such as a recommendation to avoid something that you would like to invest in).

8   Social status may not be a good indicator of honesty.

9   Do not assume that because an investment firm is regulated by the authorities they have been able to check that everything is all right.

10   The ability to rely on good due diligence on investment managers is the key to minimising exposure to risk of fraud. An authoritative post-mortem report on the Madoff affair is called "Madoff: a riot of red flags". Most private investors would not spot these red flags, but it was not by chance that few institutional investors lost money with Madoff. A challenge for private investors is to ensure that they also have access to good-quality manager due diligence.

Betrayal aversion

The Madoff fraud puts a spotlight on the relationship between advisers and clients. Investors are at their most vulnerable in their dealings with advisers, and yet establishing a bond of trust with one or more advisers is probably the most important ingredient for the successful management of wealth. Iris Bohnet and Richard Zeckhauser, respectively professor of public policy and Ramsey professor of political economy at Harvard University's Kennedy School of Government, have found that individuals systematically require a premium return to compensate for the risk that they might be betrayed by an agent who is supposed to be working for them. This premium is greater than the premium that would be asked to accept the same probability of a poor outcome where there is no likelihood of betrayal. As Bohnet has written:

> People care not only about outcomes, but about how outcomes came to be … that doesn't strike anyone but an economist – like me – as a surprise.

This highlights the importance of trust in the adviser–client relationship, and the psychological gains that flow where it is present and the psychological and possibly financial damage that results when it is not.

How much risk can you tolerate?

The assessment of investor risk tolerance is a fundamental step in designing any investment strategy, but advisers and academics approach it in different ways. Academic economists use mathematical assumptions to model risk aversion. These assumptions are attractive to them in part because they can be used in models (and also because they can be tested empirically). Meanwhile, behavioural finance stresses the importance of loss aversion rather than risk aversion, and the asymmetry of response between gains and losses which is revealed in behaviourist studies (see Chapter 2).

Wealth managers have for a long time used questionnaires to categorise their clients by their attitudes to risk-taking. These questionnaires typically cover investors' circumstances (age, family,

FIG 1.2 **Risk tolerance scores and equity market returns**
Jan 2002–May 2013

Sources: Finametrica Pty Ltd; MSCI

income, wealth, expenditure plans, and so on) as well as their attitude to risk. One problem is that questions posed by wealth managers about risk may use language and concepts that are unfamiliar to non-experts. Anecdotal evidence suggests that people who are not familiar with investments often expect a risk questionnaire to be difficult to complete. They may therefore ask their advisers to help them answer the questions. This introduces errors and also seems to introduce systematic bias, as investment advisers appear to be more tolerant of risk than their clients. For these reasons, conventional risk questionnaires may fail standard criteria for assessing people's attitudes.

In recent years psychometric profiling services have developed to address these concerns, making use of focus groups to make sure that their questions are easily understood. For example, Finametrica, an Australian consultancy, has built up a database of over 520,000 responses from around the world to its questionnaire, which itself grew out of research by psychology academics in the United States. These responses reveal some interesting patterns. For example,

Finametrica reports that the pattern of responses does not vary much by country; individuals' tolerance for risk is, on average, fairly stable over time; women tend to be more cautious than men (which is important for investing family wealth); and investment professionals tend to be more tolerant of risk than their clients (who in turn tend to be marginally more tolerant of risk than the population as a whole). The database also shows quite a wide variation of responses for individuals around these average characteristics.

The finding (which is repeatedly found) that investment advisers are on average more tolerant of risk than their clients may help to explain instances of investors saying to their advisers: "I didn't realise we were taking that much risk." This greater tolerance of risk might be interpreted as reflecting advisers' greater understanding of investment risk than that of their clients. Separate survey findings (also from Australia) suggest that investor education (for example, through attendance at seminars) has little impact on the risk tolerance of investors, even though it can be effective in persuading employees to save more for retirement. This suggests that investment advisers may think it reasonable to take more risk than most people would wish, not because they have a better understanding of investment risk, but because their nature is to enjoy the proximity to volatile markets. It seems that cautious people probably cannot be educated out of their disposition to be cautious, and it also seems likely that well-designed psychometric testing may help to categorise the risk appetite of investors better than ad hoc questionnaires.

However, a single score on a risk-tolerance questionnaire, even a well-designed one, will not be an adequate guide to an investor's willingness or capacity to take risk. An investor is likely to have different financial accounts for different purposes: one or more may be critical to achieve and another purely aspirational; one may be for a short-term objective and another for a long-term one (such as pension saving). A well-designed risk score might provide a starting point for discussing risk-taking, but it will not give the differentiated answers that are probably needed, nor will it cope with the different ways that investors respond to the experience or threat of losses, sometimes by increasing risk-taking (see Chapter 2).

Attitudes to risk and the financial crisis

A suggestion that investors became much more risk averse during the financial crisis of 2008 would be accepted as self-evident by many economists. Risk asset prices declined because investors were no longer as comfortable holding them; in other words, they became more risk averse. An alternative explanation is that prices fell because earnings expectations declined, justifying lower stock prices (and also wider spreads between the rates at which companies and creditworthy governments borrow). But the spike in the VIX index of stockmarket volatility in 2008 (see Figure 4.1) indicates that the stockmarket became more risky, and so investors with a given degree of risk aversion might reasonably feel uncomfortable with their existing allocations to risk assets unless they had a strong view that the increase in risk was a temporary phenomenon. These alternative perspectives are important for investors, and those who have benchmark allocations to risky and cautious assets will typically find themselves underweight risk assets after a decline in equity markets. These investors may then rebalance back to benchmark weights, but if they do this they will be taking on more risk when others wish to take less (see Chapter 4).

These considerations contrast with the data that emerge from psychometric tests, which suggest that investors' tolerance for risk was, on average, surprisingly stable during the financial crisis, although there are indications that their assessment of stockmarket risk was increased. (In other words, they might be equally willing to tolerate risk, but less willing to tolerate stockmarket risk, because it had increased.)

As with much in finance, the relationship between assessments of risk tolerance, risk aversion and loss aversion (see Chapter 2) remains an unresolved issue.

Know your niche

The style of involvement in decision-making is one of the most important things that investors need to decide. How hands-on or hands-off do they wish to be, and what are their preferences and special areas of investment expertise? This is a natural starting point for discussions between any investor and a new investment adviser.

Some investors like to devote much time and personal effort to their investments. Others prefer to delegate as much as possible to someone they trust. Neither policy is inherently superior, so long as keen investors have grounds for believing that their interventions are likely to add value (or to save value), and disinterested investors are sure that their advisers properly understand their investment objectives and that a reliable process of review has been established.

Successful entrepreneurs often have specialist skills that put them in a privileged position in the assessment of new business opportunities in their specialist areas. This role as potential informed investors is likely to open doors to investment opportunities that are not available to others. But it will be unclear how these investments should fit into an overall investment strategy and how the entrepreneur should weigh the risks.

Such investors need to consider whether and how far to diversify away from their niche area to provide a downside layer of protection (see Chapter 2), or a safety net for at least part of their wealth. How much should be allocated to such rainy-day investments depends on personal circumstances, preferences and willingness to tolerate extreme disappointment. For example, there is great scope for disappointment from individual venture capital investments, even when skilfully selected. For successful venture capitalists, it is likely that the risk of an individual investment failing is greater than the likelihood of that investment being a runaway success. But one runaway success will more than pay for several failures. One temptation for specialist investors will be to try to diversify into related areas. In these cases, a quiet review of the behavioural biases that commonly affect decision-making could prove invaluable (see Chapter 2). Investors should ask themselves the following questions:

■ Am I moving away from my natural habitat where I am confident of my "edge"?
■ Do my skills and specific expertise translate to this new market?
■ Will I have the same degree of control?

■ Do I have the same degree of confidence in my access to information and in my feel for these new businesses?

If an investor cannot be confident of replicating the ingredients of success that were successfully used in the original niche, there will be no basis for expecting the extra performance needed to justify the risk that goes with this pattern of concentrated private investments. In any event, an investor should ask whether this new venture provides the diversification of risk that is being sought. It may be better to seek a professionally managed approach to financial investments for part of the overall wealth. If all goes well, it is most likely that the "natural habitat" investments will perform better than the diversified investments. But this simply reflects the old saying that to become wealthy, it is necessary to concentrate expertise, but that to conserve wealth, it is necessary to diversify. However, risk concentration where there is no information advantage is a recipe for ruin.

Wealthy individuals are often entrepreneurs, and their own businesses will often represent the bulk of their wealth. Although the risks and opportunities of each business will vary considerably, when considering overall investment risk, it is usually appropriate to treat the business, which will typically be a private company, as if it represents a concentrated exposure to equity market risk. A mistake that is often made is to allow familiarity with a business to cloud perceptions of that business's intrinsic risk. Just because it is not possible to observe the volatility of the stock price of a private company does not mean that its value is not highly volatile. Whether a company is quoted or unquoted, an investor's familiarity with it – even the knowledge that the company is well managed – is no guide to its lack of volatility or risk as an investment.

Successful entrepreneurs often have such investments dominating their risk profile. Allowances need to be made for this when setting investment policy for financial investments that are held separately from the business. Typically, and depending upon financial needs, this will result in cautious recommendations for such investments, even if the investor is tolerant of financial uncertainty. Not surprisingly, most investors are concerned to conserve as well as to accumulate, to have a layer of downside protection as well as upside potential.

War chests and umbrellas

Where financial investments are being managed alongside business investments, they may constitute a liquid war chest to help fund future new opportunities, which may arise at short notice. In this case, the time horizon is likely to be short, with a premium put on liquidity and the stability of capital values, no matter how tolerant of risk the investor might be in other contexts.

Alternatively, a family with a volatile business may wish to build up a rainy-day umbrella fund, either to help the business through tough times which the family expects to be short-lived, or to provide an alternative source of income should the business fail. Many family-business investors have learned not to trust the umbrella of loan facilities willingly extended by banks during good times to be available when it starts raining seriously and have therefore arranged financial "umbrellas" from their own resources. In such cases, a low-risk umbrella investment strategy would be expected to include a significant allocation to investment grade bonds, no matter how risk-tolerant their risk profile assessment might be.

Base currency

Most investors have no difficulty defining their base currency. This is the currency of their home country: the currency in which they measure their wealth and in which they formulate their expenditure plans. Anything outside this base represents foreign currency and entails a risk of adverse fluctuations against the base currency.

The position is more ambiguous for many investors. Most private investors in Latin America, the Middle East and parts of East Asia use the US dollar as the accounting currency for their investments. But a convenient accounting currency is not necessarily a base currency. For many of these investors, the role of the US dollar will be different from the role it plays for a purely domestic US investor. Meanwhile, there are now tens of thousands of expatriate international executives, many of whom have earnings and residency in one currency and nationality and perhaps also retirement plans in another. This ambiguity alters the benchmark for measuring success or disappointment from investment returns. It is also particularly important in constructing appropriate investment strategies to meet particular commitments in different currencies. Consider, for example, a European working in New York, subject to severe earnings volatility and with alimony payments in euros, or a financially constrained foundation with commitments to support projects in more than one country. In both cases, the concept of base currency and currency risk management need addressing.

Discussions with international investors whose investments are typically accounted for in US dollars suggest that this currency ambiguity is rarely considered an important issue in Latin America or Africa, but it is recognised as a potential issue in the Middle East and is regarded as a material concern by many investors in Asia. Asian investors may have their investments reported and measured in US dollars, but they are concerned by any marked depreciation of the US dollar against the yen, the won or other Asian currencies. One practical and easy way to address this is to diversify holdings of cash across currencies in a way that approximately meets their particular needs. For example, the Monetary Authority of Singapore has for many years pursued a policy of stabilising the value of the Singapore dollar against a basket of currencies of Singapore's major trading partners and competitors. In other words, account is taken of fluctuations in the yen, the euro, sterling, other Asian currencies and the US dollar. Likewise, international families may feel more comfortable with their safe-harbour investments, especially cash, spread among currencies in which the family has obligations, rather than exclusively in the US dollar.

2 Understand your behaviour

Insights from behavioural finance

During the past 30 years research by experimental psychologists has enormously enriched economists' understanding of how we take decisions. These insights have differed markedly from the assumptions that underlay the traditional models of economists and finance academics. They matter for a range of reasons, of which the most important for this book is the prediction that in many instances we are inclined to take worse decisions than the models of traditional finance would predict. An understanding of these weaknesses ought to help us to take better financial decisions.

These advances led to the development of behavioural finance, which provides a framework that enables us to explore and understand investor preferences, and to delve into the biases that affect how we take decisions and how these may cause us to deviate from the textbook assumptions of how rational investors ought to behave. An appreciation of these influences is a prerequisite for making sure that investors adopt appropriate investment strategies.

Traditionally, economics and finance have focused on models that assume rationality. There is an old story about economists that highlights the difference between the two approaches:

An economist [was] strolling down the street with a companion. They come upon a $100 bill lying on the ground, and as the companion reaches down to pick it up, the economist says: "Don't bother – if it were a genuine $100 bill, someone would have already picked it up."

The economist's theoretical prior belief tells him that the anomalous observation must be a data problem. The behaviourist, however, would want to examine the evidence, in other words to conduct an experiment before concluding that the bill was probably a fake, without any prior belief one way or the other. This is a profound difference in approach which has important implications for investment advice.

Traditional models in finance can be caricatured as follows: "If investors are rational, and if markets are efficient, then investors ought to be behaving as follows." Almost all investors have been shown these models, for example in the "risk" and "return" trade-offs of an "efficient frontier" analysis, which implicitly assume that markets are "well behaved" and "efficient", that investors should prefer diversified to undiversified portfolios of risky investments, and that they should view the risk of losses consistently with their attitude to the opportunity for gains. Since the financial crisis of 2007–09 such models have been the subject of increased criticism, but they remain useful (and are used to provide illustrations of policy alternatives in Chapter 5). However, investors should have some understanding of their potential weaknesses. A simple illustration will suffice. Many people buy lottery tickets; they expect to lose money, but they hope to gain riches. Traditional finance implicitly finds this behaviour inefficient. Nevertheless, it can be rational as it provides the best legal way to have at least some chance (however remote) of securing riches in the short term. If you do not buy a lottery ticket, it is certain that you will not win. An understanding of our willingness to gamble in some predictable circumstances and to overpay for insurance in others can help us to manage our finances better (see below).

Behavioural finance uses research from psychology that describes how individuals actually behave, and applies those insights to finance. This has led to two major streams of research. The first concerns how investor behaviour might not accord with the textbook concept of the efficient rational investor. The other is how less than fully rational investors may cause market prices to deviate from their fundamental values. The first strand of work, how investors behave, is used to look at how investment strategy should accommodate what investors want. The second, how investors' behaviour may affect how markets function, is used in Chapter 6 to look at whether active investment managers are likely to find it easier to outperform (for which the short answer is "no").

Recognition of the contribution that behavioural analysis is making in financial economics was reflected in 2002 with the award of the Nobel Prize in Economics to a professor of psychology, Daniel Kahneman (who won it jointly with Vernon Smith). This work, much of it developed jointly with the late Amos Tversky, a cognitive and mathematical psychologist, has been summarised and updated in Kahneman's retrospective tour de force, *Thinking fast and slow*. It developed from a series of experiments that led to strong conclusions about the biases of intuition that affect how individuals take both instinctive and even thoughtful decisions and how they form preferences. A good understanding of investor preferences is critical in giving investment advice, and an understanding of investor biases is important in understanding how investors may respond to particular events or developments. If biases are weaknesses that could injure the interests of an investor, investment advisers should not pander to them. This indicates, for example, a need for investor education. But investors and their advisers should be aware of these biases since they will help determine reactions to a range of predictable market developments.

Investor biases

Psychologists have documented systematic patterns of bias in how people form views and take decisions, which Kahneman has described as "biases of intuition". Although the primary research did not usually involve investors or investment decisions, it is directly applicable to investments. These biases influence how we form investment opinions, and then how we take investment decisions. For example, the observation that most car drivers think that they are better-than-average drivers reflects a general characteristic of optimism and wishful thinking. It would be naive to think that this characteristic did not affect our investment views. Furthermore, people are systematically overconfident, tending to put too much faith in their own intuition. Overconfidence in turn is reflected in confirmation bias, whereby we show too ready a willingness to accept as proof any information that reinforces our existing views, and also in self-attribution, for example attributing to our own innate ability and unusual skill any success that we may enjoy. Individuals who are unusually well paid might interpret this as evidence of their own unusual ability, for instance.

Correspondingly, self-attribution leads to a natural tendency to attribute any disappointment to bad luck rather than a lack of skill. Investment examples of this would be provided by most accounts of investment manager underperformance that an investor might have heard: outperformance reflects skill, while underperformance reflects bad luck. This is also associated with hindsight bias, whereby individuals are sure, after the event, that they expected whatever happened to happen: "It was obvious it was going to happen, wasn't it?" Or, if the outcome was a bad outcome: "It was a disaster waiting to happen." Unfortunately, the future is rarely so clear.

A similar bias is representativeness, or stereotyping, whereby individuals are too quick to conclude that they understand developments on the basis of too little information. For example, in 100 years of stock and bond market performance history, five separate (non-overlapping) 20-year periods can be observed (which is a small sample). Subject to the periodicity of the data, any number of overlapping 20-year periods can also be constructed – for example, 20 years to last year, 20 years to the year before last, and so on. This will help to slice and dice the data more finely and enable more fancy statistical analysis. Despite this, the inescapable fact is that we do not have many 20-year observations of performance to conclude much (purely using performance numbers) about, for example, the likelihood of stocks outperforming bonds over 20-year periods.

There are more sophisticated techniques that can be used to get a handle on the same issue, but it remains common to draw strong conclusions from small data sets when that is the only evidence available. In such circumstances, it is safer to be circumspect about any conclusions drawn from limited data.

Another bias (probably just displayed) is conservatism, which arises when it is widely recognised that the available data are insufficient to support strong conclusions. In this case, it is a common error to place too little weight on the available evidence, or even to disregard it and to rely solely on prior expectations.

Yet another bias is "anchoring", whereby we gravitate towards a quantity that has been suggested before addressing the appropriate answer in our particular case. One common example would be the proportion of financial wealth that an investor ought to invest in the stockmarket; inevitably the answer will be strongly influenced by what the investor is told the norm is. This is understandable (though often not appropriate). Anchoring is a surprisingly widespread phenomenon, and it can easily lead to us being misled.

A further bias is belief perseverance, which concerns the evidence that people cling to prior opinions for too long when confronted with contrary evidence that would be sufficient to convince equally talented newcomers to the field. In this way, individuals demonstrate a reluctance to search for evidence that contradicts their previous views, because they are reluctant to write off past investments in their own human capital, despite it being clear that they are partly obsolescent.

Biases often represent mental shortcuts (called "heuristics" by academics), which we use to avoid having to process large quantities of information. These shortcuts may derive from an established opinion of how markets work. For example, many investors expect to be able to identify good managers who will outperform. Sceptics, however, are more likely to ascribe outperformance to transient luck, and may be puzzled by apparent evidence of good managers. These differences in "received wisdom" can lead to shortcuts which cause some to think that much more analysis is needed before a decision is taken and others to readily conclude that the appropriate course of action is self-evident. This type of shortcut will have led some to feel comfortable that they had found a good manager in fraudster Bernie Madoff.

Increasing complexity (for example of investment products) makes it more likely that decisions will rely on shortcuts because of the difficulty of processing all the available information. The practical alternative to using shortcuts may often appear to be indecision. But where a decision appears to have relied on such a shortcut and the decision goes wrong, hindsight can be embarrassing.

An alternative, increasingly common among institutional investors, is the adoption of a set of "investment beliefs", widely supported by the fund's decision-makers, which summarises a coherent view of the opportunities offered by markets and whether the fund is well-placed to exploit them (see Appendix 3). This can facilitate considered and coherent decision-making. All investors, large and small, need to consider whether their own views of how markets function might lead to shortcuts and whether they might compromise or improve their own chances of investment success.

Even when investors are able to sit back and consider potential biases dispassionately, there is no escape from the danger of regret risk. Regret is the emotion individuals feel if they can easily imagine having acted in a way that would have led to a more favourable outcome. Early behavioural studies emphasised that regret from taking action that was subsequently unprofitable is usually felt more acutely than regret from decisions to take no action that were subsequently equally costly. A typical investment example would be the different reactions to a fall in the price of investments. If it is a recently acquired investment, there is generally more regret than if it is a long-standing investment. For investors, this leads to the common (almost universal) dilemma of how and when to implement new investment decisions, even if investment risk arguments point to the desirability of immediate implementation (see Chapter 5 for a discussion about the issues involved in implementing investment strategy changes).

A theme of some research is that regret about a disappointing outcome following a change in strategy may be reduced if the decision was justified. This may lead to a distinction between regret about bad decisions and regret about bad outcomes. These do not always go together: sometimes bad decisions do not lead to bad outcomes. Other research also indicates a tendency to move away from decisions that have recently had disappointing outcomes. Nevertheless, if an unprofitable investment decision was unjustified, the investor will blame himself (or the adviser). However, if an investment decision was justified, the investor may regret the decision or its timing but should at least understand why it was taken.

Thus good process should not only lead to more considered (and, hopefully, better) decision-making, but also support stability and confidence in the existence of a "steady hand at the tiller". This should help control the potentially harmful effect of some of the biases that can influence investment decision-making. One of the best ways to manage the impact of these may be to draw attention to them and discuss their potential impact before important investment decisions are taken.

Investor preferences

If investor biases should be managed, investor preferences should be respected and reflected in investment strategy, in so far as it is both feasible and sensible.

There are two particular areas of investor preference that have been highlighted by behavioural finance. The first (perhaps not surprisingly) is loss aversion, which Kahneman has described as "the most significant contribution of psychology to behavioural economics". In behavioural finance, loss aversion fills the role of risk aversion in traditional finance. The second is mental accounting, which reflects the way in which investors assign sums of money to different actual or notional accounts for different purposes with varying degrees of risk tolerance depending upon the importance of achieving the particular objective. For example, an individual's summer vacation money will be in a different mental account (and probably a different actual account) from pension savings.

Loss aversion

Traditional finance assumes that investors behave rationally and evaluate the risk and potential return of investment strategies in terms of their expected utility or satisfaction. There are different ways of calibrating utility, but they all have the characteristic that they represent assumptions about how investors should be expected to express preferences. They have the additional characteristic that they can be modelled mathematically, which is convenient for modellers. Much less convenient is the widespread evidence that these rational utility models do not reflect how people view the prospect of financial gains or losses.

This has been reflected in prospect theory, which is built upon a wide range of experiments showing that people will take quite large risks to have some chance of avoiding otherwise certain losses, but that they are quick to bank any winnings. Investment banks tap into this investor preference through sales of highly profitable principal-protected structured products, which provide downside protection with the prospect of some combination of leveraged positive returns. In other words, they offer a seductive combination of "little fear and much hope". This relationship between the disutility or dissatisfaction that comes from losses and the utility or satisfaction that comes from gains is captured in the so-called coefficient of loss aversion, which across a wide range of experiments has come out at a value of around two. This measures how much more highly investors weigh losses than they weigh gains. Loss aversion is most commonly expressed in terms of a comparison of absolute gains and losses, but it also applies to gains and losses relative to a benchmark.

These experiments have highlighted the importance of how a question is framed or asked as a determinant of the reaction to it. The choice of a benchmark becomes of great importance by helping to "frame" expectations for performance and whether an investor should be pleased or disappointed with an investment result. An investor, for example, may be disappointed that a fund has lagged well behind the performance of the stockmarket, whereas the manager may try to persuade clients to be happy that the fund has shown some growth in value. How expectations are set at the outset for an investment can become as important as the subsequent performance in determining whether an investment is judged to be successful.

A related challenge arises from the inconsistency between the wish to have stable, or at least protected, investment values, and the desire to have a stable income that is financed by those investments (see Chapter 5). These wishes are incompatible, because only long-dated, high-quality government bonds, which are volatile, can guarantee a stable income over time. This highlights the need for investors to be educated as well as asked the relevant questions, framed in an appropriate way.

The "fourfold pattern" of attitudes to gains and losses

Kahneman and Tversky's prospect theory, which is based on experiments into how individuals choose among risky alternatives, is commonly represented by a quadrant such the one below.

	Big gains	Big losses
High probability	Sell winners to lock in substantial but smaller than expected gain	Reject opportunity to crystallise existing losses, run risk of even larger losses to have at least some chance of avoiding likely big loss
Low probability	Buy lottery ticket to have chance of big win	Buy insurance to avoid small chance of big loss

The top left quadrant indicates a preference to accept less than the expected value of a successful gamble to lock in a certain gain. In the investment world, this translates into selling winning investments after a run of good performance.

The bottom left quadrant is the temptation to buy lottery tickets, even though the most likely result by far is the loss of the cost of the ticket. In the investment world, this too translates into the surprisingly large demand for structured products that offer large payouts in the event of plausible but unlikely events.

The top right quadrant is the tendency to hold onto lossmaking investments to avoid the pain of realising losses. This offers some hope of recouping losses, at the risk of incurring even bigger ones. In Kahneman's words, when confronted with only bad options, "we were just as risk seeking in the domain of losses, as we were risk averse in the domain of gains".

The bottom right quadrant is where investors openly buy insurance, to avoid the small risk of some loss.

Mental accounting and behavioural portfolio theory

A division of investments between safety-first, cautious accounts to meet basic needs, and more aggressive "aspirational" accounts to meet less critical or simply more distant objectives is one of the predictions of the mental accounting framework of behavioural finance. This approach is not found anywhere in the traditional finance textbooks but it is common (some would say common sense) in everyday experience, as the following examples illustrate.

The subsistence farmer

Subsistence farmers often grow two types of crops: food for the family and cash crops with volatile prices. Growing food represents the safety-first portfolio. The allocation of land to growing food is determined first by basic needs, such as family size. The remaining land is allocated to the cash crop, which is the more speculative opportunity to raise living standards – in other words, the aspirational portfolio.

The champion poker player

Greg "Fossilman" Raymer gave this account of how he and his wife kept their "aspirational account" separate from their essential "safety-first" cash when he started out on his successful career at the poker table:

> I started getting steady wins, but I was now married, and [my wife] was becoming increasingly concerned about the time I was spending on it. She'd also hear horror stories about players bankrupting their families. In the end we made a deal: I was allowed a $1,000 poker bankroll on condition it stayed separate from our savings. And if I lost it all, I'd never play again. It never got to that.

The central bank foreign exchange reserve manager

Even central banks demonstrate this layering of investment resources. The first purpose of a central bank's foreign exchange reserves is to fund whatever market intervention might be necessary to defend the exchange rate of the national currency. This means investing in high-quality, highly liquid, short-dated securities, in particular US Treasury securities. This is the safety-first portfolio. Central banks also often hold substantial reserves of gold bullion. These are intended to have a different, longer-term capital preservation and confidence-building role, which sets them apart from short-term liquid reserves.

In recent years a number of central banks accumulated unprecedented levels of foreign exchange reserves, far in excess of the likely need to support their currencies in the short term. These excess reserves have often been separated from the short-term liquid reserves and been used to fund government-owned sovereign wealth funds (see Chapter 4). The long time horizon for investing sovereign wealth funds gives them a different set of objectives and attitude to risk from central bank reserves. Sovereign wealth funds represent a national aspirational portfolio. The investment of central bank foreign exchange reserves and the accompanying sovereign wealth fund parallels the layered pyramid of behavioural portfolio theory.

Investment strategy and behavioural finance

Each of these examples, from the champion poker player to the central bank, shows a natural process of segmentation of risk-taking, with separate allocations to different accounts, each with distinctive risk tolerances and time horizons dictated by particular objectives. Above all, this segmentation provides an easy-to-monitor, keep-it-simple management information system for individuals and institutions.

This mental accounting also helps to discipline future behaviour by highlighting deviations from decisions that have already been taken. For example, in a family context, someone might say, "no, we will not use that money to buy a new car, it's our pension savings"; or, in an institution, "no, we can't use that cash to finance a private equity opportunity, it is our ready cash to pay pensions".

Traditional finance does not segment financial resources in this way. It treats all a family's financial resources or all a pension plan's resources as a unified whole and seeks a total wealth-efficient solution to considering risk, return and investment strategy. It also considers money to be fungible (cash in this account is the same as cash in another account if it is owned by the same person and has the same tax status). Furthermore, and this is of great importance, traditional finance takes into account the relationships, for example, correlations, that may exist between the investments and the objectives or obligations of the different accounts. Separate accounting, with separate strategies designed independently for each account, would ignore these relationships. This can be a major inefficiency in the widespread practice of mental accounting. Mental accounting helps financial resources to be targeted for different purposes. Each person will have a different risk tolerance for achieving different objectives. Some goals are critical, but others are just nice to have. Decisions will be influenced by regulations that impinge on taxed and tax-exempt accounts, current-generation resources and trust or other tax-efficient accounts for future generations, and philanthropic accounts.

A more general example of mental accounting is quoted by Meir Statman and Vincent Wood in *Investment Temperament*, when they describe the pattern of responses to the following question in the Fidelity Investments Asset Allocation Planner:

If you could increase your chances of improving your returns by taking more risk would you:

1 *Be willing to take a lot more risk with all of your money*
2 *Be willing to take a lot more risk with some of your money*
3 *Be willing to take a little more risk with all of your money*
4 *Be willing to take a little more risk with some of your money*

Overwhelmingly, the respondents indicated a willingness to take either a lot or a little more risk with some of their money. This indicates a preference to segment or layer risk-taking, which is generally considered to be at odds with the traditional risk–return trade-off commonly presented to investors. This addresses the performance and risk of the total portfolio, which would presume taking either a little or a lot more risk with all of the money. However, if a traditional efficient portfolio comprises a mixture of a holding of risk-free assets and an allocation to market risk, these responses would make sense in terms of being willing to shift some resources out of a safe-haven investment and into a market risk portfolio (see Chapter 5). In other words, the responses could be consistent with traditional finance as well as behavioural portfolio theory.

Parameter uncertainty and behavioural finance

Investors often like to test the reasonableness of major decisions from different perspectives before committing themselves. This is a rational way to proceed with decision-making when faced with uncertainty about the reliability of models or approaches. One of the themes that pervades this book is that the parameters used in financial models are subject to marked degrees of uncertainty, with some elements more uncertain than others. There is nothing new about this.

Even in the traditional model of rational markets and rational investors, investors have not generally faced a unique solution to their investment problems, although that may be what they were offered. Quantitative analysis may provide supposedly unique answers to asset allocation problems, but the investment markets have rarely (see Chapter 3) provided such clear answers. Instead, our understanding of the uncertain relationships between markets has always involved a trade-off between broadly appropriate alternative investment strategies which appear to lie within the range of what is best described as the "fuzzy frontier".

This means that in any particular situation there will always be strategies that are demonstrably inefficient or that involve a clearly inappropriate risk profile. There will also be a range of strategies that are each broadly appropriate, given our current state of knowledge of markets and investors' attitude to risk. This can give a surprisingly wide scope for the investment preferences of principals or fiduciaries to be reflected in investment strategy, while still staying consistent with the overriding desire to adhere to their goals and objectives. It also makes it more likely that investors will find that independent ways of presenting strategy, such as the behaviourist-layered pyramid approach, provide intuitively attractive cross-checks on the traditional quantitative approach.

The idea of a fuzzy frontier can be traced back to work on uncertainty in scientific measurement dating from the 1960s. Much of the uncertainty in measurement that we know exists cannot be adequately captured by statistics. This has potential applications in many different fields. One of its starting points is that we often do not know precisely how to categorise items that are being analysed.

This was reflected in a debate over 20 years ago about whether US quoted multinational corporations with US boards of directors but extensive overseas operations were really US companies. This was captured in the title of a 1990 article in *Harvard Business Review*, "Who Is Us?", by Robert Reich, a former US labour secretary. In reality, this is an issue that the staff of any investment firm wrestle with every day. Mechanical rules have to be applied, but rules differ from one investing institution to another, often in ways that purists would dispute, resulting in apparent arbitrary differences in investment allocations. Leading index providers have disagreed about whether South Korea is an emerging or a developed market. Investors buy UK stocks to gain exposure to a developed market, but is a Kazakh mining company or an Indonesian coal miner listed in London a UK exposure, or is an Israeli technology company listed on NASDAQ a US exposure? In high-level summaries of portfolio allocations, should a convertible bond be classified as debt or as equity? In finance, these classification issues are routinely put to one side in investment analysis, and yet they undermine the precision with which policy conclusions can be drawn.

Traditional finance, behavioural finance and evolution

In recent years steps have been taken towards synthesising traditional finance with the insights from behavioural finance, but there is much further to go before an integrated approach is agreed which combines both the rigour and comprehensiveness of "traditional" finance and evidence-based assumptions about investor behaviour from behavioural finance.

Some things are already clear. First, it is important for investors and their advisers to benefit from the insights of behavioural finance to understand better the influences on their own decision-making and preferences. Advice and strategy can then be adapted to accommodate that. This does not provide an excuse for ignoring the fundamental principles of diversification, correlations between different investments or the need to tailor policies to the time horizon of investment objectives. Equally, it would be arrogant to suggest that it is always poor practice for individuals to purchase the investment equivalent of lottery tickets, as this may be an efficient way of maximising the chances of acquiring riches. Furthermore, behavioural finance helps advisers gain a better understanding of how investors take decisions, why investors' portfolios are structured as they are, how investors are likely to respond to any instance of disappointing performance and the nature of their strong preferences.

As Statman writes in *Behavioral Portfolios: Hope for Riches and Protection from Poverty*:

> *We might lament the fact that people are attracted to lotteries, or we might accept it, and help people strike a balance between hope for riches and protection from poverty.*

Andrew Lo, Harris & Harris Group professor of finance and director of the Laboratory for Financial Engineering at MIT, puts it more starkly when he writes in *The Adaptive Markets Hypothesis* that "for all financial market participants, survival is the only objective that matters".

Against this background, the most important first step may be to start discussions of investment strategy with an assessment of whether an investor has sufficient wealth to guarantee survival. In other words, does the investor have sufficient resources to hedge against the risk of shortfall from critical objectives by investing in liability- or objective-matching high-quality government bonds? In the years after 2008, the era of ultra-low interest rates meant that the answer for many was "no". Survival, in terms of meeting what previously seemed reasonable expectations (for example, in terms of retirement income or retirement date), cannot be guaranteed and risk-taking, and the danger of worsening shortfalls, cannot be avoided. How such risk-taking might best be structured is discussed in the next chapter.

3   Market investment returns

THE FINANCIAL MARKETS should be seen as a place to protect and grow wealth, not as a place to grow wealthy. This chapter looks at expectations and uncertainties for future equity and government bond market returns. An important message is that the start of this century has set the tone for less favourable equity returns than were enjoyed in the 20th century and for modest returns to be earned from creditworthy government bonds. But the main qualification remains that even over long periods of time, we are unclear how markets are going to behave.

Traditionally, domestic Treasury bonds and bills have been considered free from credit risk and safe havens for investors. This has been a cornerstone of much modern portfolio theory and practice, but it has been shaken by the government debt crises that flowed from the credit crunch of 2007–08. Despite this, appropriately interpreted, it is a foundation that remains largely intact (see Are governments risk free? below).

Inflation-linked government bonds are an innovation that can provide an important degree of security for cautious long-term investors. But the extraordinary monetary easing after early 2009 led to negligible rates of interest being paid on all types of creditworthy government bonds. This has posed severe challenges for cautious investors, for whom the cost of security has often been too high. An unwelcome degree of risk-taking and standard-of-living uncertainty became unavoidable as the security of income from government bonds became too expensive.

Sources of investment performance

In a country with a creditworthy government, investment performance can be described as coming from six sources:

1 **Treasury bill yield.** The short-term (less than one year, and typically 1–6 months) risk-free rate of interest.

2 **Inflation-indexed government bond yield.** The long-term inflation-risk-free rate of interest. It is unclear whether these inflation-indexed bonds need to offer a premium return over Treasury bills.

3 **Conventional Treasury bond yield.** The long-term nominal risk-free rate of interest. This rate of interest is subject to the risk of unexpectedly high inflation. It should include a premium over inflation-linked bonds to compensate for expected inflation, and probably also a margin above this for the uncertainty of that inflation (but see below).

4 **Market risk premium.** The compensation that any rational saver should seek in return for putting money or future income at risk of loss. The market provides this reward for bearing "market risk". This is reflected in the equity risk premium (the amount by which equities are expected to outperform bonds or cash) and the credit risk premium (the extra yield paid on corporate bonds to compensate for the risk that a company might default – see Chapter 8). Less obviously, market risk premiums seem to be offered in return for accepting various types of insurance risk and also for different types of equity risk (for example, small-company risk separately from equity market risk). These are discussed in Chapter 7 (equity investing), Chapter 9 (hedge funds) and Chapter 11 (real estate).

5 **Investment manager skill.** Generates investment performance (or alpha) that is separate from the performance of the market (or beta). Frequently, investment performance that managers attribute to their skill (which is an expensive, scarce commodity) gets confused with aspects of market performance (which can be accessed inexpensively).

6 **Noise.** Introduced to investment performance by unskilful

managers of investors' portfolios. Noise is often described as "alpha" when it is positive. (Sceptics have described alpha as "the average error term".) Distinguishing noise from skill is one of the most difficult tasks for investors. There are always likely to be more unskilled "noise" managers with marketable track records than skilled managers who, in addition to being skilled, also have a marketable record at any point in time. Noise will normally bring some extra volatility; it will also incur fees and distract investors, wasting their valuable time.

This summary simplifies matters considerably, by ignoring cross-border investment in government bonds and by assuming that all investors have an unambiguous base currency, which as discussed in Chapter 1 is not the case. Nevertheless, this provides a useful introduction to the building blocks of investment performance. The first three sources can be accessed easily and inexpensively by anyone, through direct holdings of government securities (or through funds, including exchange traded funds, which hold only government securities). Equity market risk can also be accessed inexpensively through index funds or exchange traded funds. Some investment markets and some aspects of market risk premiums (for example, private equity – see Chapter 10) can be accessed only if the investor is willing to take a view on investment manager skill. The sources of hedge fund performance are discussed in Chapter 9.

The pattern of returns available from exposure to market risk can also be re-engineered through "structured products" which contain combinations of embedded options with exposure to particular markets. These do not generate performance, but they can provide insurance (which must be paid for) against the risk of disappointing outcomes in ways that may suit investors.

Are government bonds risk-free?

The idea that government bonds are free of credit risk is routinely used as a building block in designing investment strategies, but it seems to be at odds with ample evidence to the contrary. The highest rating assigned by the credit-rating agencies (see Chapter 8) is AAA, which denotes a debt of the highest creditworthiness, when in the words of Standard and Poor's, the issuer is "judged to be of the highest quality, subject to the lowest level of credit risk". Nevertheless, credit-rating agencies frequently assign ratings to sovereign and other central-government debt which imply some degree of risk that the government's obligations will not be honoured; in recent years one or more of the three leading rating agencies has rated the domestic central-government debt of the United States, Japan, France, the UK, Italy, Spain and Ireland below AAA. Furthermore, modern credit markets enable investors (or speculators) to buy or sell insurance contracts, called credit default swaps, which can give a market assessment of the likelihood of a government defaulting on its debt, and can track fluctuations in market assessments of a government's creditworthiness (although the credit crisis highlighted counterparty issues with these contracts). Most obviously, there is a history of governments defaulting on their international and (but less frequently) domestic debt.

Surveys of the historical experience of defaults by governments (see Appendix 4) have sometimes misinterpreted market refinancing of sovereign debt – when a government exploits a contractual opportunity to redeem a loan and refinance it at a lower interest cost – as a *de jure* default, which it is not. Between 1952 and 2008 there seems to have been no instance of the central government of a developed country failing to honour the nominal face value of its marketable debts, although there have been examples from emerging markets (most notably Russia in 1998–99, and the forcible termination of US dollar or inflation indexation of debt in a number of Latin American countries in the 1980s), as well as Greece in 2012.

Debasement of government debt through inflation has been a characteristic behaviour of over-indebted sovereign governments since time immemorial, and it is a risk faced by holders of the debt of any government. But it is also clear that developed-market (and many emerging-market) sovereign governments can be counted on to take honouring the face value of their marketable debt extremely seriously and, at least in respect of their unindexed domestic obligations, they should always have the means to ensure that they can meet those obligations.

Not surprisingly, when governments do default, there seems to be a hierarchy of risk exposures, with foreign-currency-denominated or linked and inflation-indexed obligations more vulnerable than unindexed domestic debt. For this reason, the proportion of sovereign debt that is denominated in foreign currency or which is indexed is a useful credit risk indicator.

Sovereign risk and "a country called Europe"

An important financial difference between a sovereign and a local government is that, if it needs to, a sovereign government can debase its currency to meet its obligations, which are fixed in its own currency, but a local government does not enjoy this degree of freedom. This means that an over-indebted sovereign government has the scope to try to devalue its way out of a domestic debt crisis but an over-indebted local government does not.

This is not a new insight, and for some European countries, the opportunity to replace the discredited temptation to devalue and to accommodate fast inflation, and the high interest rates which came with that freedom, with a new regime with the discipline of a fixed exchange rate, apparently tight fiscal-policy guidelines, and a tie-in to low rates of inflation and interest, was seen as a major attraction of European currency union ahead of its introduction in 1999. This involved some voluntary yielding of financial sovereignty, and the credibility of monetary union depended on an expectation that this was irreversible.

For government bond investors this meant (though scant attention was paid to it at the time) the substitution of inflation risk with the credit risk that a national government might be unable to honour its obligations. In the euro zone, member countries have their own government bond markets, and efforts are made to co-ordinate fiscal policy between member countries, but there is no dominant euro-zone fiscal policy or the issue of collective euro-zone government debt, underwritten by the euro-zone taxpayer – although there have been steps towards this with financing arrangements put in place after 2009. For euro-based investors, it follows that the choice of a safe-harbour government bond is more judgmental and nuanced than for investors from other countries. But this has parallels with US investors, who must weigh the tax and creditworthy status of different municipal bonds, which form core long-term "safety-first" holdings in many personal portfolios (see Chapter 5).

Safe havens that provide different kinds of shelter

If investors take no risk, they should not expect to receive a premium return. But one investor's safe-haven may be a risky investment for another:

- For a short-term investor, domestic Treasury bills represent the minimum risk investment that provides capital protection over the short term.

- For an individual, a bank or an insurance company wanting to secure an income, domestic Treasury bonds give that security for the lifetime of the bond. Treasury bills that mature every three or six months are risky for this purpose as they are immediately vulnerable to cuts in interest rates which a Treasury bond, if held to maturity, is not. The risk from these bonds is that inflation may pick up (and, separately, that interest income may have to be reinvested at lower yields). Figures 3.1, 3.2 and 3.3 show how the pre-tax income yield on offer for ten years to buy-and-hold investors in ten-year Treasury bonds has compared with the

FIG 3.1 **Income yield from 10-year US Treasury notes and 3-month Treasury bills**
% per year, Sep 2004–Oct 2013

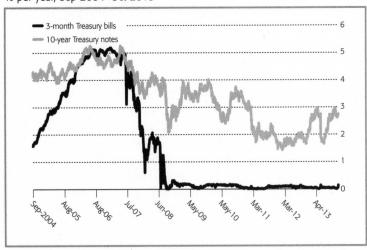

Source: www.ustreas.gov

FIG 3.2 **Income yield from 10-year UK gilts and 6-month Treasury bills**
% per year, Sep 2004–Oct 2013

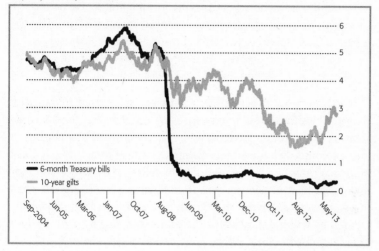

Source: www.bankofengland.co.uk

FIG 3.3 **Income yield from 10-year euro-zone AAA Treasury bonds and 3-month Treasury bills**
% per year, Sep 2004–Oct 2013

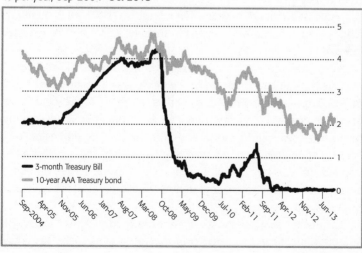

Source: www.ecb.int

yield on offer for the next three months for holders of Treasury bills for the United States, the UK and the euro zone.

■ An individual who wants a secure income that is also protected against inflation can use inflation-linked Treasury bonds. These provide the low-risk investment, insuring against adverse inflation and adverse real interest-rate surprises, but the illiquidity of inflation-linked markets is a concern.

Each of these investors has a different safe-haven investment: Treasury bills for the short-term investor; conventional fixed-income Treasury bonds for the investor who is not concerned about inflation (most commonly an insurance company with contracts to pay fixed monetary amounts); and inflation-linked government bonds for the prospective pensioner who is concerned about inflation. Each investor takes a risk when they venture outside their own safe haven. Often they will feel they have little choice, but they need to consider how and whether they will be rewarded for taking that risk.

Which government bonds will perform best?

In the examples above, the insurance company does not need to be paid a premium yield by the taxpayer to be persuaded to hold Treasury bonds, nor does the pensioner to hold inflation-linked government bonds. This means that it is unclear how much premium return, if any, should be expected from government bonds, whether indexed or not, over cash.

So different groups of investors have their own separate natural or preferred habitats in different segments of the government bond market. From time to time this can affect the shape of the yield curve (that is, the pattern of yields offered on government bonds of varying maturities – see Figures 3.4, 3.5 and 3.6). This can sometimes make it hard to rationalise the differences in interest rates that a government pays to different groups of investors. The barriers that can limit attempts to arbitrage away apparent pricing anomalies are looked at in Chapter 6.

The normal shape of the yield curve has been an area of extensive, and often inconclusive, research in macroeconomics. The historical pattern is clear on two things. First, there has normally been an

FIG 3.4 **US Treasury conventional and real yield curves**
% per year, October 21st 2013

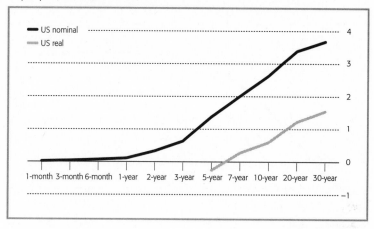

Source: www.ustreas.gov

upward-sloping yield curve – in other words, longer-dated Treasury bonds have offered higher yields and returns than shorter dated government bonds, in particular Treasury bills. (See Appendix 1 for

FIG 3.5 **UK Treasury conventional and real yield curves**
% per year, October 18th 2013

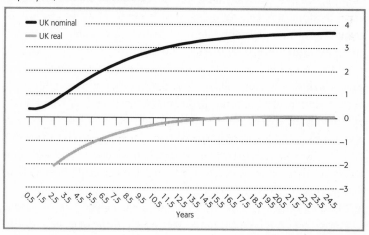

Source: www.bankofengland.co.uk

FIG 3.6 **Euro-zone AAA rated Treasury conventional yield curve**
% per year, October 18th 2013

Source: www.ecb.int

definitions of Treasury bonds and Treasury bills.) Second, the extent of this premium varies over time. This is often described as the term premium that short-term investors need to be offered to tempt them to buy longer-dated bonds (because such bonds are subject to price volatility). But insurance companies do not need to be paid a term premium because longer maturities provide their "natural habitat", and investors may in any event wish to hold government bonds because they are, or at any rate have been (see Chapter 8), the best and most liquid diversifier of equity market risk.

Since the introduction of the markets in inflation-linked government bonds (see below), there has been growing emphasis on the premium in conventional government bond yields as an inflation risk premium. Pensioners should not normally buy conventional bonds unless they offer compensation not only for the expected rate of inflation, but also for the risk that the actual rate of inflation might be higher than the rate that is expected. This is the inflation risk premium. (This ignores taxation issues, which are important in deciding between different types of government bonds.) Long-term investors who are primarily concerned with securing a stable standard of living will feel more comfortable holding conventional government bonds when they have greatest confidence in inflation being kept within the target set by the central bank. If not, they will need to believe that there is sufficient premium in the yield on conventional government bonds to compensate for the threat to their standard of living posed by an uncertain inflation rate.

A market expectation for inflation can be deduced from the difference between yields on conventional government bonds and the yields on these indexed bonds. This is the so-called "break-even" inflation rate. (If inflation turns out at this rate, an investor will get, approximately, the same return from holding indexed government bonds as from conventional treasuries of the same maturity.) But whether the break-even rate really is a market forecast for inflation is controversial.

Is the break-even inflation rate the market's forecast?

Inflation-indexed government bonds are now available in each major financial market. They were introduced in the UK in 1981 and since then they have been made available in Australia (1985), Canada (1991), Sweden (1994), the United States (1997) and Japan (2004), with government issues in the euro zone from France (1998), Italy and Greece (2003), and Germany (2006). A number of emerging markets, including India, Brazil, Israel and South Africa, have also made use of inflation-linked bonds. They now represent an instrument whose characteristics investors in each country should understand. In the United States, these bonds are known as Treasury Inflation Protected Securities or TIPS, and that acronym is used here to refer to any inflation-linked government bond, not just those issued by the US government. The pattern of 20-year inflation-linked and conventional US and also UK Treasury bond yields and the implied 20-year break-even rates of inflation are shown in Figures 3.7–3.10.

Those unfamiliar with inflation-indexed bonds are advised to check the difference in yields from conventional and index-linked issues of government bonds. Break-even inflation rates can be deduced from any table of government bond prices and yields (and are regularly published in the *Financial Times*). TIPS are indicated by the letter "i" in tables of US Treasury bond yields and

FIG 3.7 **US Treasury 20-year yields**
% per year, Jul 2004–Oct 2013

Source: www.ustreas.gov

FIG 3.8 **US 20-year "break-even" inflation (difference between 20-year Treasury and TIPS yields)**
% per year, Jul 2004–Oct 2013

Source: www.ustreas.gov

FIG 3.9 **UK 20-year gilt yields**
% per year, Sep 2004–Oct 2013

Source: www.bankofengland.co.uk

FIG 3.10 **UK 20-year "break-even" inflation**
% per year, Sep 2004–Oct 2013

Source: www.bankofengland.co.uk

the same classification rule is used, for example, for French and German government issues linked to inflation. The break-even rate of inflation is affected by a number of technical factors, which may mean that it is not a true market forecast for inflation. These include the following:

■ An inflation risk premium. This would cause, if it exists, the break-even rate to be higher than the market's forecast for inflation.

■ In the United States and other countries, but not the UK, TIPS provide an insurance against deflation as the bonds will be redeemed at the higher of par or that value plus their accumulated indexation. In times of low inflation or deflation, this can cause differences in break-even inflation rates implied by new issues and long-standing bonds even if they have the same maturity date. (In the UK, persistent deflation could cause an issue to be redeemed at less than par.)

■ Taxation differences. These can distort the relationship between inflation-linked and conventional government bonds. Tax treatment of inflation-linked bonds differs among countries. In the United States, for example, taxable investors must pay tax on both the real yield and the inflation accrual. So when inflation (or expected inflation) increases, a fall in TIPS' prices is needed to keep the after-tax real yield unchanged, and vice versa for reductions in inflation expectations. By contrast, in the UK income tax is levied only on the coupon of inflation-linked government bonds, not on the inflation compensation on the outstanding principal. So UK taxable investors may have an incentive to hold shorter dated index-linked bonds, as their tax treatment is more favourable than that of short-dated conventional bonds. To the extent that the prices of inflation-linked bonds are driven by taxable investors rather than tax-exempt investors, this can influence the break-even inflation rate.

■ Liquidity differences. Inflation-linked government bond markets are generally less liquid than conventional government bond markets. Investors value the option to be able to buy and sell investments at negligible cost, which is available from liquid government bond markets, and so the inflation-linked bond yield may contain a premium to compensate for its comparative illiquidity. This premium is likely to vary over time, and may at times be strongly influenced by the demand of long-term investors, who do not intend to trade their holdings.

■ Regulation and valuation rules for tax-exempt pension funds and insurance companies. These can cause concentrations of demand for particular segments of the conventional and inflation-linked markets, leading to valuation anomalies which require particularly long time horizons to arbitrage. This can be reflected in differences in break-even inflation rates over different maturities (and can represent investment opportunities for long-term investors who are guided by their own financial needs rather than arbitrary rules or benchmarks).

■ Biases in the measure of inflation used to index indexed bonds. Such biases are reflected in the break-even rate of inflation. For example, in the UK index-linked gilts are compensated for changes in the retail price index (RPI), and a combination of a different index weighting methodology and different coverage causes the RPI to increase by around 1% per year on average faster than the internationally comparable consumer prices index, although the difference is quite volatile. A consultation with interested parties (largely investors) to gauge support for a move towards international standards of measuring inflation found, not surprisingly, little support for change, which would have led to a fall in investment values. As a result, in the UK government bond market real interest rates are materially higher, and the break-even rate of inflation materially lower, than they appear to be.

These factors can cause the break-even rate to differ from an inflation forecast and these differences vary between countries, over time and even between maturities of bonds. The break-even rate is a readily available, crude "rule of thumb" for a market forecast of inflation, but these other factors need weighing before taking an investment decision. If a long-term investor has strong views that differ from the apparent market rate of inflation, these views can influence how the investor moves away from the safety of inflation-linked government bonds in implementing strategy. Investors whose safe-harbour investment is an inflation-linked government bond should have a strategic position in conventional government bonds if they expect conventional bonds to provide an adequate reward for expected inflation, including a margin for uncertainty.

What premium return should bond investors expect?

It is not normally in doubt that creditworthy governments will make the payments that are due on their debt, but how these payments on different types of government debt relate to each other is still unclear.

We know from the international comparison of 22 markets undertaken by Elroy Dimson and Paul Marsh, both emeritus professors of finance at London Business School, and Mike Staunton, director of the London Share Price Database at London Business School, that from 1900 to 2012 US long-dated bonds delivered a premium (geometric) return over Treasury bills of 0.8% a year and that the average for 21 countries outside the United States since 1900 was 0.5% per year. However, it is unclear how much premium, if any, should be expected from inflation-linked government bonds over Treasury bills. The experience to date is strongly influenced by the monetary policy background and the tax regime in the countries concerned and is too short to be conclusive.

John Campbell, Morton L. and Carole S. Olshan professor of economics at Harvard University, Robert Shiller, Arthur M. Okun professor of economics at Yale University, and Luis Viceira, George E. Bates professor at Harvard Business School, in their 2009 study "Understanding Inflation-Indexed Bond markets" highlight a number of different factors influencing the relationship between conventional and inflation-linked government bonds. Although there are good reasons to expect conventional government bonds to outperform index-linked over long periods, there are contrary influences that could cause them to underperform. Campbell, Shiller and Viceira conclude that the experience of recent years of marked short-term volatility and very low yields for inflation-linked government bonds does "not invalidate the basic case for these bonds, that they provide a safe asset for long-term investors".

The place of safe-harbour government bonds in strategy

The conclusions in deriving assumptions for modelling investment strategy (developed further in Chapter 5) can be summarised as follows:

- Inflation-linked bonds should provide a benchmark for long-term investors just as Treasury bills provide a benchmark for short-term investors.
- It is reasonable to assume that they will provide no premium return over Treasury bills in the medium term.

In the absence of inflation surprises, conventional bonds are likely to provide some inflation risk premium over inflation-linked bonds, but this may average no more than 0.25% per year. However, there may be an illiquidity premium in yields on inflation-linked bonds which offsets this. In the UK, biases in the official measure of inflation mean that UK real interest rates appear unusually low in comparison with other countries but, despite this, conventional gilts (UK government bonds) may outperform inflation-linked gilts by only a small margin in the future.

The most cautious long-term investors may have an anchor holding of inflation-linked bonds, but at times of lesser inflation uncertainty (or greater confidence in the monetary authorities' ability to restrict the range of future inflation), high-quality conventional bonds are likely to replace inflation-linked bonds as the core holdings of many long-term investors. This reflects both their greater liquidity (and so lower transaction costs and flexibility), a possible inflation risk premium and the convenience of their greater regular income distribution.

The equity risk premium

The Triumph of the Optimists is the title that Dimson, Marsh and Staunton gave the first edition, published in 2002, of their path-breaking review of returns since 1900 from stocks, bonds and cash in 17 countries (which has since been extended to 22 countries). Their message was that equity investors had done better than they should reasonably have hoped in the 20th century and that they should expect the 21st century to be less generous for long-term equity investors. As if on cue, the new century started terribly for equity investors, and despite a strong recovery after 2008, by December 2012 the total return on world equities in US dollars, after allowing for inflation, was just 1% ahead of the end-1999 level, and for most investors, after allowing for fees, trading costs and, for many investment accounts, taxation, would have been significantly behind. According to the Dimson, Marsh and Staunton data, 2008's total return, before fees and expenses, of −37% for US equities was the second worst calendar-year performance ever recorded for the United States; and for the world excluding the United States, 2008's performance of −43% was the worst on record. (Rolling 12-month data for the 1930s indicate much worse experiences in 1932.) For the ten years to December 2008 the return, again before expenses and also before allowing for inflation, for the US market was −0.6% a year, the first negative ten-year return since the 1930s; it was not until 2010 that the ten-year return was positive again.

So what performance should equity investors expect and how does it relate to the performance from bonds and cash? This is an area of great controversy and therefore uncertainty. This uncertainty matters and needs to be reflected in the design of investment strategy.

The starting point is history. In recent years much academic research into historic market performance has been published. The original pioneers in this were Roger Ibbotson, a professor in the practice of finance at Yale School of Management, and Rex Sinquefield, co-founder of money managers Dimensional Fund Advisors, who in 1976 jointly published long-run databases of carefully constructed returns data for the United States back to 1926. Shiller has extended this back to 1871. In the past few years this US work has been substantially extended, most notably by the Dimson, Marsh and Staunton international research.

The data conclusively show that, apart from two notable exceptions, in all countries covered by Dimson, Marsh and Staunton's work equities have, over the longest periods measured, outperformed both government bonds and Treasury bills and so risk-taking has eventually been rewarded. The two exceptions are Russia, where investors in stocks and bonds effectively lost everything in 1917, and mainland China, where investors lost almost everything in 1949. The more general and familiar pattern is highlighted in Figures 3.11 and 3.12, which show historic investment market performance from the perspective of investors with the US dollar or the UK pound as their base currency. Table 3.1 gives a summary of the performance and risk as revealed by the Dimson, Marsh and Staunton annual data

FIG 3.11 **US cash, government bonds and stockmarket cumulative performance**[a]

$, after inflation, 1900–2012, Dec 1899=1

a Performance before all costs, fees and taxes.
Source: Dimson E., Marsh P., Staunton M., 2013

FIG 3.12 **UK cash, government bonds and stockmarket cumulative performance**[a]

£, after inflation, 1900–2012, Dec 1899=1

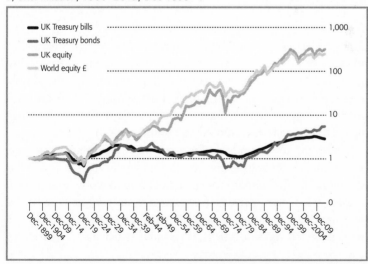

a Performance before all costs, fees and taxes.
Source: Dimson E., Marsh P., Staunton M., 2013

for 22 countries from 1900 to 2012, showing results for the world (as measured by these 22 countries) and the United States and the UK, the two most important national markets over the past century. In Table 3.1 the data incorporate the impact of the losses in Russia and China (Russia represented around 6% of world equity market capitalisation in 1899, while China was much smaller).

TABLE 3.1 **Long-run market performance and risk[a]**
After inflation but before all fees and expenses, 1900–2012

	Performance[b] % per year			Volatility % per year			Maximum cumulative decline %		
	World[c]	US	UK	World[c]	US	UK	World[c]	US	UK
Treasury bills	–	0.9	0.9	–	4.7	6.3	–	−46.5	−49.7
Bonds	1.8	2.0	1.5	11.5	10.3	13.7	−72.3	−62.7	−72.9
Equities	5.0	6.3	5.2	17.5	20.1	19.8	−60.2	−59.5	−70.6

a After inflation but before fees and expenses.
b Geometric annualised returns. Including impact of inflation on volatility of returns.
c World bond index is weighted by GDP; world equity index is weighted by capitalisation; world index returns and volatility are shown in dollars.
Source: Dimson, E., Marsh, P. and Staunton, M., 2002 and 2013

Recent experience and a close examination of the data reveal that this pattern of equity outperformance has sometimes taken a long time to assert itself. Figure 3.13 shows there have been long periods when equities have not outperformed cash or bonds. This applies not only to individual small markets, which are not well diversified, but also to the United States and the rest of the world.

Figure 3.13 shows underperformance by equities relative to long-dated bonds from 1980 to 2012 for the US equity market, from 1986 to 2012 for the UK, and from 1968 to 2012 for the world in aggregate. These are long-term periods in anyone's lifetime. Figure 3.14 shows the cumulative performance of equities relative to government bonds for a range of countries; there is nothing unusual in government

FIG 3.13 **Cumulative performance of equities relative to long-dated government bonds**
1899–2012

Source: Dimson, E., Marsh, P. and Staunton, M., 2002 and 2013

bonds failing to outperform equities over long periods. Figures 3.15 and 3.16 show the 20-year excess returns from equities over cash (Treasury bills) and long-dated Treasury bonds from the United States, the UK and the world, as measured by the 22 countries covered by the Dimson, Marsh and Staunton research. The figures indicate that the long-term underperformance by equities relative to government bonds in recent years had parallels in the 1930s and 1940s

Table 3.2 shows performance of equities, government bonds and cash separately for the longest periods to 2012 over which equities have underperformed government bonds. This shows that these instances reflect not the weakness of equity market performance but the unusual, and surely unrepeatable, performance of government bond markets. Equity market performance has not over these periods been unusual relative to cash nor in absolute terms (after inflation). A repeat of such performance over similar numbers of years by government bonds from the low level of bond yields in late 2013 is almost inconceivable, and although the returns from equity markets

FIG 3.14 **There are no free lunches: cumulative performance of equities relative to long-dated government bonds in leading markets**

Source: Dimson, E., Marsh, P. and Staunton, M., 2002 and 2013

FIG 3.15 **20-year equity risk premium over Treasury bills**
% per annum, 1919–2012

Source: Dimson, E., Marsh, P. and Staunton, M., 2002 and 2013

FIG 3.16 **20-year equity risk premium over government bonds**
% per annum, 1919–2012

Source: Dimson, E., Marsh, P. and Staunton, M., 2002 and 2013

shown in Table 3.2 are mostly higher than would on average be expected, they are comfortably within the range of likely outcomes.

So much for history: what matters for setting strategy is what we expect for the future. The majority view is that the 20th century was kinder to equity investors than they should reasonably have expected, and that the 21st century is likely to be pay-back time (because a margin of last century's performance was brought forward or "borrowed" from the future). The broad story is that a significant part of the outperformance of stockmarkets in the 20th century was because they started cheap and ended expensive, and that the process of becoming more expensive explains a significant part of their historic outperformance of both cash and bonds. Translating this into expectations for the future is impeded as there is disagreement about the normal level of the market, for example in relation to company earnings.

Some look for valuations of the stockmarket to revert towards the average from the past (see Chapter 4). However, others suggest that we should expect the stockmarket to be priced more expensively than on

TABLE 3.2 **Longest periods ending December 2012 of equities underperforming long-dated government bonds**[a]

	Geometric return % per year	Excess over cash % per year
US: Dec 1980–Dec 2012		
Cash	1.6	
Treasury bonds	7.2	5.4
Equities	7.1	5.3
UK: Dec 1986–Dec 2012		
Cash	2.5	
Treasury bonds	5.8	3.2
Equities	5.5	3.0
World: Dec 1968–Dec 2012		
Cash	0.9	
Treasury bonds	4.9	4.0
Equities	4.6	3.6

a After inflation and before fees, transaction costs and taxes.
Source: Derived from Dimson, E., Marsh, P. and Staunton, M., 2002 and 2013

average in the past because investors can now easily invest at less risk and less expensively because of the wider use of pooled funds, and especially index funds and well-diversified exchange traded funds. If investors can access the market less expensively, that raises the equity risk premium for those investors. There is apparent consensus that bond returns in recent decades have been unsustainable, as yields have been driven to historic low levels, and that going forward bond performance will be disappointing, either because bond yields will recover (as the markets are predicting) and so prices will tend to fall, or because yields will stay low for a long period and so provide a modest return. There is a range of views as to where government bond yields will stabilise. In the interim, for equities to be expected to perform poorly relative to bonds, they would need to be thought expensive in 2013.

At the turn of the century finance experts differed on prospects for the superior return that should be earned from equity investing, and those differences show no sign of abating. There is increasing (but not consensus) agreement that medium-term prospects need to take some account of whether the market is cheap or expensive at the outset. A variation on this is that since market risk evidently fluctuates, investors should want and expect a higher risk premium when the market is more volatile. This may coincide with times that the market is less expensive, but it might not. Although this sounds like common sense, there is also agreement that it is difficult to exploit valuation indicators to earn higher returns, and there would be quite wide support for the idea that it is fruitless to adjust expectations used in long-term planning except when the stockmarket appears to be either unusually expensive or unusually cheap. Another complication is that the relevant expected equity risk premium will vary from one investor to another. For example, if the margin over Treasury bills or bonds at which investors can borrow for a mortgage increases, they may find it more attractive to prepay their mortgage rather than invest in equities for their pension.

Lower estimates of future returns are produced by researchers who believe that the stockmarket is expensive. A survey of the future geometric average annual returns from equity investing (measured as a premium over the risk-free rate) in 2001 ranged from zero to 7%, with an average of just below 4%. There is increasing agreement that at some times the risk premium may be higher than at other times. A more recent range of projections would be similar, with the average close to 4%. But this is by no means universally agreed. In 2011, Rob Arnott, chairman of Research Affiliates, an investment manager, wrote:

> This brief history lesson illuminates that the much-vaunted 4–5% risk premium for stocks is unreliable and a dangerous assumption on which to make our future plans. In our view, a more reasonable analysis would suggest 2–3%, which is the historic risk premium absent the rise in valuation multiples in the past 30 years.

Dimson, Marsh and Staunton, in their 2013 Credit Suisse Global Investment Returns Yearbook, say "we infer that investors expect an equity premium (relative to bills) of around 3–3½%" as a geometric average for world equities, and conclude that a reasonable premium for investing in long-dated government bonds is close to 1% per annum. This would mean that they infer that the expected equity premium return over government bonds is a bit over 2–2½%. By contrast, a rather more optimistic prospect is offered by Peng Chen of Morningstar Investment Management, who in 2011 projected a 20-year geometric average return from US equities of 7.6%, a premium of 3.3% per year above 20-year US Treasury bonds and 5.0% per year ahead of Treasury bills. These approaches involve various ways of projecting the different sources of return that comprise the equity market return, and adjusting for factors that cannot be relied on in the future (such as the market becoming ever more expensive).

Corporate finance asks a different but related question: what market rate of return above the rate guaranteed by the government is required by businesses to tempt them to invest? Pablo Fernandez and Javier Aguirreamalloa, together with Luis Corres, all of IESE Business School at the University of Navarra in Barcelona, have published the results of internet surveys of assessments of required rates of return from academics, investment analysts and business executives. Their 2012 survey produced over 7,000 responses from 82 countries, of which 52% were from five countries: the United States, Spain, Germany, the UK and Italy. These show a noticeable pattern: the median responses from developed countries tend to be grouped between 5% and 6%, while for emerging markets they most commonly lie between 7% and 9%.

The standard MBA corporate finance textbook, *Principles of Corporate Finance*, by Richard Brealey, Stewart Myers and Franklin Allen, provides a sceptical view of this debate. As the authors point out:

> *Many financial managers and economists believe that long-run historical returns are the best measure available ... out of this debate only one firm conclusion emerges: Do not trust anyone who claims to know what returns investors expect.*

This perspective reflects a view that the pattern of stockmarket returns is essentially a random walk – that is, a matter of rolling the dice from one period to another. As mentioned above, there is though increasing support for the view that the level of the stockmarket (and the level of bond market prices) can tell us whether returns will be higher or lower in the period ahead. This is considered in more detail in the next chapter.

This debate does not much affect the likelihood of next year's equity market performance being disappointing. However, it does have a large impact on the prospects for wealth accumulation from equities over long periods, particularly the potential for disappointing returns from equity markets over extended periods. The one thing any investor can do to raise their expected returns from equity investing is to be vigilant about the fees that they pay; this also has a large impact on wealth accumulation over extended periods of time.

Equity risk: don't bank on time diversifying risk

The size of the equity risk premium would be of less concern if it was true that equities are "less risky" for long-term investors than for short-term investors. This is a separate area of debate with strong differences of opinion – and therefore much confusion – among investors. But what are the experts saying?

The longer the time horizon the more likely it is that stockmarket indices will outperform bonds or cash, simply because on average stocks are expected to perform better. Furthermore, the longer the period the more likely it is that this cumulative outperformance will translate into an increasingly large proportion of the initial investment. Long-term investors in equities should expect to do better on average than investors in bonds or cash, and the longer the period of time, the better in monetary terms they should expect, on average, to do. So long as equity investors are offered a positive risk premium, which more than outweighs the extra investment management fees they pay, this should be uncontroversial.

The real issue is the risk of disappointing results over longer periods of time and how this can compound into an increasingly large shortfall, and how strongly investors should be assumed to want to avoid the pain caused by such shortfalls. This has always been a central focus of finance, and it has been brought into even sharper focus through the work on loss aversion in behavioural finance. The experimental work on loss aversion discussed in Chapter 2 suggests that investors are probably twice as sensitive to the prospect of losses as they are to gains.

For long periods (up to 20 years or so), the risks of equities underperforming long term bonds and cash are not negligible, even though equities are, on average, expected to outperform bonds and cash by a wide cumulative margin. Figures 3.14, 3.15 and 3.16 show this vividly and more persuasively than would a quantitative model whose assumptions will always be subject to debate, and therefore doubt.

Table 3.3 shows the results of just such a modelling exercise in which 2,000 possible outcomes for equity markets have been simulated by replicating the summary characteristics of how the US markets have behaved since 1900. Of course, actual experience is only one of many possible outcomes. The table shows a range of outcomes, from the disappointing 5th percentile outcome, through the median or 50th percentile outcome to the favourable 95th percentile outcome, and it shows these simulated results over 5, 10 and 20 years. It also shows that in at least half of the modelled scenarios equities far outperform bonds and cash over each period, with the potential in strongly favourable markets for substantial outperformance. Nevertheless, the 5th percentile unfavourable outcome for equities is shown lagging behind cash and bonds over each period.

In recent years, there has been growing agreement that the standard statistical assumptions underlying Table 3.3 understate short-term risk (crashes happen more often than the models assume) and might overstate long-term equity risk. This is because a body of academic research supports the widely held view that, to some extent, markets "overreact" (in relation to the standard assumptions underlying the table). If this is true, then if investment returns have been above average, they are likely subsequently to come down, and if they have been below average, they are likely to increase. This process of overreaction, where good market performance is expected to be followed by poorer performance, is called "mean reversion". A result of this is that equity markets would vary less over time than

TABLE 3.3 **Does time diversify away the risk of disappointing equity market performance?**

	100% Treasury bills as low-risk strategy			100% Treasury bonds as low-risk strategy		
	5 years	**10 years**	**20 years**	**5 years**	**10 years**	**20 years**
$100 in low-risk strategy "becomes", after inflation[a]	105	110	121	111	123	152
$100 in all equity strategy "becomes"[b]						
95th percentile	263	482	1,305	263	482	1,305
50th percentile	135	182	331	135	182	331
5th percentile	69	69	84	69	69	84

a 50th percentile outcomes for bonds and Treasury bills shown.
b Using the North American convention of counting percentiles from the most disappointing outcomes.
Source: Author's calculations based on historical volatilities and returns using Dimson, Marsh and Staunton data for returns, after inflation, for US stocks, bonds and cash, 1900–2012

traditional models would suggest. If this is true, stockmarket volatility measured over, say, decades or 20-year periods would be "less" than would be expected if we were simply to extrapolate short-term volatility. However, the degree to which it is the case is controversial, particularly among academic researchers.

The simple, easy-to-use modelling that underlies Table 3.3 (and many savings planning exercises) has been widely criticised. But these approaches continue to be used, partly because there is no agreement on how to replace them. However, the weakness of these models needs to be reflected in how wealth planning is presented. An expectation that a risk-based strategy is likely, but not certain, to achieve an objective is often reassuring enough. If investors want more certainty (for their "safety-first" portfolio – see Chapter 2), the underlying investment strategy needs to be based on hedging using tailored inflation-linked or conventional government bonds. Often the honest message is that the price of such insurance is too high, and many investors have little choice but to live with a significant degree of uncertainty.

FIG 3.17 **Frequency of equity outperformance of bonds, overlapping 5-year periods**
%, 1900–2012

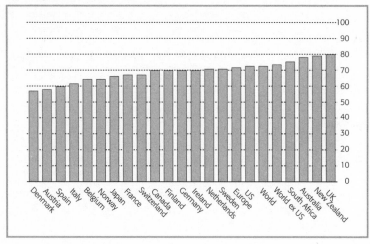

Source: Dimson, E., Marsh, P. and Staunton, M., 2002 and 2013

FIG 3.18 **Frequency of equity outperformance of bonds, overlapping 20-year periods**
%, 1900–2012

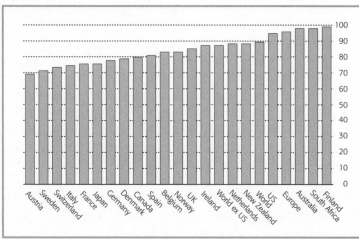

Source: Dimson, E., Marsh, P. and Staunton, M., 2002 and 2013

At present, the best guide to the risk of equities underperforming cash or bonds is given by examining the historical data. As discussed above, the prevailing view of finance academics is that the 21st century is likely to be less favourable to equity markets than the 20th century was. Furthermore, allowance needs to be made for the drag of investment fees and transaction costs and, where relevant, for tax. So a reasonable assumption would be that the incidence of disappointing equity markets will be higher in the 21st century than it was in the 20th. The first decade was certainly consistent with this.

The international pattern for equities underperforming bonds over rolling five-year and 20-year periods is illustrated in Figures 3.17 and 3.18. These show that for US and world equities over the past 109 years, stocks have outperformed bonds in just over 70% of rolling five-year periods. For periods of 20 years, the frequency of equities outperforming bonds rises to 95% for US equities and 89% for world equities, although it is lower than 80% in almost half of the individual countries with a full track record. As recent experience shows, the risk of equity strategies underperforming safe-haven investment strategies over long periods needs to be taken seriously. These are not remote events to be dismissed as exceptional bad luck: these things happen.

4 How should and how do investor strategies evolve?

Model investment strategies

The debate about what returns to expect from the stockmarket is partly a debate between those who think that stockmarket performance over time can best be explained as a statistical "random walk", where forecasting is pointless but on average risk-taking gets rewarded, and those who think that market returns are mean reverting, with higher than average returns being followed by periods of disappointing returns and vice versa. This debate has important implications for the design of investment strategy and the role of long-term model allocations between stocks, bonds, cash and other asset classes. These are sometimes called "strategic asset allocations" or "policy portfolios". The role of such models, and how they help to differentiate between investors with different appetites for taking risk, is discussed in Chapter 5, but an important feature is that they anchor actual investments around the model allocations, no matter what is happening in markets.

In 2003 Peter Bernstein wrote an article in the *Economics and Portfolio Strategy* newsletter titled "Are policy portfolios obsolete?" This question has probably become more relevant with the passage of time. In 2008, adherence to fixed long-term asset allocation models led many investors to experience declines in investment values that exceeded their worst-case expectations. In 2003 Bernstein wrote: "Investment policy in today's environment should be opportunistic, to be played more by ear than by rigid policy allocations." He went on to quote Keynes, who wrote in 1924:

[The] long run is a misleading guide to current affairs. In the long run we are all dead. Economists set themselves too easy, too useless a task if in the tempestuous seasons they can only tell us that when the storm is long past the ocean will be flat.

Underlying the criticism of fixed long-term investment strategies is a belief that analysis can tell us whether markets are cheap or expensive, and that when a market is expensive the risk of losing money is increased. Few claim to be able to predict when a market will correct, but they do not doubt that markets do eventually correct, or that they revert to their average relationships. A similar but slightly different criticism of long-term strategy models is that markets experience different regimes or environments and that investment policy ought to respond to the different market conditions that they represent.

The notion of different market climates can best be illustrated by looking at how stockmarket volatility has fluctuated over the years, and of how the pricing of the stockmarket has evolved. Figure 4.1 shows the leading indicator and measure of stockmarket volatility, VIX, from 1990 to 2013. It highlights both the extraordinary increase in stockmarket volatility in 2007–09 and also how benign the market environment appears to have between 2003 and 2007. Since VIX reflects option pricing, it indicates fluctuations in the cost of insuring against a stockmarket crash, this being low when VIX is low and high when VIX is high. Figure 4.1 also shows what would be described as regime changes. Almost any investment strategy had a much higher risk of exceeding some threshold tolerance for negative returns in the more volatile environment of 2008–09 than when it was more moderate. This suggests that investors who are particularly sensitive to the risk of losing money should attempt to return towards their safe haven of government bonds or cash when market volatility increases. One practical issue with this is that a sudden increase in market volatility is likely to have been caused by a sudden fall in prices, making such a response a reaction to recent losses.

FIG 4.1 **VIX indicator of US stockmarket volatility**
Jan 1990–Oct 2013

Source: www.cboe.com

Risk-taking and portfolio rebalancing

At times of market turmoil, measures of volatility increase and the value of risk assets falls. Any investor who has benchmark allocations to risk assets and conservative assets (see Chapter 5) will then be underweight risk assets but overweight safe assets. In these circumstances, investment advisers – who, as discussed in Chapter 1, may enjoy taking risk more than their clients do – often recommend rebalancing back towards the strategic allocations and, for example, taking profits on government bonds and reinvesting the proceeds in risk assets. At times of great stress in markets, opportunities to rebalance will be greatest. At such times, this counter-cyclical policy is not for the faint hearted. It provides liquidity to distressed sellers and increases risk-taking in "bad times" when risk premiums may be unusually high. If markets tend to overreact and "mean revert", this added risk-taking will be a source of added value

Automatic rebalancing is a natural role for a long-term investor, but it is a way of taking more risk when others wish to take less (or avoid taking more) as market volatility increases. It is a mechanism for selling government bonds (and liquidity) when their price is high and buying government bonds (and maintaining liquidity) when others are increasing their exposure to illiquid assets. It is also a way for investors to anchor policy to a previously agreed strategy that was justified with reference to past long-term averages for market risks, which are unlikely to reflect the circumstances at the time of the rebalancing.

The argument that markets overreact and then revert towards trend or even overshoot in the opposite direction is closely related to the arguments in favour of a value style of equity investing (see Chapter 7). A persuasive analysis in this tradition is that developed by Andrew Smithers, chairman of Smithers & Co, and Stephen Wright of Birkbeck College London. They have built on the analysis of the late James Tobin, formerly the Sterling professor of economics at Yale University, who suggested that the stockmarket valuation of a company should be related to the replacement value of its assets minus its liabilities.

Figure 4.2 shows this measure, called Tobin's Q, of stockmarket value since 1900. The horizontal line shows its average value, highlighting an unprecedented peak at the end of the 1990s and a sharp decline in 2000. The dip between 2007 and 2008 is less than might have been expected because of the substantial write-offs of capital in the dominant financial sector during the credit crisis. This is only one indicator, but it provides a warning sign that when Q has been well above average, subsequent performance is more likely to be disappointing, and when Q has been well below average, subsequent performance is more likely to be good. If this is accepted, model allocations to equities should reflect market valuations and not be cast in stone. Over the ten years after the ratio reached the three most extreme lows since 1900, the US equity market performed strongly, whereas following the peaks of 1929 and 1999 performance was poor.

Figure 4.3 shows Robert Shiller's cyclically adjusted price/earnings ratio, also known as CAPE, or the "Shiller PE". The Shiller PE is the ratio of the inflation-adjusted level of the S&P composite stock price index to the inflation-adjusted ten-year moving average of the reported earnings of the companies in the index. Shiller made considerable

FIG 4.2 **Tobin's Q: ratio of the market value of US corporate equity to replacement cost**
1900–Mar 2013

Sources: Wright, S., Smithers, A., Shiller, R.; US Federal Reserve, updated

use of this indicator of stockmarket value in his book *Irrational Exuberance*, the publication of which in early 2000 coincided with the peak overvaluation, as indicated by Figure 4.3, since stockmarket records began. The Shiller PE focuses on the valuation that the stockmarket places on the ten-year historic stream of corporate earnings, whereas Tobin's Q is measuring the relationship between a company's stockmarket valuation and its net worth. Nevertheless, the two measures show essentially the same story (compare Figures 4.2 and 4.3). Shiller and Smithers both use their metrics to describe stockmarket overreaction and reversion to the mean. Shiller, for example, includes a chart relating the value of the Shiller PE to the subsequent ten-year performance of the stockmarket: for well over 100 years, high levels of the Shiller PE have tended to be followed by relatively poor stockmarket performance, and low levels of the Shiller PE by better-than-average performance.

With hindsight, few would dispute the importance of the message these two indicators give at extremes of valuation, and this emphasises the benefits of being able to adjust strategy. In the

FIG 4.3 **S&P 500 "Shiller" price/earnings ratio**
1881–2013

Source: Shiller, R., *Irrational Exuberance*, as updated, www.econ.yale.edu/~shiller/data.htm

interests of designing a more profitable forecasting tool, some have suggested adjustments (for example, in calculating the Shiller PE, by taking account of the trend in earnings rather than their average level, after inflation). Others look for reasons why the normal value of the stockmarket might be higher today than in the past (for example, as discussed in Chapter 3, since investors can much more easily and cheaply acquire a diversified exposure to the market, the stockmarket may be a less risky place to invest). Nevertheless, at extremes of market valuation, Tobin's Q and the Shiller PE have both proved to be reliable indicators of subsequent stockmarket performance.

The equity market is not alone in showing valuations revert towards trend. Figure 4.4 shows for the United States, the UK and the euro zone the difference between the yields on single A-rated investment grade debt indices (see Chapter 8) and indices of government debt (Germany in the case of the euro zone). Differences between the indices mean that the comparisons in Figure 4.4 are indicative rather than exact measures, but corporate bond yields provide another indicator of value that seems to range between periods of offering too little reward for risk-taking (as immediately before the credit crunch)

FIG 4.4 **Spread between single A credit indices and highest-rated government bond indices**
% per year, Dec 1998–Sep 2013

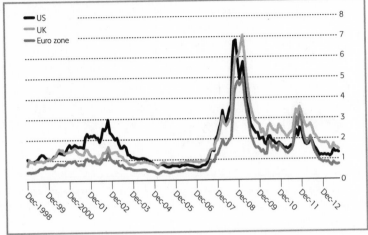

Source: Derived from Barclays index data

and periods of offering the prospect of generous risk-adjusted returns. This is discussed further in Chapter 8.

Figures 4.1–4.4 reflect the incidence of booms and busts in risk asset markets. Advice to avoid speculative excess is easier to give than to implement successfully. In practice, success does not come easily to professional investment managers who seek to time markets, and some consultants have at times given up trying to identify managers who can add value in this way. The equity bear market of 2008–09 was much more severe than that of 2000–02, which followed a boom in technology, media and telecoms stocks, but with a few notable exceptions, the 2008–09 equity bear market was much less well anticipated in advance. The buoyant credit markets in 2005–07 were much more commonly seen as offering inadequate prospective returns than were equity markets. The difficulty of anticipating events presents a major challenge for investors, and it echoes a comment made in August 2002 by Alan Greenspan, then chairman of the US Federal Reserve. Looking back on the unwinding of the late 1990s equity market boom, which he had anticipated by publicly voicing concerns about "irrational exuberance" over three years prior to the market peak in early 2000, at a level 80% higher than when he gave his warning, Greenspan said:

> As events evolved, we recognised that, despite our suspicions, it was very difficult to definitively identify a bubble until after the fact – that is, when its bursting confirmed its existence.

Greenspan's comments should encourage people to be modest about their ability to call markets successfully. This sense of modesty encourages some to argue that long-term investors should stick close to their strategic asset allocations and buy-and-hold equities through thick and thin. The reasoning behind this recommendation is that market timing is hazardous and, for many advisers, equities are less risky for long-term investors. John Campbell and others agree that equities seem to be less risky over long time horizons than is suggested by their short-run volatility because equities "mean revert". If this is correct, Campbell argues that investors should overweight equities when they are expected to perform better than average and underweight them when they are expected to do worse than average. Many would say that this is "easier said than done, except after the event".

Following 2008, the more usual concern was the dilemma of how to react to unusually low government bond yields. "Quantitative easing" by central banks was initially designed to relieve financial market distress in 2008–09 and then evolved into supporting the economy (and, in the euro zone, of relieving the crisis in peripheral government bond markets). The US Federal Reserve and the Bank of England acquired in excess of one-quarter of the US and UK national debts respectively (while the European Central Bank and the Bank of Japan greatly facilitated their lending to banks). In the United States and the UK, these bond-buying programmes (including in the United States purchases of mortgages by the Federal Reserve) were intended to reduce the yields on low-risk assets and so lower the cost of borrowing, whether for mortgages or for business. In the process, existing holders of Treasury bonds were enticed to sell, and presumably to buy higher-risk assets instead. Quantitative easing was

FIG 4.5 **US Treasury 10-year constant maturity yields**
% per year, Jan 1962–Sep 2013

Source: US Federal Reserve

a policy intended to force cautious investors to take more risk than they would normally wish to, and in so doing Treasury bond prices were forced higher. Figure 4.5 shows ten-year US Treasury bond yields over the 51 years after 1962: between April 2012 and April 2013, these averaged 1.8%, compared with an average of 6.7% over the previous 50 years. Central bank purchasing of large segments of the Treasury market was an evident distortion that was to some degree responsible for these extraordinarily low bond yields. The dilemma for investors was how to respond to this distortion, and how long would it take to unwind.

Set against this background, Bernstein's criticisms of buy-and-hold approaches to wealth management look even more relevant. The price of an investment should matter, and there is a price at which it makes sense to exchange the assurance of a high-quality government bond for a cheaper, less well-suited or less secure substitute. The first steps may be the easiest, as portfolio rebalancing leads to sales of government bonds. However, many advisers will suggest going beyond this and scaling back considerably exposure to the security of government bonds. One of the biggest problems facing investors who accept this is that no one knows how much Treasury yields have been influenced by central bank purchases (though various estimates exist) or how much continuing influence on yields will be felt by the presence of the US Federal Reserve and Bank of England as long-term holders of Treasury bonds. In other words, no one really knows the "fair" price for a Treasury bond. This is a major difficulty for those investors who were persuaded to sell their core holdings of government bonds, because they were too expensive, but who need to decide when to return to the assurance of Treasury bonds.

The years since 2007 have radically altered the investment environment for any investor. Bernstein's call for investment policy to be "opportunistic, to be played more by ear than by rigid policy allocations" surely applies to such a change in the investment landscape. In practice, the broadest patterns of asset allocation have not changed markedly for different groups of investors in the five years after 2007, although there have been important changes in detail, often continuations of trends which were evident before the global financial crisis, rather than arising in response to it.

The evolution of wealth and its investment since 2002

Table 4.1 shows estimates of the wealth of selected categories of investor in 2002, 2007 and 2012; Table 4.2 shows their allocation to different broad categories of investment. Table 4.1 is not comprehensive – for example, it does not include insurance companies – and some of the data (for example, for global private clients) unavoidably involve a significant degree of estimation, exchange rate fluctuations can distort the data, and there is some overlap between the categories. Nevertheless, Table 4.1 gives an indication of broad trends in the evolution of wealth.

The highlight of Table 4.1 is the contrast between the rapid accumulation of wealth by all categories of investors in the five years to 2007 and its slow growth, for most investors, in the subsequent five years. The shortfall from previous expectations will have been worse than suggested by the change in value of investment funds. The reduction in long-term interest rates between 2007 and 2012 will have

TABLE 4.1 **Indicators of global investable assets**

Total assets, $bn

	2002	2007	2012
Global private clients	27,200	40,700	46,200
Global pension funds	14,259	24,680	28,279
US employer-sponsored defined contribution pension plans	1,120	2,516	2,865
US individual retirement accounts	1,061	2,306	2,470
US endowments	225	411	406
Sovereign wealth funds	634	2,355	4,118
Central bank foreign-exchange reserves	2,408	6,704	10,951

Five-year growth in total assets, %

	2007	2012
Global private clients	50	14
Global pension funds	73	15
US employer-sponsored defined contribution pension plans	125	14
US individual retirement accounts	117	7
US endowments	83	−1
Sovereign wealth funds	271	75
Central bank foreign-exchange reserves	178	63

	2002	2007	2012
Average yield on 20-year US Treasury bonds, %	5.4	4.9	2.5
Average yield on long-dated US TIPS, %	3.1	2.3	0.2

Sources
Global high net worth financial investments: Capgemini and Merrill Lynch Wealth Management "World Wealth Report" 2003; Capgemini and RBC Wealth Management "World Wealth Report" 2013. "High net worth" refers to individuals with at least $1m financial wealth
Global pension funds: Towers Watson "Global Pension Asset Study" 2012. Data refer to a sub-sample of the seven largest pension fund markets, Australia, Canada, Japan, Netherlands, Switzerland, UK, US
US employer-defined contribution pension plans and individual retirement accounts: The Investment Company Institute, www.ici.org/research/stats
US endowments: NACUBO-Commonfund Study of Endowments 2012; NACUBO Endowment Study 2002, 2007
Sovereign wealth funds: Institutional Investor's Sovereign Wealth Center, www.sovereignwealthcenter.com
Central bank foreign-exchange reserves: IMF, "Composition of Foreign Exchange Reserves". Gold holdings are excluded from these totals
Bond yields: US Federal Reserve

halved the income they could safely withdraw without undermining their fund's capital. Allowance for inflation would have reduced this still further. In this environment investors will have felt severely constrained. By the summer of 2013, a recovery in bond yields had noticeably increased sustainable income levels for investors. The two categories of investor whose wealth increased substantially in the five years to 2012 were sovereign wealth funds (see below) and central foreign-exchange reserves (which in aggregate were twice the value of SWFs at the end of 2012). The increase in assets of SWFs was driven by buoyant oil and gas revenues. The impact of the quite sudden arrival of a new, rapidly growing group of substantial investors may have been to support the prices of those assets they particularly wished to hold (listed equities and alternative investments, see below). This is turn will have brought forth additional investment opportunities.

What is a sovereign wealth fund?

Sovereign wealth funds (SWFs) are government-owned investment funds, and they typically arise from persistent balance-of-payments and budget surpluses when a country's foreign exchange reserves become much larger than necessary to meet their traditional role, which is the maintenance of foreign exchange stability. Some investment funds that are owned by regional governments are also commonly classified as SWFs.

SWFs are often funded from the sale of non-renewable mineral wealth, such as oil and gas. The investment strategy of a SWF has a much longer time horizon than that of a country's foreign exchange reserves. Reserve management typically focuses on highest quality short- or medium-term government securities, whereas SWFs invest for the longer term and seek to earn a risk premium by investing in a broad spectrum of both risky and more cautious investments.

One characteristic of SWFs is that they have shown that they can grow from modest beginnings to a large size over a relatively short period of time. This differentiates them from other institutional investors, such as insurance companies and traditional pension funds, whose importance in an economy tends to evolve more gradually.

TABLE 4.2 **Pattern of asset allocation by global investors**
%

Global high net worth financial investments

	2013[a]
Equities	26
Fixed income	16
Real estate[b]	20
Alternative investments	10
Cash/deposits	28

Global pension funds

	2002	2007	2012
Equities	50	55	47
Bonds	38	28	33
Other	9	15	19
Cash	3	2	1

US employer-sponsored defined contribution pension plans

	2002	2007	2011
US equities	57	52	43
International equities	7	17	13
Listed equities	64	69	56
Hybrid[c]	11	16	22
Bonds	12	9	15
Cash	12	6	6

US individual retirement accounts

	2002	2007	2011
US equities	51	46	38
International equities	8	17	13
Listed equities	59	63	51
Hybrid[c]	10	17	20
Bonds	15	10	19
Cash	16	10	10

US endowments

	2002	2007	2012
Listed equities	50.2	47.4	31.0
Fixed income	23.4	12.9	11.0
Alternatives	24.3	37.4	54.0
Cash & other	2.2	2.2	4.0

Sovereign wealth funds (equally weighted averages)

	2002	2007	2012
Listed equities	42.6	46.7	46.7
Fixed income & cash	48.1	40.7	29.3
Alternatives	9.4	12.6	24.0

a March.
b Excludes primary residences.
c Also known as balanced funds; they include equities and bonds.
Sources: As for Table 4.1

Table 4.2 gives a broad indication of asset allocation of private clients, pension funds, endowments and sovereign wealth funds in 2012 or early 2013 and indications of changes in allocations between markets in the five years before the global financial crisis, and in the five years after its onset in 2007–08. Before drawing conclusions about the degree of change suggested by the table recall that all investments have to be owned: when one investor decides to sell, another buys, although it might take a change in price to complete a transaction. This makes it unlikely that aggregated investment data such as those in Table 4.2 will show marked shifts in allocations, except as a reflection of price changes, or over time, as the supply of different types of investment changes in response to market demand.

Table 4.2 shows moves before 2007 into listed equities by pension funds and US individual retirement savings plans (where the move was focused on international equities) and then away from listed equities by the same investors in the following five years. The data for the asset allocation for wealthy individuals are taken from the Capgemini, RBC Wealth Management and Scorpio Partnership Global

HNW Insights Survey of March 2013. The broad pattern it reveals, which is consistent with earlier surveys carried out before the financial crisis using a different methodology, is the well-diversified and generally cautious deployment of much private wealth. In early 2013, cash and deposits represented over 20% of the financial wealth of millionaires worldwide, with such caution characterising investors of all levels.

One common theme across different categories of investors, which was evident before 2007, is the increase in allocations to alternatives, the catch-all category for unlisted investments including real estate, hedge funds and private equity. US university endowments have led the way in this trend, and their importance (particularly that of the Harvard and Yale endowments) in setting trends in global asset allocation far exceeds their size (comparable to many large pension or insurance funds). David Swensen, the long-standing chief investment officer at Yale University, published *Pioneering Portfolio Management: An Unconventional Approach to Institutional Investment* in 2000, highlighting the attractions of investing in alternatives. This provided a reference book for what has become known as the "endowment model" for asset allocation, with the prospect of superior diversification enabling enhanced returns for the same level of risk. This has been an important influence on advice given to institutional investors around the world both before and since the financial crisis. The experience during 2008–09 of investors in illiquid alternatives highlighted the potential for large adverse swings in cash flow from programmes in illiquid investments in "bad times" (when the demand to meet commitments may be surprisingly high, and the cash flow generated by the investments surprisingly low). Nevertheless, the prospect of earning attractive excess returns from alternative investments continues to be reflected in growing allocations to alternatives by all categories of investors, with the "endowment model" of asset allocation having morphed in some consultants' recommendations to both institutional and private clients into multi-asset or hybrid funds, sometimes called "diversified growth funds", which embrace a growing range of alternative and mainstream asset classes.

Liquid alternative investments

Much private wealth has a shorter and less predictable time horizon than institutional wealth. This helps explain why private investors are likely to be less willing than institutional investors to make long-term commitments to illiquid investments. As one wealth manager quoted in the Money Management Institute's 2012 annual report put it:

> We don't use private equity much. This is great for Yale or Harvard. But it is illiquid, and clients just don't get it. Death and divorce are too disruptive.

Many private investors are nevertheless persuaded of the merits of a liquid, marketable variation on the "endowment model" of asset allocation, and a number of alternative assets are available in highly liquid investment vehicles. These include a new breed of "hedged mutual funds", which have grown rapidly in popularity in North America and Europe. These typically focus on liquid hedge fund strategies, including long-short equities, currency strategies, and commodity or managed futures funds (see Chapter 9) and comprise liquid underlying investments. Furthermore, in real estate and private equity, although the underlying investments are illiquid, real estate investment trusts (REITs) and listed private equity funds give investors ready access to these markets, but with the scope for large variations in the premium or discount of the market price to the assessed value of the underlying investments (see Chapters 8 and 9). In addition, Chapter 9 discusses the development of liquid hedge fund strategies, which seek to replicate, at low cost and with high transparency, the risk and return characteristics of the average hedge fund. They can also be used to target sources of risk and return which are not available in equity and bond markets, and which provide one of the traditional reasons for investing in hedge funds.

Alternative assets do not need to be illiquid, and are not the exclusive preserve of institutional investors. According to the Money Management Institute, US mutual funds and exchange traded funds (ETFs) that focus on providing hedge fund or commodity-based investment strategies grew from $117 billion in 2007 to $368 billion by March 2012.

The opportunity for improved diversification by accessing different types of systematic risk (see Chapter 9) is one of the expected benefits of investing in alternative assets, and is a principal insight of the "endowment model" that should be available to investors in "liquid alternatives". However, three of the further benefits institutions hope to gain by investing in alternatives may not be readily available to investors in their marketable alternatives. The first is a liquidity premium: when investors buy a private (that is, unlisted) investment they should do so on the understanding that they are acquiring it on better terms than if the investment was highly liquid. Readily marketable versions of the endowment model should not be expected to offer this benefit (although they might, particularly if they trade at a discount). A second advantage that institutional investors hope to secure is access to unusually skilled managers, for whom there may be restricted access. A third, and most important, benefit is that large investment funds ought to have an advantage in securing advantageous fee terms, which will not be available to a much smaller investor.

However, one of the central lessons of 2008 was that in "bad times" the correlations between risk assets increase noticeably, and that although alternatives – whether liquid or illiquid – may offer some diversification from equities, despite the increase in correlations, that is scant consolation in "bad times". If you really want to diversify performance risk in bad times, or to hedge your liabilities, keep a significant part of your wealth in government bonds. Risk assets do not achieve either of these objectives: they are risk assets.

In subsequent chapters other significant trends in asset allocation are highlighted. There is a global trend to lessen the home bias in equity investing; there has been a rapid move away from investing in funds of hedge funds; and most of all, many investors around the world, having sold US Treasury and mortgage bonds to the Federal Reserve and UK government bonds to the Bank of England at historically high prices, are wondering at what yield to buy back the assurance offered by government bonds.

5 The time horizon and the shape of strategy: keep it simple

An appropriate role for strategy models

This chapter discusses investment strategy models for investors with different tolerances for shortfall risk and with different time horizons for investing. One of the great insights of modern portfolio theory, which should be used in designing model portfolio strategies, is the portfolio separation theorem of the late James Tobin. Tobin suggested that the degree of investor risk aversion only influenced the allocation of an investment strategy between risky and cautious investments. As Willem Buiter, global chief economist at Citigroup, wrote in 2003 in an appreciation of Tobin's contribution to economics:

> This is an important and beautiful result, which is not done justice by Tobin's own summary: "Don't put all your eggs in one basket". Indeed, Tobin's remarkable result is better summarised as "regardless of your degree of risk aversion and caution, you will only need two baskets for all your eggs".

A great deal of damage was done to investors' wealth in 2007–09 because investment advisers lost sight of this essential principle, partly because they thought they had discovered new and improved ways of diversifying investment portfolios which falsely offered the benefits of security at higher rates of return. (See Appendix 4 for further comments on the portfolio separation theorem.) One dilemma facing investors in the second decade of the 21st century is how to benefit from Tobin's insight while making some adjustments to allow for the historic low rates of interest paid on high-quality government debt. Cautious advisers choose to stay quite close to Tobin's insight.

Asset allocation models: an essential discipline

Chapter 4 opened with a criticism by the late Peter Bernstein of fixed asset allocation policy models. Bernstein's policy portfolios are what others call strategic asset allocations or high-level benchmarks. He argued that the usefulness of such model allocations is undermined by fluctuating market volatility and changes in investment opportunities as market prices change. Despite this, many investors – including the largest sovereign wealth funds, university endowments and public pension funds, as well as large investment houses which advise a wide range of investors and many boutique investment firms – make use of formal or informal policy portfolios. These provide a framework against which the management of investments is anchored, often within pre-agreed limits. They help to express an attitude to risk-taking (even though it is known that market volatility fluctuates), and in particular an attitude to the division of investments between safe-harbour and risk assets. They also express an attitude to liquidity and provide a context for a review of investments and investment opportunities as well as performance.

The role of anchoring is particularly important: an investment adviser may think that safe-haven government bonds are undesirably expensive, and may recommend moving quite a long way from the allocation and duration of the benchmark allocation into other assets. These different investments will introduce new risks, but, if the adviser's forecast is correct, they should reduce the exposure of a capital loss being incurred on expensive bonds. The policy portfolio provides a benchmark against which to measure that decision. It also provides an anchor to drag investments back towards the model if the pricing "anomaly" subsequently corrects. Policy asset allocation models provide an important discipline for any investor to keep investments in line with a previously agreed approach, to judge moves away from that agreed approach and sometimes to anchor limits by investment managers from that policy in pursuit of tactical market opportunities.

This chapter discusses investment strategy models for long-term and short-term investors with different tolerances for disappointment risk. In each of these models, government bonds or Treasury bills provide an anchor for the strategy. The weight given to them is driven by the appetite for risk of the investor. Risk assets are represented by allocations to equities. Whether equities alone represent the most efficient way of gaining access to premium returns needs to be assessed in the light of market valuations and expectations for performance, risk, and correlations from different asset classes at a particular point in time. It will be normal to invest in a range of risk assets including, for example, credit. These opportunities are discussed in Part 2. But no matter what an adviser believes about the predictability of market returns or which asset class is cheap or dear, a cautious investor will be keener on having safe-haven assets than an aggressive investor, and a cautious long-term investor will be more interested in government bonds than a short-term investor, who will want more cash.

When safe-haven investments are themselves expensive, cautious investors face a particular problem. They need to decide how much to pay for what is in effect insurance and how much risk to incur by moving away from the safe haven. For cautious long-term investors, bond ladders can be particularly useful in these circumstances (see Laddered government bonds below).

Short-term investment strategies

For short-term investors, the safest strategy is to have 100% of their investments in Treasury bills, or highest quality money-market funds. The "war chest" or "umbrella" fund might be considered a short-term portfolio (see Chapter 1). Short-term investors are absolute return investors. Their focus is immediate and they have no need to hedge against risks in the future. Although the textbook benchmark against which success should be judged is the performance of Treasury bills, the reality is that achieving a positive investment return provides a line in the sand that matters above all else to short-term investors.

Moving strategy away from the safe haven of cash (Treasury bills) brings both the hope of a better performance and the fear of a disappointing outcome. Initially, it is simplest to constrain investment choices to the traditional areas of stocks, bonds and cash.

How safe is cash?

The anchor investment for short-term investors is cash. Cautious investors who want more security should hold more of it. Investment books, such as this one, often proceed as if cash was always invested in Treasury bills. This is rarely the case. One of the most shocking features of the credit crunch's early stages in 2007–08 was the sudden erosion of confidence in cash investments held at banks and in money-market funds. This was coupled with uncertainty about the attitude of governments to bank failures and the extent of government deposit insurance. It was a ripe environment for crowd behaviour by savers as they responded to rumours of impending bank failures.

The first major collapse was that of a British retail bank, Northern Rock, in September 2007. Its online cash withdrawal service was overwhelmed and customers formed long lines in the street to remove their savings. It was the first run on a British retail bank since 1866. One year later, in September 2008, a $64 billion US money-market fund, Reserve Primary Fund, "broke the buck" by marking down its unit price to 97 cents following losses caused by the failure of Lehman Brothers, a global financial services firm. As a result, within days investors withdrew over half the assets managed by the fund, and the US authorities moved to shore up confidence in money-market funds by providing a temporary guarantee to underpin their value. There were other signs of sudden loss of depositor confidence in banks. But concerns about the security of bank deposits were allayed by the clarification of deposit guarantee schemes, and in particular by the growing understanding shortly after September 2008 that deposits at major banks would be protected, not least by the steps taken to bolster bank capital. It remains the case that unguaranteed cash investments in banks need careful due diligence.

No all-seasons short-term strategy

A focus on managing short-term negative return risk has to respond to changes in the level of interest rates. The rate of interest provides a performance cushion which is reduced when rates are low. Thus short-term investing is made easier by higher interest rates when (somewhat) more aggressive strategies can be pursued with no increase in measured risk of incurring a negative return. In this particular context, investing is made more hazardous by low interest rates, when it will be natural to stay closer to the safety zone (cash).

TABLE 5.1 **Unaggressive strategy: negative return risk varies as interest rates move**
%

10-year Treasury yield	1	2	3	4	5
Calculated probability of negative return[a]	42.0	33.3	25.8	19.3	13.3

a Calculated probability of a negative return in a calendar year for an unchanging, unaggressive ("capital protection") strategy, as described in Table 5.6. See comments in text about risk of underperformance.
Source: Author's calculations

This means that there is a tension between standard "one-size-fits-all" model asset allocations and the focus of short-term investors on their absolute performance. The problem with the standard approach is not that groups of clients do not face similar investment risks and opportunities – they normally do. It is rather that a one-size-fits-all approach takes no account of market conditions. At higher rates of interest, it is appropriate for an unaggressive short-term investor to consider accepting more investment volatility. This means that the illustrative short-term stylised model allocations should be seen for what they are: allocations which might be appropriate if bond yields are around 3.0%, but otherwise they should be considered subject to revision, particularly for unaggressive investors.

Do bonds provide insurance for short-term investors?

The answer is sometimes yes and sometimes no. The normal pattern is for equity markets and bond markets to be positively correlated with each other. When equities do well, bonds tend to do at least quite well. At times of crisis and flight to quality, however, the relationship has often broken down as investors flee to government bonds. During the stockmarket declines of 2008, the volatility of long-term government bonds provided an invaluable lever to offset the declines in equity markets. But the scale of the insurance "payout" depended critically on the size of the allocation to bonds and the duration of those government bonds. Cash, the safe haven for short-term investors, provided little help. This paralleled the experiences of the 2000–02 equity bear market. But at other times in the past, for example during the sustained increase in inflation expectations during the 1960s, equities did well while bonds were eroded by inflation and suffered a gradual increase in yields. There have been several years when fixed income suffered negative returns while equities performed strongly.

In times of crisis, bonds normally appreciate, but (even for longer maturities) not necessarily by much, and not by as much as equities fall. Aspects of the historic record since 1987 are summarised in Tables 5.2 and 5.3. It is evident from the experience of the months of October 2008 and February 2009 that equity market setbacks do not necessarily coincide precisely with strong performance by the US Treasury market (see Table 5.2). However, Table 5.3, which records the worst calendar year experiences of US equities, shows that in those years the US Treasury market performed strongly with, as expected, long-dated bonds performing strongest.

TABLE 5.2 **Bond diversification in months of equity market crisis**
Total return performance, %

	MSCI US Index	MSCI World Index	Barclays US Treasury Long Term Bond Index	Barclays US Treasury Intermediate Term Bond Index	Barclays US Aggregate Bond Index
Oct 1987	−21.3	−19.6	7.3	3.0	3.6
Oct 2008	−17.1	−16.3	−3.3	0.7	−2.4
Aug 1998	−13.9	−13.8	4.5	2.0	1.6
Sep 2002	−11.3	−11.0	4.2	1.9	1.6
Feb 2009	−10.2	−8.9	−1.0	−0.4	−0.4

Note: Data sorted by worst monthly performance of MSCI US equity index, January 1987–September 2013.
Sources: Barclays; MSCI

TABLE 5.3 **Bond diversification in years of extreme equity market performance**
Total return performance, %

	MSCI US Index	MSCI World Index	Barclays US Treasury Long Term Bond Index	Barclays US Treasury Intermediate Term Bond Index	Barclays US Aggregate Bond Index
2008	−37.1	−38.3	24.0	11.4	5.2
2002	−22.7	−23.8	16.8	9.3	10.3
2000	−12.5	−9.6	20.3	10.3	11.6
1989	31.4	24.7	18.9	12.7	14.5
1997	34.1	22.9	15.1	7.8	9.7
1995	38.2	20.0	30.7	14.4	18.5

Note: US equity and bond performance during the best and worst three years for the MSCI US equity index between 1987 and 2012.
Sources: Barclays; MSCI

Table 5.3 looks "quite good" for supporting the insurance role of bonds. However, the overall message regarding the insurance role for bonds is that it sometimes works but not always, and furthermore that US Treasuries provide better insurance than corporate bonds and other components of the Barclays Aggregate Index (see Chapter 8).

The other message is that the relationship between different maturities of bonds is generally predictable, with the longest dated (and most volatile) US Treasuries appreciating most in periods of stockmarket crisis. But this does not always happen. When it does not, the shape of the bond yield curve can shift markedly, which argues for diversified exposure to bond maturities. Long-dated bonds are unquestionably much further away from a short-term investor's safety zone than short-term bonds and so are much more risky. But the payout of short-term bonds is much less when fixed-income markets are providing insurance.

So the process for short-term investors should be first to decide how much risk they want to take, and then to make sure that risk-taking is itself diversified across asset classes. Offset equity exposure with at least some fixed-income exposure, not in this case for income but for insurance. But do so knowing that this is one of those insurance policies with loopholes in the small print.

Are you in it for the long term?

The purpose of wealth, however large or small, is to fund expenditure in the future. This might be tomorrow or it might be in 40 years' time, but the time horizon for most investment objectives cannot be described as short term. For long-term investors who are concerned to target a minimum standard of living, or, for an endowment, a minimum level of disbursements, the strategy should not target a particular level of wealth. Wealth is a means to an end, but not the end in itself. The sufficiency of wealth is best examined from the perspective of the level of income or disbursements that the wealth can support.

Time horizon for private and institutional wealth

The income that a defined-benefit pension fund or an insurance company is obliged to disburse can be modelled by actuaries years in advance with a reasonable degree of accuracy. There are issues with the uncertainty surrounding these projections and whether this has increased with corporate change and with greater life expectancy. But these issues are of an order of magnitude different from the uncertainty surrounding the spending of much private wealth.

The obligations of endowments and charities (and also sovereign wealth funds) are again different in nature. Their spending is constrained by what they have, by the bequests or inflows that they receive, and by the need to balance the interests of today's beneficiaries with those of tomorrow. This need to ensure equitable treatment in making allocations between different generations of beneficiaries is a particular concern for "perpetual" endowments, such as college foundations, and some sovereign wealth funds, whose investment strategy needs to assume that the foundation will last "for ever".

The increase in wealth of tax-exempt endowments with both professional investment management and successful fund-raising offers the prospect of accumulation that is bounded only by their endowments' fund-raising capacity. David Swensen of Yale University gives a revealing account of the differing evolution of the Yale, Harvard and Carnegie Institution investment funds since the early 20th century. In 1911, Carnegie and Harvard had funds of around $23m while Yale had around $12m. By June 2012, the Carnegie Institution's investment portfolio, which devotes itself to supporting scientific research, had more than kept pace with inflation, with an endowment of $989m. However, this was dwarfed by Harvard's $30.7 billion and Yale's $19.3 billion. The reason for this scale of difference is not superior investment management but the much greater access of the university foundations to new bequests.

Private wealth is different. Families continue from generation to generation, but family wealth gets spent. There is little scope for the intergenerational exponential wealth accumulation that may be enjoyed by educational foundations. Private wealth is consumed, dissipated in fees, paid in taxes, or donated (as with the Carnegie family wealth) to charitable foundations. If this did not happen, the parsimonious among the wealthy could become stupendously wealthy. For example, in the 113 years to December 2012, the cumulative return from US equities after inflation, but before all costs, taxes and fees, was 6.3% a year. This implies that a very wealthy family with perhaps $20m in 1900, equivalent to around $500m in today's prices, could have an inherited fortune of almost $500 billion if it had been invested in the diversified US stockmarket, and if that family had consumed nothing apart from what they earned independently of that wealth and had contrived to pay no taxes or investment management costs. Such a scale of inherited wealth does not seem to exist. Wealth is inherited, but it is also spent or disbursed.

There is often little predictability in the spending plans of individual family members. This creates asset-planning issues that do not affect institutions. By contrast, the purpose and strategic direction of endowments and institutions are legally fixed by trust deeds or equivalent documents. With families, strategic objectives and actual disbursement of wealth can evolve at short notice, sometimes in surprising directions. This introduces uncertainty into the time horizon for the management of private wealth, which has few parallels for endowments or institutional investors. However, a change in regulations for pension funds and insurance companies (there have been many since the late 1990s around the world and more are under consideration) can have a sudden impact on the time horizon of institutions.

In setting strategy, the importance of different points on the time horizon for an investor needs to be clarified. For family wealth, the objective is not normally precisely defined. Sometimes there are clear dates associated with particular financial goals which can easily be benchmarked using government bonds; in other cases, wealth is explicitly needed for opportunities (or contingencies) which may arise in the short term. But usually this is not the case and plans often need to evolve as circumstances change and as more information becomes available. However, this should not be used as an excuse for assuming that such investors are, by default, short-term investors, as the adoption of a medium- or longer-term investment strategy could well help protect the purchasing power of their investments.

Long-term investors

Long-term investors have much greater flexibility than short-term investors to make adjustments to improve the likelihood of meeting financial objectives. Long-term investors are not just at the mercy of the investment markets and their initial choice of investment strategy. Depending on the investor's circumstances, financial disappointment "along the way" often leaves time to elicit a response, which provides extra degrees of freedom that reduce risk in the ability to meet objectives. For example, there may be time for a revision to the investment strategy, or for an individual to postpone retirement or to reduce current expenditure. For an endowment, there may be time for a drive to raise additional bequests, and for a pension fund, time to raise the level of regular pension contributions. These options provide flexibility for the long-term investor that is not available to the short-term investor. For any individual or foundation (or perhaps pension plan) that relies on a regular injection of savings or contributions to fund future financial needs, variations in these sources of income are often a much bigger source of risk and opportunity to meet expected commitments than are market conditions.

Financial planning and the time horizon

Short-term investors have a clear focus on total return as a measure of the success of their investment strategy. Long-term investors will often focus on the same measure. However, as discussed in Chapter 3 this is understandable but wrong. For example, it is common for individuals to have a target for accumulated savings before they feel able to retire. Over quite short time periods an amount that was broadly appropriate can become inadequate if long-term interest rates fall. The key is not the absolute amount of savings, but the ability of that amount, if cautiously invested, to support the intended level of retirement income. This leads to a focus on shortfall risk rather than the risk of generating a negative return. The benchmark for measuring shortfall is the performance of the appropriate "safety-first" strategy, and so shortfall risk is the risk of underperforming that strategy.

This is well understood and reflected in financial advice and the "laddered" bond portfolios of many cautious private investors in North America. It is much less common, however, in the generic advice given to investors elsewhere. Internationally, it is common for private wealth holdings of bonds to be of short duration. Often this reflects concerns about the potential impact of inflation and a desire to avoid the risk of short-term negative returns from volatile assets, even if they are government bonds guaranteed to deliver a set amount at a given date in the future.

Outside the United States, it is widely believed that long-term bonds are inappropriate as investments for cautious private investors for whom the emphasis should, it is argued, be on controlling absolute volatility and short-term capital preservation. However, this is the appropriate focus only for cautious short-term investors. An error that often accompanies failure to design risk-taking strategies appropriate to an investor's time horizon is to confuse this time horizon with risk tolerance. The two should be treated separately. There are cautious long-term investors and there are aggressive short-term investors.

"Safe havens", benchmarking, risk-taking and long-term strategies

The ability of government bonds to "lock in" objectives (by avoiding the danger of having to suffer less favourable interest rates at a later date) means that they have a benchmarking role in setting strategy for long-term investors. Where financial objectives can be precisely specified, the benchmark is a series of government bonds that would provide a stream of income to match the objective. Where they are long term, but not specified, the best benchmark and "safe haven" is a long-dated government bond.

A "safe-haven" investment strategy quantifies how much wealth is needed today to secure or to "hedge" with reasonable certainty a particular objective at a chosen date in the future. Alternatively, it can tell you how much can, with confidence, be accumulated by that date with a given level of initial investment.

For cautious long-term investors, long-term bonds should normally dominate the investment strategy. However, when interest rates are very low, cautious investors need to venture out of their comfort zone and take more risk than usual. For more aggressive investors, the holding may be much smaller, but government bonds will still provide a reference point for comparative measurement of the chosen investment strategy.

This core reference role for longer-dated highest quality bonds is needed because they enable cautious long-term investors to hedge the risk to their future income and standard of living from adverse movements in interest rates. Reductions in interest rates should be of little concern to a pensioner, or someone approaching retirement, who has followed a sufficiently funded and properly implemented cautious long-term investment strategy.

The danger of keeping things too simple

However, for many investors, an overriding desire to "keep things simple" may encourage them to indicate that they are content to be considered as short-term investors, even though their objectives are longer term. This is the option to be treated as "absolute return" investors, for whom the safe-haven investment strategy is to be 100% invested in cash.

The danger is that these investors will miss two important differences between short-term and long-term investing. The first is the focus that long-term investors must have on the price level and inflation uncertainty. The second is that such investors will also fail to distinguish between a reduction in the price of future security (a fall in government bond prices) and a reduction in the market's assessment of an investment's quality.

Declines in prices are sometimes good for you

Sometimes you can be sure that a financial loss can be reversed. Pensioners living off the income generated from a well-constructed ladder of high-quality government bonds can respond to a fall in the market value of their investment portfolio following an increase in bond yields with composure. It should be of no concern. A creditworthy government issuer will keep them in the style to which they are accustomed. However, individuals who suffer a similar fall in investment value as a result of a downgrade in the creditworthiness of a corporate or even government bond, on which they are relying for pension income, might reasonably suffer sleepless nights, because there is less assurance that they will get paid.

For a short-term investor who wishes to realise objectives in the near term, either reversal should be viewed as if it might be a permanent loss which could need to be realised. For a long-term investor, only the credit downgrade should be of concern. It might be said that it is not the credit downgrade that should concern the pensioner, since it is only a default that leads to a loss of income. But this is a classic case of the dangers of mismeasuring risk. Investors lose sleep over their ability to support their future standard of living a long time before most downgraded corporate bonds default. A bond ladder comprising corporate debt that stretches many years into the future is more likely to suffer worrying credit downgrades at some stage than actual default.

Volatility which is reflected in a reduction in government bond prices reduces the cost of buying future income. This is unambiguously good news for anyone saving for a pension or a college education, for an endowment investing new money to meet future needs, or for a sovereign wealth fund trying to balance the interests of today's beneficiaries with those of tomorrow. For all these investors, higher real interest rates mean both lower bond prices and being able to meet more of tomorrow's needs with each new investment.

To achieve success as a long-term investor, this distinction between good and bad price declines should be accepted and reflected in how an investor responds to financial reverses. This is invaluable for private investors, who often regard any loss as if it is bad news, when it may represent an opportunity to lock in access to higher future income.

A lack of clarity about financial goals can encourage investors to focus on inappropriate time horizons. The one predictable consequence of this is inefficiency in the implementation of strategy. An example of this occurs if private investors, whose appropriate focus is on the long term, behave as short-term investors. They will fail to appreciate their vulnerability to changes in long-term interest rates and to the gradual erosion of inflation. Any change in long-term interest rates is likely to be misinterpreted, with positive performance arising from only partial exposure to falling interest rates being seen as "good performance" (it is not, it is poor, because it only partially hedged the fall in interest rates and should have been better), and negative performance owing to partial exposure to rising interest rates being seen as "poor", when underexposure to the safe haven of long-term bonds may (depending on the interest-rate sensitivity of existing investments) offer an opportunity to secure a higher future income with existing resources.

A financially disciplined endowment fund or institution managing cash flow obligations over a number of years is less likely to make these errors. The issue is that where the financial constraints are not naturally tight, market competition is not available to ensure that wealth is efficiently managed. Instead it requires deliberate decision-making and appropriate governance to make sure that a proper focus is maintained on the objectives that are suitable for the time scale of each investor.

Unexpected inflation: yet again the party pooper

The distinction between good and bad declines in prices, which draws on academic research on equity markets discussed in Chapter 7, is a useful device to help long-term investors understand the importance of the passage of time for the success of the investment strategy. It also helps differentiate between short-term and long-term investors. Strictly, so-called good declines in prices refer primarily to the prices of government inflation-linked bond yields, such as TIPS (Treasury Inflation Protected Securities). The reason is that a fall in conventional government bond prices which reflects an increase in inflation expectations (rather than an increase in real interest rates) is not good news for an investor, for it indicates an expected irrecoverable devaluation in the worth of all nominal bond investments. This is the process that explains why, in most countries for which there are data, bonds provided disappointing returns in the 20th century.

"Keep-it-simple" long-term asset allocation models

"Diversify, diversify" asset allocators often say. However, in designing low-risk strategies, which should always be the starting point for asset allocation, the first step should be to design the best hedge to neutralise risks of failing to meet objectives. For some investors it is conceivable that this could be achieved through a single holding in a particular government bond. An example would be the acquisition of a long-term inflation-linked government bond whose maturity date coincides with when a young child's university expenses are expected to be payable. Diversification becomes an issue as an investor moves away from this "best hedge". Any such move needs to be made efficiently, which will call for diversification of avoidable risks.

The short-term asset allocation models (see Tables 5.5 and 5.6 at the end of this chapter) are rooted in the intellectual breakthroughs of the 1950s, and given the flood of advances in finance since then could be described as "antediluvian". They provide an easy shortcut to thinking about managing the risk of losing money. They assume that markets are "well behaved" (which they are not), they deal with a single period (which is an unusual focus for an investor), and they assume that wealth is a goal in itself and not a means to an end.

So what does a long-term investment plan look like, and how should it be structured? It is not a wealth plan – it is a long-term income or spending power plan. An income plan needs to take account of your financial and other assets, your likely earnings, your financial obligations and your spending plans. The first step will be to establish a base case to see if you are able to "hedge out" your obligations and plans, given your current resources and current levels of interest rates. To do this, financial advisers need to be able to access sophisticated modelling tools that enable investors to match the profile of their investments with the likely schedule of their payment obligations in a way that highlights the low risk (but high expense) of following a "fully hedged" investment strategy. It should show how the expected cost may fall (with an accompanying danger of accumulating a shortfall from financial objectives) as strategy moves away from the fully hedged position.

A flavour for the differences in strategy from the short-term models is shown in Table 5.4 and Figure 5.1. The focus is now on the risk of shortfalls from the fully hedged strategy instead of the risk of negative returns. So instead of showing the expected return and its trade-off

TABLE 5.4 **Stylised model long-term strategies, with only stocks, bonds and cash**

	Unaggressive ("income protection")	Moderate	Aggressive
Equities	25	60	80
Long-term conventional government bonds	50	40	20
Cash	0	0	0
Inflation-linked government bonds	25	0	0
Expected surplus (% per year)	1.2	2.6	3.5
Volatility of surplus	7.6	12.9	16.8

Source: Author

FIG 5.1 **Stylised surplus risk and opportunity for long-term investors, stylised approach**
Expected surplus, % per year

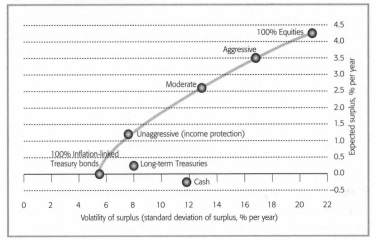

Source: Author's calculations

with the volatility of that return, the focus is on the expected surplus or deficit in meeting objectives, as compared with the minimum risk of a full hedging investment strategy. The "model strategies" for long-term investors are shown in Table 5.4. Note that Figure 5.1 assumes that even a most cautious long-term strategy is likely to involve a risk of falling short of financial objectives.

Should long-term investors hold more equities?

The discussion about stockmarket bubbles in Chapter 4 reintroduces the question of whether stockmarket risk is reduced with time. For if booms and busts in the stockmarket predictably follow each other, it may be possible to profit from this pattern. However, if we doubt our ability to time markets, even though we believe in market cycles, this predictable cyclical nature of equity returns will reinforce the case for a somewhat higher allocation to equities for long-term investors (which is incorporated in Table 5.4).

A number of studies, notably by Jeremy Siegel in *Stocks for the Long Run*, have suggested that over long holding periods (for example,

30 years or more) an investor might be more sure, or at least less uncertain, of what after-inflation performance to expect from equities than from conventional government bonds. This builds on the experience of the 20th century, when the impact of unanticipated inflation made cash and bonds much riskier for holding wealth over long periods than shorter-term experience would suggest. The evidence that Siegel uses to support this comes primarily from the United States, but it also appears to be supported, almost without exception, by international data. Taken together, these would suggest skewing, at least to some extent, the investment strategy allocation for long-term investors towards equities and away from bonds for cautious as well as aggressive investors.

However, he makes clear that although this model does reflect the effect that unanticipated 20th century inflation had on the investments in conventional government bonds and cash of cautious investors, it does not incorporate the potential role of inflation-linked government bonds.

The introduction of inflation-linked government bonds has changed the ground rules for long-term investment strategy in the 21st century. Long-term investors may have medium-term as well as long-term objectives, and often, especially with private wealth, unexpected opportunities or requirements to draw down investments arise. Taken together with the insights of behavioural finance into loss aversion, this suggests that it is now neither necessary nor desirable to recommend high equity allocations for long-term cautious investors. However, if long-term cautious investors have confidence in the equity mean reversion story, especially if they have access to other sources of income, they might reasonably hold more equities than would be recommended for cautious investors with a short time horizon.

Inflation, again

There is no role for cash in the long-term models in Table 5.4. This is because cash is volatile relative to the safe haven (inflation-linked bonds) and it normally offers no performance advantage. At the same time, the future relationship between inflation-linked bonds and conventional government bonds is sensitive to views on inflation.

It should be assumed that these inflation risks cannot be properly reflected in any set of modelling assumptions, and that it will be necessary to rely heavily on judgmental opinions. Furthermore, the judgments of "experts" should probably not count for more than the views and experiences of informed investors on issues such as inflation expectations. However, the apparent views of the financial markets on the break-even rate of inflation should always be used as a point of comparison.

Views on expected inflation and the uncertainty about future inflation should be reviewed from time to time with the help of some simple "what-if" illustrations for the price level at different dates in the future. In the stylised model for long-term investors shown in Table 5.4, a key decision will be the extent to which the holdings of government bonds should be in the form of inflation-linked or conventional bonds.

Laddered government bonds: a useful safety-first portfolio

A bond ladder is a portfolio of bonds with staggered maturity dates. It secures a stream of income for years ahead, and it reduces the risk of sudden changes in that income resulting from interest-rate changes. As each bond matures, it will need to be reinvested at prevailing interest rates and this exposes the income from the ladder to a margin of uncertainty. But this reinvestment risk applies only to an individual rung of the ladder as it matures. It can take judgment out of timing movements in long-term interest rates and reduce uncertainty in a pensioner's future income. Spreading maturities allows more reinvestment opportunities and less exposure to regret at the terms with which any particular bond was reinvested. A greater number of bond issues also enables effective management of different types of risk exposure (see below).

The danger of having to reinvest at lower interest rates than prevailed when the maturing bond was purchased could have been avoided if a life annuity had been purchased instead of a bond ladder (though complicated tax issues arise if the annuity is purchased with taxable savings). However, the laddered approach is more appealing to many investors than a life annuity as it gives greater control over their wealth and avoids the need to lock in a single long-term rate of interest on the day they purchase the life annuity. Although a ladder does involve reinvestment risk, it also offers reinvestment opportunity, namely the chance to reinvest at more favourable interest rates at a later date.

This can provide an element of inflation protection to retirement income. If individuals decide to buy a fixed-income life annuity rather than invest in a bond ladder, they will be wholly exposed to any unexpected increase in inflation for the rest of their lives. However, if an increase in inflation is expected to persist, bond yields will be higher, and the rungs on a fixed-income bond ladder will be reinvested at the new higher rate of interest. If an investor expects interest rates to rise, but is not sure when they will, having to reinvest maturing bonds allows income to be "averaged up" if rates do rise over time. If the objective is to secure a steady income, this prospect of securing a higher income should matter more than the temporary dips in capital value of the existing bonds as rates rise ahead of maturity.

This degree of inflation compensation is incomplete and less effective than what could be offered by inflation-linked government bonds. Furthermore, reinvesting a conventional maturing bond will always, if there has been any inflation, support a lower standard of living than when the bond was first purchased. Nevertheless, this partial element of inflation compensation in a bond ladder, in conjunction with the flexibility and discretion that it leaves the investor, will be an appealing feature for many investors.

A bond ladder is designed to mitigate interest-rate risk and it should encourage a proper understanding of the distinction between good and bad declines in prices. This is because an investor will find it easier to respond to a fall in government bond prices as an opportunity to lock in higher income when the next rung on the ladder matures. However, if the cause of the decline in investment values was a downgrade in the credit quality of a component rung, the result is likely to be, at least, a worried investor until the bond matures.

For this reason, ladders should be constructed from government (including high-quality municipal) bonds. With good-quality longer-term corporate bonds there is always the risk of a deterioration in credit quality, and this risk obviously increases with longer maturity bonds. When constructing a long-term bond ladder designed to provide dependable income, it is safest to assume that there is no such thing as a blue-chip, entirely reliable corporate credit risk. For example, a US dollar corporate bond ladder built up in the initial years after 2000 would probably have included large exposures to several then highly rated financial institutions, including banks as well as AIG, an insurance company which had to be rescued by the US government in 2008. (See Chapter 8 for how corporate credit risk evolves over time.) An investor who wishes to take advantage of the higher yields available from assuming credit risk should follow a professionally managed approach to investing in credit risk and forgo the concept of a bond ladder. Investors can see sample portfolios (for example, mutual fund portfolios) of the most highly respected fixed-income portfolio managers. These will show that credit risk is well diversified with modest exposures to individual institutions. A bond ladder gives much less opportunity for such diversification.

In practice, building a bond ladder of high-quality bonds to generate a secure flow of income stretching over a number of years is mostly associated with the US municipal bond market. This immediately introduces credit-quality concerns. Building a bond ladder involves a series of choices (which may be more limited than would be wished) and usually trade-offs between what is desirable for a buy-and-hold approach to investing and what is available. Bond ladders need to be constructed with care, taking account of the tax status of different issues, credit risk, the existence of call options that enable the issuer to repay the bond early, and the costs that may be incurred if the investor decides to sell the bond before its final maturity date.

Bond ladders, tax and creditworthiness: the case of US municipal bonds

At the end of March 2013, US state and local authorities had outstanding obligations in the form of different types of municipal bonds of $3.7 trillion, making the "muni" market approximately one-third of the size of the US Treasury market. The market is highly diverse with, according to a 2012 Securities and Exchange Commission (SEC) report, close to 44,000 state and local issuers and over 1m different municipal bonds outstanding in 2011. This heterogeneity contributes to illiquidity in the market (see below). The municipal bond market is attractive to US taxable investors because interest on municipal bonds is generally exempt from federal income tax and from state and local tax in the issuing state. (Interest on US Treasury and government agency bonds is subject to federal income tax but exempt from state income taxes.) This makes the municipal bond market a natural habitat for the taxable savings of US private investors. According to the SEC, individuals owned around 75% of outstanding municipal bonds in 2011, with around 50% held directly and 25% held through mutual funds (or other investment vehicles, such as closed-end funds or exchange traded funds – ETFs).

There are the two main types of tax-exempt municipal bonds: general obligation bonds and revenue bonds. General obligation bonds are backed by the full faith and credit of the issuer and are usually supported by the issuer's tax-raising powers. By contrast, revenue bonds are serviced from specific projects or businesses that have been funded by the bonds. If the project fails to generate sufficient income to service the debt, the bondholders have no access to other sources of revenue of the issuing authority. Other highest quality municipal bonds include those where the original issue is "refunded" or collateralised, for example with US Treasury securities.

Before the 2007–08 credit crisis, as well as having tax advantages, investment in municipal bonds was aided by the role of the insurance companies, with just under 60% of the value of new issues in 2004–07 being insured, according to the SEC. Following the credit crisis, insurance companies have greatly reduced this service and in 2009–11 the proportion of the value of new issues insured fell to an average of 17%. This has coincided with growing concerns about the credit quality of issuers, increasing both the burden of due diligence on investment advisers in recommending specific municipal bonds to investors and the attraction of investing in mutual funds managed by well-resourced teams of analysts. It has also shifted perceptions of creditworthiness: revenue bonds which are secured by predictable high-quality projects or business activities have become relatively more attractive as the role of insurance has declined and doubts about the "full faith and credit" of some issuers backing general obligation bonds have increased (see below).

In 2009–10 a new type of municipal bond was issued, encouraged by federal government subsidies: the "Build America Bond" or BAB. However, unlike most municipal bonds, BABs are not exempt from income tax, and so are of more interest to institutional investors keen to diversify their exposure to new issuers than to taxable private client investors.

Rules of thumb are normally used to compare tax-exempt municipal and Treasury bonds, such as a comparison of the difference in yields with the investor's tax rate. (Inaccuracies with this approach arise because of interest coupon reinvestment risk and the tax that has to be paid on the coupon of the taxable bond.) A key indicator is the ratio of the yield on highest quality municipal bonds to that on US Treasuries of similar maturity and a comparison of that ratio with the investor's tax rate. An indication is given in Figures 5.2 and 5.3.

In practice, a number of factors need to be assessed for individual municipal bonds:

- The creditworthiness of the issue.
- The availability of credit enhancement, such as insurance or collateralisation.
- Liquidity and the ease of selling a bond in the market. For Treasury securities this will not be a factor, but for many municipal bond issues the transaction costs can be considerable.
- Whether the municipal bond issue has call provisions that enable the issuer to repay the bond early, at par or at a specified premium to par. Call provisions undermine the usefulness of a bond as part of a ladder intended to secure future income, because the bond will be called when it suits the issuer, not the investor. Call provisions always undermine the interests of investors and provide a valuable option for the issuer, so a callable bond should offer investors a higher yield than a non-callable bond.

Several of these factors help to explain why the municipal bond

FIG 5.2 **Comparison of municipal and US Treasury long-dated bond yields**
% per year, Jan 1992–Sep 2013

Source: Barclays

FIG 5.3 **Long-dated municipal bond yields as a percentage of US Treasury yields**
%, Jan 1992–Sep 2013

Source: Barclays

market has often traded at higher yields than might be expected by simply making a comparison with the US Treasury market and prevailing tax rates. This was exacerbated after 2007 (see Figure 5.3).

The dramatic change in the relationship between US Treasury and municipal bond yields in 2008 was one aspect of the flight to liquidity and quality in financial markets. Historically, losses from the municipal bond market have been modest. Moody's, for example, reports that the one-year default rate for Moody's-rated municipal issuers was a low average of 0.030% for the five years to end 2012, compared with just 0.009% for 1970–2007. By comparison, in Chapter 8 research is cited which reports an average annual default rate on corporate bonds of around 1.5% over 150 years (with actual losses, after allowing for amounts recovered for investors, around half that amount). Even after the 1994 bankruptcy of Orange County, California, municipal bond investors were repaid in full, with reassurance meanwhile having been provided to investors by insurance companies standing behind a number of the bonds that would otherwise have been at risk.

The changed relationship between yields on municipal bonds and yields on Treasury securities primarily reflects increased concerns about the creditworthiness of state and local issuers. It also reflects the withdrawal of insurance for municipal bonds and increased illiquidity in the municipal bond market. In its initial stages in 2008 and 2009, the spike in yield differentials (see Figure 5.3) was exacerbated by forced selling by leveraged investors in the illiquid municipal bond market. Creditworthiness concerns have been heightened by the well-publicised financial difficulties of a number of municipalities, downgrades by the rating agencies since 2008 and the July 2013 bankruptcy filing by the City of Detroit, with debts in excess of $14 billion.

These issues present challenges for advisers constructing bond ladders that are intended to provide dependable income over many years for investors. The preferred way to establish a ladder is gradually, over time, as part of the process of portfolio diversification, for example by diverting cash flow from earnings or asset sales in the years before retirement and buying individual bonds from time to time. There are always concerns that the best yield is not being achieved, but this is not a sufficient reason to delay laying the foundations for a secure income. In establishing the bond ladder, credit risk can be managed but it cannot be avoided (unless, arguably, the ladder comprises only US Treasury issues). It is normally tax efficient to focus on municipal bonds issued by the investor's home state, as these will be exempt from state as well as federal income tax. However, states such as Florida and Nevada do not levy personal income tax, making their municipal bonds attractive for out-of-state investors seeking to diversify issuer risk. Furthermore, investors may choose to pay out-of-state income tax to allow further diversification of issuer risk. Revenue bonds provide a further source of diversification, which for more secure "essential revenue issues" (typically tied to utility earnings) can attract high credit ratings. Revenue bonds include niches where unusually attractive yields with little credit risk may persist because the issues are too small to be arbitraged away by large-scale investment, but may suit individual buy-and-hold investors. This is an area where due diligence by a skilled adviser can pay dividends.

Historically, the difference between US Treasury and municipal bond yields has been most marked for longer maturities. As a result, the term structure of the municipal bond market has often been steeper than that for US Treasuries. This is a most attractive feature for a laddered, buy-and-hold approach to investing in municipal bonds.

Municipal bond ladders: the impact of the credit crisis and ultra-low interest rates

Since 2008, investors in the US municipal bond market have been buffeted by the demise of insurance, concerns about the credit quality of issuers and ultra-low interest rates. Investors have responded to this by altering how they invest in municipal bonds. The first effect has been on unadvised retail clients, who – when they buy individual bonds – seem increasingly to have bought shorter maturity highest quality issues. A second effect has been to encourage reliance on third-party due diligence (particularly following the demise of insured bonds) and so a greater investment in managed accounts and municipal bond funds, including ETFs. In turn, the managers of such bond funds, conscious of the need to honour redemption demands, have a strong preference for more liquid, high-quality – but not necessarily short maturity – municipal bonds. This has left a significant segment of the municipal bond market where advised investors can find high-quality, relatively inexpensive but illiquid municipal bonds which are best suited for a buy-and-hold-to-maturity investment as part of a bond ladder.

At each month-end between September 2012 and April 2013, the redemption yield on the Barclays 20-year municipal bond index was less than 3%, and it averaged 2.8%. This posed a challenge for investors who needed to reinvest the proceeds of maturing bonds from a bond ladder. There was anecdotal evidence of investors looking for short-term liquid homes for their cash, such as short-dated municipal bond mutual funds, while agreeing with their advisers threshold yields at which they would consider re-entering the market to rebuild a dependable source of medium- or long-term retirement income. Such yields appeared to have started to be met in the summer of 2013. However, the overriding message from the period of ultra-low interest rates should be that the mechanism of a high-quality bond ladder is a good way to secure retirement income. The more generous income yields on offer in previous years, and maintained for the life of the bonds, would have avoided precipitous declines in investors' income for many years. This is the core value of a government bond ladder comprising high-quality issues with staggered maturity dates. Many cautious pensioners elsewhere in the world, suffering diminished income from their investments after 2008, would have benefited from the advice given to large numbers of their American counterparts, who faced essentially the same issue of how to secure a reasonably stable retirement income.

What's the catch in following a long-term strategy?

At the time of writing, the "worst" month for the US TIPS market was October 2008. In that month the yield, according to the US Treasury, on long-dated (ten-year-plus) TIPS increased by 0.6% to 3.4%, and the Barclays Capital index of this part of the market showed a monthly performance of –10.7% (in May and June 2013 results almost as "poor" were recorded). For an investor funding a pension plan from regular cash contributions to inflation-linked government bonds, such an increase in yield and reduction in price, if taken in isolation, is clearly good news as it enables each contribution at the lower price to purchase more pension entitlement. This is at the heart of the distinction between good and bad price declines. For cautious long-term pension investors who were continuing to contribute to their savings plan, the October 2008 increase in real yields and fall in bond prices should not have been a concern, even though with hindsight they may regret not postponing purchases until the higher yields were on offer. But it is normally wishful thinking to believe that they might have been able to succeed at such market timing.

However, the most important feature of short-term and long-term models is that there is a fundamental difference in strategy design for cautious long-term investors and cautious short-term investors. These are not small differences that can be ignored: there is an essential difference between stabilising the income that can be generated from an investor's wealth, the objective for a cautious long-term investor, and stabilising the value of that wealth, the objective for a cautious short-term investor.

Market timing: an unavoidable risk

Whatever strategy is being followed, from time to time it is likely that investors will be persuaded of the need to change investment direction. But the process of changing strategy is fraught with risk for investors. There is often little advice available on how to decide when to change strategy. For larger institutional investors, investment managers and consultants provide much advice on how to insure against bad outcomes and how to manage transactions costs once an investor has decided when to change strategy. However, there is little profit for an adviser in answering the key question: "When?" But for all investors this is a crucial issue in managing investments.

Implementing strategy change involves unavoidable market timing. You know you have to get from A to B, but how to get there, and particularly when to get there, requires judgments about market timing. These have to be balanced against the knowledge that your investment risk profile is not what you want it to be (which is why you want to change strategy).

A simple rule to follow is that if investors decide that their risk profile is too aggressive, they should move to the new, more cautious strategy promptly, perhaps allowing a small amount of time for trying to predict market movements, but with little confidence that this will add much value. Such investors should not let seeming confidence in short-term market forecasts extend the period during which their risk profile is inappropriate. This is easily stated and perhaps more easily applied in the case of an institution rather than an individual or a family. This is because discussions about risk tolerance are rarely separated from views on market prospects in discussions with families.

However, for all investors, within each four- or five-year period there is a significant chance that circumstances may force a change of direction. The obvious group of investors for whom this might not apply is well-resourced "perpetual" endowments (such as some sovereign wealth funds, university foundations and charitable endowments). Adjustments to strategy involve taking views on markets and, typically, a significant degree of regret risk.

The real issue is not that market timing cannot be undertaken skilfully or profitably: it can. There are some investment managers whose skill in market timing has manifested itself over time. But these track records are not built by one-off "bet the ranch" decisions on the timing of corrections to inappropriate risk profiles. They are carefully managed and, within limits, diversified. Changing strategy is different. There is normally no way to diversify the investment decision or to give meaningful time to profit from the correction of perceived market anomalies.

It is often suggested that phasing implementation of a change in investment strategy from one asset class to another is the best way to proceed if an investor has to change strategy. The investor is likely to feel more comfortable with this approach. But the strong argument in favour of immediate implementation of change is that if an investor has decided that the risk of the current investment strategy is excessive, any delay extends unnecessary risk-taking. When faced with the need to make such a decision, there are always reasons why now is not the best time to act.

Some "keep-it-simple" concluding messages

The model allocations described in this chapter are simplified and will often need tailoring to suit an individual investor's needs as well as to market circumstances. But they give a flavour of what strategy might look like if the available investments comprised only cash, domestic conventional government bonds, domestic inflation-linked government bonds and diversified equities. In many cases, appropriate "keep-it-simple" strategies, consisting only of these investment classes, can be constructed for the financial needs of investors. Actual investment holdings can then deviate from these to reflect, within agreed limits, views on the cheapness and dearness of markets.

In practice, most investors will spend much more time focusing on the detail of implementation, which involves departures from this keep-it-simple approach. How much should go in hedge funds? Isn't finding the right manager more important than the right hedge fund strategy? Surely value will outperform growth? Is high yield too risky? What about emerging markets? And so on.

Despite the time that most investors spend on these issues, the most important one is the extent to which obligations or spending plans are hedged and future income secured. The keep-it-simple framework is more than adequate to address these fundamental issues. What is often thought to be the more exciting material about the different asset classes is covered in the second part of this book. When reviewing these more exciting and sophisticated opportunities, a key question to keep asking is: how will this product perform in "bad times" when reliable diversification will be most important to me?

The chance of a bad outcome may be higher than you think

What is a "bad outcome" or "minimum acceptable return" (MAR) for short-term investors? A cautious short-term investor will be less tolerant of short-term losses than an aggressive investor. For unaggressive short-term investors, it has been arbitrarily assumed that the measured risk of a negative return of worse than −5% in any particular year should be no greater than one in 20. This is the target MAR. For moderate risk short-term investors, the MAR is assumed to be −10% and for aggressive short-term investors −15%. In principle, any figure can be selected, but whatever it is, the calculated probability of breaching may be only one in 20 in any particular calendar year; however, over five years, for example, the probability of breaching the guideline in at least one of these five years will be more than one in five. If, as is most probable, the investor's portfolio is monitored more frequently than once a year, say at the end of each month, the probability of at least one breach, measured on the basis of rolling 12-month periods, will be closer to 50%. (Note that the MAR probability refers to the chance of an outcome worse than the specified parameter in a particular calendar year.) These things happen and are not surprising, even if you think that a one-in-20 risk is a remote risk. A real problem for advisers is that investors may think that such a poor outcome is unlikely to happen, which places a particular responsibility on investor education.

Having selected these tolerances for losses, in theory we can design short-term model strategies that give the best prospect for wealth generation, given these guidelines. These would be the conventional efficient portfolios that are optimal for each indicated level of risk-taking by short-term investors. Efficient portfolios give the best possible trade-off of expected risk and expected return. For any given level of risk-taking there is, in theory, only one optimal portfolio. It would be impossible to achieve higher expected returns with no increase in risk and it would be inefficient to pursue the same returns, but at higher risk. In practice, the uncertainties discussed in Chapters 2 and 3 mean that this does not work since we cannot precisely model uncertainty. We may expect that a particular outcome is unlikely, but we generally do not know with any precision how unlikely that result is.

A consequence of this is that these indicated MAR risk figures can support a range of very different strategies, and the intention would often be to manage the strategy to a lower level of risk-taking than indicated by the MAR. Consider the three illustrative short-term strategies, using only stocks, bonds and cash, shown in Table 5.5, which have stylised allocations to stocks increasing from 20% to 50% and then to 75%. The allocation of non-equity investments is divided between over-ten-year US Treasury bonds and cash.

TABLE 5.5 **Model short-term investment strategies, with only stocks, bonds and cash: historical perspective**

	Unaggressive strategy	Moderate strategy	Aggressive strategy	Treasury bills	Government bonds	US equities
Asset allocation						
Equities	20	50	75	0	0	100
Bonds[a]	20	50	25	0	100	0
Cash[a]	60	0	0	100	0	0
Performance Dec 1900–2012, % per year[b]	5.6	7.8	8.7	3.9	5.0	9.4
Historic volatility	4.8	11.1	15.2	2.8	8.8	19.9
"Value at risk" (apparent 1 in 20 chance of return of this, or worse, in any one calendar year)[c]						
	−1.9	−8.4	−12.5	0	−8.8	−17.6
Extreme results since 1991 using Barclays and MSCI monthly data						
Worst 12 month result	−7.5	−20.5	−32.5	0.1	−12.5	−43.1
Best 12 month result	16.9	34.6	42.7	6.5	31.9	53.4

a Indicative allocations between bonds and cash for short-term investors sensitive to duration of bond benchmark.
b Geometric averages.
c See text comments on risk of more frequent occurrences of disappointing returns.
Sources: Underlying data sourced from Barclays; Dimson, Marsh and Staunton; MSCI

Table 5.5 shows the average return for each strategy based on the historical performance of market indices, before all fees and expenses, since 1900 using data from Dimson, Marsh and Staunton. It also shows, based on historical relationships, the sort of returns that might be expected in a disappointing year. For example, the moderate strategy indicates that a return of −8.4%, or worse, should be expected with no more than a one-in-20 chance in any particular year. The back-testing of results using monthly data since 1991 shows that much larger negative returns would have been recorded in the recent past with

TABLE 5.6 **Model short-term investment strategies, with only stocks, bonds and cash: forward-looking perspective**

	Unaggressive strategy	Moderate strategy	Aggressive strategy	Treasury bills	Government bonds	US equities
Asset allocation						
Equities	20	50	75	0	0	100
Bonds[a]	20	50	25	0	100	0
Cash[a]	60	0	0	100	0	0
Expected return[b]	3.5	5.0	6.0	2.5	3.0	7.0
Historic volatility since 1900	4.8	11.1	15.2	2.8	8.8	19.9
"Value at risk" (apparent 1 in 20 chance of return of this, or worse, in any one calendar year, based on "expected relationships")[c]						
	−4.1	−11.7	−16.3	0	−11.2	−21.8

a Indicative allocations between bonds and cash for short-term investors sensitive to duration of bond benchmark.
b See text for derivation of expected returns.
c See text comments on risk of more frequent occurrences of disappointing returns.
Source: Author

such a "moderate" strategy, with market indices pointing to a negative return of 20.5% in the 12 months to February 2009.

This illustrates that actual experience can from time to time be a lot worse than would be suggested by the past average statistics for overall returns and volatility. The more comforting figures are provided by routinely used modelling exercises. These suffer from severe averaging difficulties which suggest, for example, that stockmarket volatility stays at one average level. It does not, and, as 2008 demonstrated, the worst news arrives when this is least true. More particularly, the risk figures are undermined by the "surprising" frequency of extreme returns – by trending or momentum in markets, and by the fact that at times of stress, "normal" relationships between different markets may not hold.

Table 5.6 replaces the historical statistics with forward-looking statistics, based upon standard assumptions that flow from Chapter 3. The expected

FIG 5.4 **US stocks, bonds and cash: "efficient frontier" and model allocations for "short-term" investors**

Source: Author's illustrations

returns are anchored on the ten-year government bond yield, taken as 3.0%. (Cash is expected, over time, to yield 0.5% less than ten-year bonds and equities are expected to earn an arithmetic average return of 4% above ten-year bonds. Correlations and volatilities have been estimated using data since 1900.)

The lower slope of the line in Figure 5.4 indicates a slower future rate of accumulation of financial wealth that is being anticipated by most financial experts, whereas the higher slope shows average performance since 1900. These differences have a significant impact on the likelihood of achieving distant objectives.

"Models behaving badly"

We know that we should expect investment models to perform poorly from time to time, and that surprising things happen surprisingly often. But we know more than this. One thing is that at times of crisis and flight to quality, bad news infects all risk assets, and diversification among risk assets provides less protection than was hoped. Another, against which investors should also be alerted in advance, is that strategies which are intended to have modest volatility may be particularly prone to disappointing surprises.

Everyone knows that the stockmarket is volatile, and so no one should be surprised that the stockmarket suffers sharp setbacks from time to time. However, our notion of a poor investment result is conditioned by our expectation of the level of volatility that is built into an investment strategy. A shocking result for a cautious strategy is a smaller shortfall than a surprisingly poor result for a volatile strategy.

A cautious investment strategy provides a natural habitat for low volatility risk assets that offer the prospect of a surprisingly attractive ratio of performance to volatility (known as the Sharpe ratio, see Appendix 1). The fraudulent delivery of stockmarket type rewards for minimal apparent volatility was the main attraction of the Madoff scam (see Chapter 1). But many legitimate investment strategies offer attractive pay-offs between measured volatility and reward. The challenge confronting investment advisers is to assess the extent to which they understand these strategies and whether past volatility adequately captures the risks that matter to investors.

Many low volatility strategies indirectly offer insurance to someone else and are in effect option-writing strategies, which collect a steady premium most of the time but then occasionally suffer large losses. A number of hedge fund strategies fit this description, and groups of hedge funds occasionally perform poorly together (see Chapter 9). Less obviously, corporate bonds also fall into this category, since an individual corporate bond can be seen as a combination of a government bond and an option (for which a premium yield is received) provided by the bond investor to other creditors to reimburse them in the event of default. Providing this insurance becomes more of a liability to investors as equity volatility increases (as it did in 2007–08, see Figure 4.1), and so we should not be surprised if corporate bonds, as a group, perform particularly poorly when stockmarket volatility increases. Generalised increases

TABLE 5.7 **US and global capital markets: volatility and excess kurtosis**

	Oct 2000– Dec 2006	Jan 2007 – Sep 2013	Oct 2000– Dec 2006	Jan 2007– Sep 2013	Dec 2007– Oct 2008
	Volatility, % per year		Excess kurtosis		Total return, %
Barclays US Government TR	4.9	4.3	1.2	1.7	3.7
Barclays US investment grade corporate bonds TR	5.2	7.2	1.3	5.5	−14.5
Barclays Global Aggregate Credit hedged to $ TR	3.6	4.9	0.7	2.9	−8.4
MSCI USA GR	14.5	18.3	0.5	1.2	−33.0
MSCI World Ex US GR	15.8	22.0	0.3	1.1	−43.0
MSCI Emerging Markets GR	25.1	28.7	−0.1	1.6	−53.1

Note: TR means total return; GR means gross return.
Source: Derived from Barclays and MSCI index data

in risk aversion can lead to increases in the spread offered on corporate bonds, causing them to underperform government bonds by surprisingly large amounts and by amounts which more than compensate for the subsequent experience of default on corporate bonds (see Chapter 8). Many cautious investment strategies, which almost inevitably reach for yield beyond that offered on government bonds, include this type of exposure and it is a reason why cautious strategies may be prone to perform "surprisingly" poorly in "bad times", when cautious investors will particularly value safety.

The performance of corporate bonds and many cautious investment strategies in 2008–09 fit this pattern. It is now conventional wisdom that market returns are "fat tailed" and that surprising performance happens more often than volatility numbers alone would suggest. One issue is that volatility itself fluctuates, as noted in Chapter 4, and at times of high volatility it should be no surprise if the best and worst performance results look more extreme than would normally be expected. Another is that with a given level of volatility, the range, or "tails", of the distribution of returns is more extreme than would be expected (if it followed a normal pattern). This is caught by a statistical measure called "kurtosis" (see Appendix 1). Excess kurtosis has a value of zero in the normal distribution assumed by most investment models. Table 5.7 shows how volatility and excess kurtosis changed after 2006 for US markets (a similar pattern is shown by UK and euro-zone data).

The highlighted data for excess kurtosis in Table 5.7 indicate that the pattern of extreme monthly returns in capital markets was much more "surprising" in the US and global corporate bond markets than in equity markets, including those of emerging markets, even though they suffered much larger cumulative declines in 2008. This is consistent with the experience of many apparently cautious or moderate investment strategies in 2008, whose investors might reasonably have said that they had no idea that they were running so much risk. One reason for this is that before 2007 this exposure to kurtosis was not evident in the pattern of monthly returns of the previous few years. This should be expected: one thing we know is that we are most unlikely to have reliable data on the risk of an investment surprise. Yet another thing we know is that some types of investment strategy carry the risk of surprisingly poor performance even if it is not evident in the available data (and will not be shown in market tracking records). This emphasises the importance for investment advisers to think through how investments might be expected to perform in bad times as well as good and to ask whether investors are being adequately compensated for that risk.

PART 2

Implementing more complicated strategies

6 Setting the scene

A health warning: liquidity risk

The "keep-it-simple" strategies described in previous chapters should be liquid as well as simple. Almost always, when investment strategy gets more complicated it starts to embrace more liquidity risk. Liquidity is a dimension of risk which is not captured by the off-the-shelf risk models that are routinely used in managing investments. This is because it is difficult to model, not because it does not matter. Illiquidity has been described as "the most dangerous and least understood financial risk".

Investing in illiquid markets

A common error is for an investor to expect an illiquid investment to offer a premium return just because it is illiquid. This can be an expensive mistake. From an investor's perspective, the appropriate way to look at an illiquid investment opportunity is to see if it offers the prospect of a premium return that is sufficient, given the investor's circumstances, to compensate adequately for giving up the flexibility offered by liquidity. Net of fees, and given the investor's circumstances, the illiquid investment opportunity may often not pass the test.

This gives rise to two related questions: How should investors judge their appetite for illiquidity, in other words, the trade-off between the potential to earn excess returns in return for accepting the near certainty of added inflexibility that comes with increasing allocations to illiquid investments? How should investors assess the returns to be expected from a particular illiquid investment? A theme from the chapters in this book on hedge funds (Chapter 9), real estate (Chapter 11) and private equity (Chapter 10) is that investors should not assume that they will be able to earn a market return (whatever that might be) in illiquid markets unless they can convince themselves that they have an "edge" which will enable them to perform better than average. Otherwise, it is safest to assume that they will underperform. One hurdle to overcome is the high level of fees, which appears to be almost a universal characteristic of investing in illiquid markets. Another is the series of issues covered by the umbrella heading "agency issues", which refers to the informational and other disadvantages handicapping clients in their dealings with investment advisers in private markets.

Andrew Ang, Ann F. Kaplan professor of business at Columbia Business School, has analysed these and other issues that arise in trying to determine an optimal allocation to private equity and other illiquid investments. An immediate problem he identifies is that traditional "mean variance" optimiser models used to derive recommended asset allocations for investors assume that investors can rebalance their portfolios at any time, which does not apply with illiquid investments. This inability to rebalance investment allocations imposes real opportunity costs on investors, and can result in unwanted risk-taking. A particular aspect of this, which is easy to overlook in the search for premium returns from illiquid investments, is that the ability to rebalance portfolios back to a long-term strategic allocation (see Chapter 4) is a means of seeking a liquidity premium from normally liquid securities markets by providing liquidity to risk asset markets at times of crisis when others are fleeing to safety. Investors who are heavily exposed to illiquid markets will be much less able to benefit from this liquidity premium. Ang concludes that long-horizon investors do have an advantage in investing in illiquid asset classes. However, this does not mean that it is optimal for each long-term investor to hold illiquid investments.

"Liquidity budgets"

One of the lessons to emerge from the credit crunch of 2007–09 is that investors need a policy on liquidity management. This became evident as investors scrambled to respond to a situation where formerly liquid markets became prohibitively expensive to trade in, and illiquid portfolios of alternative investments generated less cash and made calls on the commitments investors had already agreed. Against this background it became important that investors should have a good balance between liquid and illiquid assets, if only so that liquid investments could be sold to raise cash; it also became evident that when the dust settled investors ought to have an explicit policy on allocations to liquid and illiquid investments.

Illiquidity in normally liquid markets

Liquid markets give investors the option to buy or sell an investment at a modest transaction cost at a time they choose at prevailing market prices; illiquid markets do not give them this option. Like any option this is valuable, though some investors will value it more highly than others. Furthermore, the value that investors put on it varies substantially over time and between investors. Investors who particularly value liquidity will need to be offered a premium rate of return before investing in illiquid assets. Correspondingly, investors should always pay less for an illiquid investment than for an otherwise identical liquid investment.

Liquid investments should provide the natural habitat for short-term investors, even for aggressive short-term investors. This is because they may need to realise investments at short notice (which is why they are short-term investors). Long-term investors can more easily accommodate illiquidity and with skill (or luck) may profit from it.

The liquidity of an investment in stocks or bonds often varies according to the size of the holding. It will normally be possible to buy or sell a marginal holding of any quoted investment at or close to its published price. But the holdings of large investment funds can represent a significant part of the available capitalisation of a security. Any attempt to establish or realise such holdings requires skill and time so as to manage the adverse "market impact" on the price of the transaction. These are circumstances in which large investors can be heavily penalised or well-rewarded for demanding liquidity from or supplying liquidity to the market. For substantial investors in many markets liquidity is at best an illusion, as the published prices provide a reliable guide to realisable transactions for only a small part of their holdings in individual stocks. This means that substantial short-term investors who really do have a short time horizon must maintain a high degree of liquidity in their investments.

The global financial crisis has shown that some markets that are usually liquid can become illiquid surprisingly quickly. When investors want to sell, which is the same as saying when they want to demand or pay for liquidity, they may be forced to delay transacting and so accept risks that they would prefer to avoid, or they may be forced to concede damaging prices that they do not wish to accept. If the intentions of large investors seeking to unwind or establish substantial positions in a short period become known to others in the market, they will always become victims of predatory behaviour by other market participants. The market never behaves benevolently in these circumstances.

Variable liquidity is both a risk and an opportunity. An alternative definition of a short-term investor is an investor who may need to demand liquidity at short notice. Short-term investors should review and limit the allocation of their portfolio to markets that might be subject to marked fluctuations in liquidity because in these markets the price of liquidity can become prohibitively high in a very short period. This is a clear threat to the achievement of short-term financial goals. Long-term investors, however large or small, can profit from these swings in liquidity, so long as they are able to use skill in "selling" liquidity. However, if they have used their long time horizon to load up on illiquid assets, they will not be able to do this, and often the best outcome will be to ride out liquidity crises without having to accept penal terms for buying liquidity when it is most expensive.

It is not only at times of crisis that these principles apply. Differences in equity transaction styles between trading desks of different investment houses reflect whether the money managers or traders demand and pay for immediate execution, which raises their "execution" costs, or whether they are content to bide their time, at the risk of missing out on the potential advantages of rapid execution. "Value" equity managers normally pride themselves on their ability to provide rather than demand liquidity. The opposite is true of momentum managers, who seek to profit from market trends.

Long-term managers with a clear sense of investment philosophy and discipline who, at the required time, have the asset allocation flexibility, will be able to exploit the occasional extreme price paid for liquidity. But for waverers, hesitation will always be reinforced by the certainty that there will be highly reputable commentators who argue that prospects have changed for the worse and that what appears inexpensive is at best fairly priced. For long-term investors for whom risk assets represent a "natural habitat", who have the good fortune (or foresight, or both) to have significant resources awaiting investment at the moment of crisis, these events can present a one-off opportunity to significantly improve their finances. But it will be a reward for taking risk when the majority wanted security.

Behavioural finance, market efficiency and arbitrage opportunities

Illiquidity indicates a breakdown of market efficiency in securities markets. Any discussion of market efficiency should start by addressing a widespread heresy, a variation of which Robert Shiller has described as "one of the most remarkable errors in the history of economic thought". This is the notion that the very existence of inefficiency in markets is a sufficient reason to expect outperformance from skilful managers. This notion is wrong. It does not follow that there must be easy rewards for skilled investors simply because markets are inefficient. The reason is that inefficiencies can be difficult to arbitrage. Correspondingly, if there seem to be no easy rewards for active managers, this is not necessarily evidence of markets being efficient. The rule of thumb is that if the existence of a market anomaly can easily be demonstrated, the safest conclusion is that there must be some difficulty in profiting from the anomaly. As Aswath Damodaran, professor of finance at Stern School of Business, New York University, writes in his book *Investment Fables*: "If you see easy money to be made in the stockmarket, you have not looked hard enough."

Barriers to arbitrage

Anomalies in the pricing of contracts that offer the same economic risks can persist even in markets which are the natural habitat of investment banks and hedge funds. One historic highly visible example of an evident arbitrage opportunity is the significant differential that existed between the share prices of Royal Dutch (traded principally in Amsterdam and New York) and Shell Transport & Trading (traded principally in London). Shares in both companies gave strictly comparable ownership rights in the same company, but Royal Dutch traded historically as much as 35% underpriced and as much as 15% overpriced compared with Shell Transport & Trading.

The Shell share price anomaly did not provide an easy profit opportunity because the anomaly could get worse. This position was resolved only after Shell announced in late 2004 that the two share classes would finally merge in 2005. The corporate announcement provided some assurance of a profitable exit within a specified time period. Often there exists no such exit strategy from a perceived anomaly which explains why it may persist.

The key to the potential persistence of these "anomalies" lies in the impediments to arbitrage which can prevent instances of irrational pricing translating into easy profit opportunities. These barriers are generally considered to be of three types.

Fundamental risk and arbitrage

The first barrier is the common danger (not present in the Shell example) that fundamental risk may undermine any effort to arbitrage away an anomaly. An example would be where one company in an industry is thought to be expensive and a similar one to be more sensibly priced. A hedge fund manager might sell the former and buy the latter, but the size of these positions will be limited because the arbitrageur will know that unexpected events could cause the expensive stock to appreciate in price and the cheap stock to decline, causing losses to both sides of the "hedge".

Once in a while a graphic illustration of an apparently good hedge resulting in large losses for hedge funds is revealed. In May 2005 Kirk Kerkorian, an American billionaire investor, announced his intention to increase his holding in General Motors (GM) stock (which increased in price), and almost simultaneously Standard & Poor's (see Chapter 8) downgraded the debt of both GM and Ford from investment grade to sub-investment grade, which fell in price. The problem was that a number of hedge funds thought they were "hedging" GM equity (which they had sold) with GM debt (which they believed to be cheap, and so had bought). The result was substantial losses for a number of hedge funds on both sides of the hedge whose prices, unusually, moved in opposite directions.

This example illustrates a characteristic of a number of hedge fund strategies: that they often provide an attractive earnings stream, accompanied by the risk of occasional substantial losses (see Chapter 9). The simple lesson from this is to make sure that a hedge is a good hedge, and to be careful how much money is invested trying to exploit an apparent anomaly. The more substantive lesson is that even the best hedges may fail, and the risk of this happening puts a limit on the scale of the arbitrage position that will be applied to correct apparent market anomalies.

To risk money on an arbitrage position, an investor must consider the time horizon for the position. A hedge fund that correctly identified in the late 1990s that "new economy" (technology, media, telecommunications) sectors of the stockmarket were overpriced relative to so-called "old economy" sectors could easily have bankrupted itself before the validity of its analysis was demonstrated by the collapse of "new economy" stock prices. This illustrates that some types of market anomaly, whose identification will always be subject to margins of uncertainty, may require such long time horizons that the investors best suited to try to exploit them will be long-term investment funds, not hedge funds. Hedge funds are not ideally suited to correct all pricing anomalies.

Herd behaviour and arbitrage

Hedge funds may in fact exacerbate anomalies in the short run. The second barrier to arbitrage is that "noise trader risk" may undermine arbitrage efforts by making an apparent anomaly even more extreme. A trend-following hedge fund, or any other short-term "momentum" manager or speculator, understanding that investors may behave as if recent past performance will continue, is more likely to follow and reinforce the anomaly than to hold out against it. There is widespread support for the idea that short-term trend following can be a profitable strategy. This can be seen as one application of the "greater fool" theory, namely a confidence that profits can be made out of "hot" overpriced investments by selling them at a higher price on a later date to a greater fool (though the trend follower will not be interested in whether the investment is overpriced, only the trend in its price). This type of trading by market insiders is probably as old as markets: academics have identified evidence of such profitable investment behaviour by market professionals during the South Sea bubble of 1720.

These patterns of investing will exacerbate irrational market trends. Success in this kind of anomaly exacerbating behaviour, like a policy of dancing by the doorway when you know the music hall may burn down, requires the ability to identify and respond more quickly than others to events that may burst a speculative bubble. On average for all investors this is a doomed strategy, but wishful thinking about their own nimbleness encourages many to stay on and enjoy the party while it lasts. A few always get out in time through a mixture of skill and luck. The random element of luck is normally downplayed, leading many to conclude that they may have the skill required to play the game next time. The one predictable result is that the market process of correcting anomalies is undermined and, for a while, made less effective.

In these circumstances it can be dangerous to bet against some apparent irregularities with more than a modest investment position. Anomalies can persist for a long time, reflecting the inability of short-term arbitrageurs (such as hedge funds) to remove the mispricing.

The role of crowd behaviour in driving investment prices away from their fundamental value requires a particular collective role for what are sometimes known as "noise traders". This needs a wide interpretation, because it does not just include the actions of uninformed investors. As well as professional investors who try to exploit momentum trends in crowds of uninformed investors, there are professional investors who feel forced to implement investment decisions that they view with deep scepticism. Such investments should be regarded as generating "noise", in the sense that there may be little fundamental investment justification for the decision. This may arise from selling pressure in illiquid markets caused by end-investors who may need to raise liquidity or whose confidence in a strategy is undermined just when the investment case for it may appear to the investment manager to be greatest.

Occasionally, noise may result from spuriously precise definitions of "prudential" regulations. More common, though, may be the impact of peer-group pressure generating herding behaviour among investors. This may be purely informal commercial risk management, where a money-management firm determines that its biggest risk is to be different from other firms. Or it may be imposed by formal or informal rules which dictate the margin of difference from the market or from other investors (this is often called relative risk or tracking error) that an investment fund may run. Where funds or managers are assessed relative to an index or relative to competitors this pressure will be present.

The herd mentality is probably reinforced by the legal backing to the "prudent person" rule, which is the benchmark for the assessment of the reasonableness of the actions of fiduciaries in many countries. The 1974 Employee Retirement Income Security Act (ERISA) in the United States defines the obligations of a fiduciary as being to use:

> the care, skill, prudence, and diligence, under the circumstances then prevailing, that a prudent man acting in a like capacity and familiar with such matters would use in the conduct of an enterprise of a like character and with like aims.

As Shiller points out, this definition tests the reasonableness of a fiduciary's decision against the standard of how a peer might behave. In other words:

> The prudent person standard refers to someone who does what most of us think is sensible. Ultimately, it must refer to conventional wisdom.

It is not clear how this standard might be improved, but the inevitable consequence is that it validates the reasonableness of crowd behaviour. As a result, the impact of this standard of care is more likely to reinforce than to correct any tendency towards market mispricing. It will encourage trades that follow and support market trends as managers control their differences from the market or the peer group of other reasonable investors, who are behaving in exactly the same way. The behaviour of pension funds responding to this pressure has in the past been likened to a parade of circus elephants following each other round in a circle, joined from trunk to tail. The honest conclusion is that institutional investors never completely break from this circle. Their fiduciaries are, rightly, always looking over their shoulder and comparing themselves with comparable funds. For private wealth there is more flexibility, which brings both more opportunity and more danger.

Implementation costs, market evolution and arbitrage

The third potential barrier to arbitrage activities is that "implementation costs" can be prohibitive. Typically, an arbitrageur needs to sell short an investment. To be able to do this, a hedge fund needs to borrow the stock from another investor so as to deliver it to the investor who has bought it. This works smoothly in textbooks and in liquid markets. In illiquid markets it can be a nightmare. This is because it is a process that is subject to administrative interruptions that can threaten investment positions. For example, if a stock lender wants the stock returned, the hedge fund's broker needs to find another investor from whom to borrow the stock. If it cannot, the hedge fund manager will be forced to buy the stock back before the anomaly has corrected (or, even worse, when it has become more entrenched).

In 2008, client selling, withdrawals of borrowing facilities and regulation changes (such as restrictions on short selling) probably conspired to exacerbate rather than correct market anomalies. At times of crisis liquidity pressures can force hedge funds prematurely to close positions, thereby exacerbating the very anomalies that they were trying to arbitrage. The 1998 Long-Term Capital Management crisis provided earlier vivid testimony to the reality that funds cannot always afford to maintain large positions that they may want to sustain for a long period. (Long-Term Capital Management was a large hedge fund that failed in 1998 as a result of the failure of arbitrage strategies of enormous size.)

These influences mean that there is no inevitable tendency for markets to become progressively more efficient. The cycles of market liquidity show that market efficiency is also cyclical. Nevertheless, the pressures to arbitrage away anomalies will always be a powerful force in any market. If a particular market arrangement is a barrier to efficiency, you can be sure that there will be great pressure to remove that impediment because there will be arbitrage profits available to those who help remove it. Today's barrier to arbitrage may not exist tomorrow, as institutional and market arrangements and instruments are continuously evolving to overcome obstacles and exploit opportunities to make money. Tomorrow there may be other anomalies, and old ones may reappear, but it would be a great mistake to underestimate what Robert Merton, the University Professor Emeritus at Harvard University, and Zvi Bodie, the Norman and Adele Barron professor of management at Boston University, refer to as "the financial innovation spiral" that works to chip away at anomalies and inefficiencies.

Institutional wealth and private wealth: taxation

The three principal differences between private and institutional wealth management are:

- the role of taxation in private wealth;
- the role of committees of fiduciaries in the management of institutional wealth;
- the contrast between the flexible spending objectives of family wealth and the precise purposes of much institutional wealth.

However, these are generalisations. Not all private wealth is subject to taxation and not all institutional wealth is exempt from taxation. Investment committees are found in the management of both private and institutional wealth. Some institutions have flexible objectives, while family philanthropic foundations have closely defined purposes and mark the boundary at which private wealth becomes institutional. Yet the broad generalisations remain valid, together with the further observation that the amounts of money represented by private wealth are normally much smaller than those of institutional investment funds.

Some advisers make far-reaching proposals for investment strategy to accommodate tax structures. Others emphasise that the benefits from many tax devices are in practice modest. Investors should be aware that given the same facts, conflicting advice may be offered. For taxable investors, minimising the overall tax bill makes less sense than trying to maximise post-tax income, given their tolerance for risk, even if it means paying more tax. Any tax-management scheme should be assessed in this light: if it is not expected to improve post-tax income, after allowing for tax advisory fees and for any special elements of risk (such as illiquidity) introduced by the proposal, it probably should not be pursued. It is worth paying more tax if it is associated with even more income.

Tax does make an enormous difference, however, by constraining the evolution of private wealth. Table 6.1 illustrates its potential impact, although the picture is much more complicated than this. It assumes that capital gains and income are taxed at the same rate, which they are not, and that each individual stock earns the same return, and ignores any tax allowances that would reduce a headline tax rate to a lower effective rate. But the simple story remains true, that income and capital gains taxes seriously undermine the rate of accumulation of private wealth and the premium offered for taking risk. In practice, the impact on risk-taking varies, as income tax particularly affects low-risk assets (bonds and cash) whereas capital gains tax particularly affects equities.

Individual taxpayers have tax-deferred accounts (for example, retirement accounts, which accumulate free of tax but withdrawals from which are treated as taxable income) as well as taxable accounts, and depending upon the jurisdiction an investor may have some tax-exempt accounts (accounts from which the investor can withdraw funds without incurring a tax penalty). Investment strategy and wealth management should take account of the different tax status of different accounts. This starts with an assessment of the sufficiency of wealth to meet future objectives. For example, a dollar in a tax-deferred pension savings account will be worth less than a dollar in

TABLE 6.1 **The impact of taxation on taxable investment returns and wealth accumulation**

Average tax rate, %	0	15	30
Expected returns, % per year			
Equities	7	6.0	4.9
Bonds	4	3.4	2.8
$100 becomes after ten years[a]			
Equities	$197	$178	$161
Bonds	$148	$140	$132
$100 becomes after ten years, today's prices assuming 2% per year inflation[a]			
Equities	$163	$147	$133
Bonds	$122	$115	$108
$100 becomes after 20 years, today's prices assuming 2% per year inflation[a]			
Equities	$265	$217	$177
Bonds	$149	$132	$117

a Assuming actual return equals expected return and that tax rate applies to annual total return with no allowances or tax shelters.
Source: Author

a tax-exempt account. At the same time, investment strategy needs to take account of the totality of an investor's wealth in each different account or "location", and the allocation of investments to different locations needs to allow for the differences in the impact of tax on different types of investment.

The impact of taxation on risk-taking needs to be kept in mind when considering the uncertainty surrounding future equity returns. But uncertainty also surrounds future tax rates and allowances. This needs to be acknowledged in the degree to which the details of today's tax rules are allowed to influence the medium- or long-term investment strategy for an investor's taxable investments. If in doubt, keep it simple (but take advice), but be particularly aware of the costs of unwinding an arrangement which is tax efficient today, but may not be tomorrow.

For a taxable investor, investment strategy never starts from a blank sheet of paper. There is always a legacy tax position that exists whenever an investor changes investment manager or adviser. This can have implications for:

■ the choice between different styles of investment management;

■ whether to have fewer or more managers or funds;

■ the desired average holding periods for investments;

■ whether to have a bias towards low turnover accounts (though the relationship between turnover and taxation will not be straightforward);

■ whether to have a bias against strategies that involve "top slicing" of all positions to rebalance or implement asset allocation decisions.

Tax overlay management services are often made available by private wealth managers in the United States. They introduce a degree of consistency and rigour into what might otherwise be a judgmental process. These services are typically model-driven and can help manage the tax consequences of a move to a new investment manager, and can also assist so-called tax-loss harvesting when a portfolio has a combination of capital gains and capital losses. These approaches can include the management of both portfolio risk and tax obligations.

To address these issues, taxable investors should consult a tax-literate investment adviser (who may be better placed to advise on strategies to optimise after-tax investment returns) as well as a tax specialist (who may have a bias towards minimising tax payments). However, in responding to tax advice, investors should always retain an overall picture of their tax status as well as their investment strategy. This is particularly important if the investor divides savings and wealth between different objectives, different risk profiles, and a mix of taxed and tax-advantaged accounts. Finally, be cautious before prolonging any excessive investment risk (such as a concentrated stock position) simply because of concern about the tax consequences of selling down a position which represents a substantial capital gain. It is better to make a gain on which you pay tax than not to make a gain.

7   Equities

The restless shape of the equity market

At the start of the 20th century, railroad stocks represented 63% of the US equity market and just 0.2% a century later. Russia, India and Austria-Hungary together represented 25% of the global equity market in 1899 and less than 1% a century later, which in the past decade has increased to 2.5%. In the past 30 years in the global equity market, the weights of Japan, technology stocks and banking stocks have risen and then fallen, and in the years since the late 1980s the weight of the emerging markets has increased from around 1% of the global market to around 13%. The scale of these changes is a powerful challenge to anyone suggesting that investors should passively accept whatever changes may occur in the market. An autopilot approach to investing in either domestic or global equities over long periods is not credible. All investors need to be responsive to changes in the structure, risk and opportunities of the marketplace.

Concentrated stock positions in private portfolios

The analysis so far has assumed that any equity exposure reflects the risk characteristics of the equity market. Frequently, though, equity holdings are concentrated in a way that increases risk-taking. Sometimes this arises from an executive's successful career with a listed company. In the United States, concentrated positions in employer stock within company-sponsored 401(k) defined-contribution pension plans used to be common, though these have declined in recent years. According to a 2013 report from Morningstar

Investment Management, almost 25% of 401(k) plan assets for companies with a market cap of greater than $10 billion were invested in the company's own stock in 1999; by 2011 this had fallen to 10%.

The prescriptions of traditional finance are clear on this issue: there is no premium return, only increased risk, offered for a lack of diversification. Increasing awareness, legislative change and the threat of litigation are moving practice in the same direction. Nevertheless, the Morningstar report shows that it was still common in 2011 for 401(k) plans to have concentrations of exposure to employer stock that exceeded the maximum levels (often 5%, or perhaps 10% for a highly focused, active portfolio) that a money manager would maintain for a most favoured stock.

Concentrated holdings within defined-contribution pension accounts are separate from the concentrated stock positions that executives may accumulate as a reward for success through corporate remuneration schemes. The pension plan holdings reflect a deliberate decision by the individual to acquire, or to retain, the stock. Executives' concentrated stock holdings reflect involvement in business through employment or entrepreneurship. The exposure was acquired to align the interests of an individual with those of the company. In an executive stock compensation scheme, if the company and the individual have been successful, significant wealth may have been accumulated. At that stage issues of wealth and risk management become relevant. They are not relevant at the outset of the process. For this reason, concern about how best to manage an executive's concentrated stock position is an "enviable dilemma".

An executive's stock position is often subject to formal or informal selling restrictions. When a restricted holding represents a substantial part of an investor's wealth, a financial adviser may recommend borrowing against the security of that holding to allow investing elsewhere. If the concentrated position is unhedged, the borrowing will not reduce risk-taking. It will increase the potential for wealth accumulation by gearing the investor's overall portfolio, but at the cost of even greater volatility of that wealth. The likelihood of a sudden diminution of wealth is increased, not reduced, by borrowing against an unprotected concentrated stock holding and investing the proceeds of that borrowing in a diversified stockmarket exposure.

Assisting in the tax and wealth management of concentrated stock positions is an important role for many financial advisers. The risks of such positions need to be taken into account when allocating other financial investments. This is because the total wealth is dominated by their volatile exposure to the equity of their business.

Stockmarket anomalies and the fundamental insight of the capital asset pricing model

Despite the extraordinary changes in the shape of the global equity market, an annually rebalanced, passive approach to investing in US, UK or global equities, if it had been available, could have performed extremely well over the past 11 decades (see Chapter 3). However, the belief that it should be possible to do "better" than to match the performance of the stockmarket is supported by a wide body of research (even though simple arithmetic tells us that this cannot be true for all stockmarket investors). This research has focused on extensive analysis of stockmarket "anomalies", which are well-established patterns of stockmarket performance that do not conform with the predictions of the original simplified theory called the capital asset pricing model (CAPM).

In its original form, the CAPM said that the performance of any stock should be expected to reflect two things: the extent to which the stock is a geared or a diluted "play" on the market as a whole; and a considerable amount of company-specific volatility. The first represents a stock's exposure to systematic risk (measured by its "beta") for which investors should expect to be compensated. An example of a stock which would be a "geared play" on the stockmarket, or a "high beta" stock, would be the stock of an equity money manager whose fee income, reflecting assets under management, would rise and fall in line with the stockmarket and whose profitability would be highly geared to this influence. Systematic risk cannot be diversified away in an equity portfolio. The second is "noise", or idiosyncratic or diversifiable risk. This should cancel out in a well-diversified portfolio, but it reflects the scope for an individual stock, or a portfolio of stocks, to perform differently from the market (or, more precisely, from the beta-adjusted market return).

There have been numerous refinements to the CAPM to reflect research indicating that there are a number of sources of risk for a particular share price in the stockmarket which can help to explain share price performance. These include interest-rate and foreign exchange exposure, corporate balance-sheet data, income and dividend information, as well as company capitalisation, industry and geographical location. An understanding of these sources of risk can help in the construction of equity portfolios, particularly if an investor has a view that a particular source of risk-taking is likely to produce good results in the period ahead.

However, the fundamental insight of the CAPM – the division of portfolio risk into undiversifiable, systematic market risk and diversifiable, idiosyncratic risk – has stood the test of time. It provides an invaluable framework for understanding how the activities of portfolio managers alter a portfolio's systematic and idiosyncratic risk exposures and so affect the performance and risk of that portfolio. An understanding of this insight, as well as its strengths and weaknesses, is an important aspect of the interface between finance theory and practical investment.

Among the weaknesses of CAPM is that it is now accepted that the original simplified theory does not fully explain the pattern of performance between different stocks. Low beta stocks, with supposedly diluted exposure to the market, do not systematically underperform the stockmarket as the original theory suggested that they should. Furthermore, stocks with smaller market capitalisation, certain measures of "value" stocks and even recently successful, "momentum", stocks have shown an apparent persistence of superior performance that is inconsistent with the simplest versions of the theory.

There are two possible explanations:

■ These patterns reflect the impact on market prices of irrational investor behaviour such as investor fashions and a widespread desire to own shares in "good" companies and to avoid "dogs" (for example, historic stockmarket underperformers). If so, the anomalies would disappear only if sufficient weight of long-term investor money recognised the irrational behaviour of other investors, leading the "rational" investors to reorganise their portfolios to profit from these anomalies. This would bid up the prices that had been expected to outperform (removing the outperformance) and depress the prices of expected laggards (improving their subsequent performance). If enough investors responded in this way, the anomalies would disappear. But if they persist, "informed" investors who are aware of the anomalies should adjust their portfolios to profit from them.

■ The old measures of risk-taking may be wrong. If this is correct, those who seek to exploit the anomalies may simply be gearing up their risk-taking. For example, small cap (see below), some categories of "value" stocks and emerging-market stocks may be riskier than they appear to be. If so, it may be rational that they should trade at a discounted price to leave room, on average, for superior performance to reflect the extra margin of risk.

If the first explanation is correct (that groups of stocks tend to be underpriced), cautious long-term investors might reasonably increase their exposure to these groups of stocks. But if the second explanation is correct, this would be inappropriate. Investors need to know that there is no agreement among finance experts on this and that when faced with uncertainty, it is reasonable for cautious investors to err on the side of caution.

John Campbell of Harvard University and Tuomo Vuolteenaho of the National Bureau of Economic Research have argued that the traditional measure of market risk exposure, beta, is clouded by combining two different measures of risk. The first is the responsiveness of a stock to a change in the market's discount rate. As explained in Chapter 5 in the discussion of "good" and "bad" price declines, a fall in price caused by a rise in the market discount rate should be recouped by faster subsequent performance. For a cautious long-term investor this is not a major source of concern. The second element is the response of a stock price to a change in expectations for corporate earnings. This is what has been described as "bad beta", because there is no mechanism for ensuring a recovery of the lost performance in response to a downgrade of earnings growth expectations.

In studies of US equity performance, it was found that value stocks and small-company stocks are more sensitive than the market as a whole to changes in market-wide earnings expectations (bad beta) than growth stocks and large-company stocks, which are more sensitive to changes in the market's discount rate (good beta). Any investor should want to receive a premium return for incurring bad beta risk, and it seems that normally such a premium has eventually been paid to value and small cap investors, but it should not be taken for granted.

"Small cap" and "large cap"

In the early 1980s, Rolf Banz published research which highlighted the surprising superior performance of smaller companies compared with larger companies. This result has been replicated on numerous occasions since for the United States, the UK and other countries, with a general pattern that the smallest, or micro-companies, have outperformed small companies, which in turn have outperformed large companies. The historic outperformance of smaller companies is the "small cap effect" or the "small cap anomaly", because, although small companies tend to be more volatile than large companies, the degree of outperformance could not be explained by the original simplified CAPM model.

A sense of the small stock "anomaly" is gained by looking at the historical performance of small and large capitalisation companies. Figures 7.1 and 7.2 make use of the comprehensive database maintained by the Center for Research in Security Prices at the University of Chicago's Booth School of Business. They contrast the performance from 1925 to early 2013 of the largest US companies (represented by the largest 10% of New York Stock Exchange listed domestic companies, as well as companies from the other leading US exchanges which are allocated to the same size bands) with the performance of small companies, indicated by those companies falling within the sixth to eighth decile bands of the same grouping. At end of March 2013 market values, this small cap band covered US companies with a market capitalisation of between $584m and $2.2 billion, while the large cap band included all companies with a market capitalisation of greater than $20.1 billion. The cumulative outperformance of small cap since 1925 is impressive, with an initial $1 investment growing (before allowing for inflation, or expenses and taxes) to $13,800 by May 2013, compared with $2,250 for an investment in the group of largest companies. (Over the same period, consumer prices increased 13-fold.) This translates into an annualised performance of 11.5% per year for the small cap stocks, compared with 9.2% for the large cap stocks (and 3.0% per year for inflation).

A similar pattern is evident from research in the UK by Elroy Dimson and Paul Marsh, although as for the United States the margin

FIG 7.1 **Cumulative total return of US small cap and large cap stocks**
Before expenses, taxes and inflation, Dec 1925–May 2013

Source: CRSP US database indices, Center for Research in Security Prices (CRSP), University of Chicago, Booth School of Business

of outperformance by small companies depends on the period chosen and the definition of small cap that is used. Their work lies behind the Numis Smaller Companies Index (formerly the Hoare Govett smaller companies index), which has measured the performance of companies within the bottom 10% of the UK market capitalisation since 1955. Over the 58 years to the end of 2012, this index gave an annualised return (before fees, taxes and other costs) of 15.5%, which is 3.2% per annum above the broad UK market, measured by the FTSE All-Share index.

Figure 7.2 shows a number of ten-year periods when small cap underperformed large cap in the United States. The most recent episode, including almost every overlapping ten-year period in the 1990s, coincided with a widespread view that the earlier observed "small cap anomaly" had indeed been corrected by heavy investment in small cap by investors bidding up prices as they tried to exploit the anomaly. In fact, since 1925, US small cap stocks have underperformed large cap stocks (on the definitions used here) during around 30%

FIG 7.2 **10-year rolling average returns for US small cap and large cap stocks**
Before fees, taxes and inflation, Dec 1935–May 2013

Source: CRSP US database indices, Center for Research in Security Prices (CRSP), University of Chicago, Booth School of Business

of all rolling ten-year periods. Such relatively frequent periods of underperformance by small stocks are sufficient to caution most long-term investors against holding much more than a significant minority of their equity investments as strategic holdings in small cap stocks.

An understanding of what is meant by "small cap" is needed before a decision can be made on allocations. For example, different small cap managers may have different investable universes of stocks. Many money managers would regard stocks in the United States or Europe of less than $2 billion market capitalisation as small cap, and a market cap range of $2 billion–10 billion as mid cap and anything above that as large cap. The index providers divide the market into proportions of the market. Large cap might be the top 70% or 80%, mid cap the next 15% or 10%, and small cap the remaining 15% or 10%. So 10% of total equity investments represents an allocation to small cap that could, if well diversified, constitute a neutral global allocation. Allocations of materially more or less than these amounts should reflect a decision to differ from the market.

With any equity investment programme, exposure to small cap stocks should be carefully monitored. It is almost always a mistake to approach small cap investing in an ad hoc, piecemeal fashion. This is more likely to be an issue with a private investor than an institutional investor, but the rule should be that exposure to smaller companies should be obtained through dedicated small-company portfolios or funds. In any event, there is a tendency for active investment managers to drift into small-company holdings (partly because they may be less well researched by competitors). For this reason, it is not sufficient to aggregate the benchmarks given to different money managers to arrive at a measure of exposure to different segments of the market. Active managers may vary significantly within loosely defined investment remits, and selected passive managers may have been appointed to manage money against index benchmarks that do not reflect the market. Wherever possible, management information should be obtained by aggregating underlying exposures to individual companies and then comparing them with the broadest possible measure of the market (see Appendix 2).

Will it cost me to invest ethically or sustainably?

Many investors have a strong preference to avoid investing in companies that transgress their personal codes of ethics or religion, so-called "sin" stocks. "Ethical" investors differ in their categorisation of sin stocks, but common industry groupings include weapons, tobacco, alcohol, gambling and pornography. A common supposition is that sin stocks will trade at a discount since they are shunned by many investors, in which case such stocks should be expected to outperform the market and ethical investors will pay a price for their ethical standards. The evidence for this is mixed, but it seems that investment managers often undermine the case for ethical investing by loading high fees onto ethical funds, which then underperform market indices and the most inexpensive index funds. But Jacquelyn Humphrey and David Tan, researchers at the Australian National University, in a 2013 *Journal of Business Ethics* article, "Does it Really Hurt to be Responsible?", have shown that responsible investing (for example, by screening out categories of "sin" stocks) need not lower expected risk-adjusted returns from investing in equities.

FIG 7.3 **Ethical investing, cumulative returns**
$, Jan 2001–Sep 2013, Dec 2001=1

Source: FTSE

The track record for ethical investing, as illustrated by the FTSE4Good series of equity indices, has underperformed the broad market since its launch in 2001 (see Figure 7.3). The FTSE4Good index provides a benchmark for investors to identify and invest in companies that meet preset criteria. The index screens out companies that are tobacco producers, weapons producers, or nuclear power operators. To be included, a company must adhere to specified standards for combating bribery, working towards environmental sustainability, ensuring good supply chain labour standards, promoting positive relationships with stakeholders and supporting universal human rights.

Analysis by the FTSE suggests that this past underperformance is explained by the company size and industry differences between the FTSE4Good index and the broad market. Specifically, the FTSE4Good index underrepresents the oil and gas, materials and utilities sectors, while overweighting technology and financials. There would seem to be no reason to expect this underperformance to continue for the indefinite future, although significant differences from market performance should not be a surprise.

Investors who favour "sustainable investment" are often not seeking to promote a particular moral code but rather to address a potential market failure, which is the likelihood that markets will fail to price appropriately externalities which impose medium- or long-term costs on the economy and society. One example would be a company that relies on inexpensive and plentiful fresh water, the supply of which is likely to become more difficult and so expensive over time, thereby undermining the company's business model. Other examples could involve waste management. Promoters of sustainable investment look to the integration of environmental, social and governance issues in investment decision-making. Some institutional investors are embracing such approaches as a way of fulfilling their desire to be responsible investors. Typically, they also anticipate that this will deliver superior risk-adjusted returns as the market gradually takes account of the costs of wasteful processes and corrects substandard governance arrangements. Such approaches have been supported by academic analysis of the corporate and social responsibility engagements with US companies between 1999 and 2009 by a leading institutional investor. This found that shareholder action by this large investor to improve the governance standards of companies on average does subsequently lead to an improvement in share price performance.

Don't get carried away by your "style"

Equity investment managers have particular investment approaches and philosophies, which lead to differences in style of investing. These characteristics are often as ingrained as any personal belief. Investors need to know and understand these differences. They will often find that some approaches are more appealing than others because of the sort of person they happen to be. Investors should be careful not to let these preferences result in unwitting risk biases in their investment strategy.

Philosophically, value and growth managers are quite different. Value managers have in common that they believe that markets repeatedly overreact as investor enthusiasm or alarm becomes detached from investment reality. As a result, value managers are contrarian individuals who are likely to make a virtue of implementing unfashionable investment decisions. Their analysis suggests that market prices oscillate around their fair values and that the turning point, when valuations become extended, is unpredictable. Value managers will try to persuade their clients that what is required is patience, as eventually the strategy is sure to be rewarded. In practice, clients are particularly attracted when a value manager has experienced recent good performance. This is when a value manager would naturally want to caution that such performance cannot be sustained indefinitely and that lean times might lie ahead.

The particular vulnerability for value managers who believe that "what goes around, comes around" is changes in long-term macroeconomic relationships. According to Sir John Templeton, a notably successful investor, "The four most dangerous words in investing are 'it's different this time'." But sometimes, particularly in the prospects for individual companies, things are different, for either good or ill. A growth manager is likely to criticise value managers for looking back and not identifying potential. For growth managers, analyses of technological and commercial change, and how this can transform the earnings prospects of individual companies, provide the cornerstone of their pursuit of new investment opportunities and understanding of business prospects. A growth manager's portfolio will consist of a variety of such investment prospects.

A crucial discipline for any manager will be when to sell out of a profitable investment position. This will often be much more instinctive for a value manager than for a growth manager, with the likelihood that a value manager may sell a profitable investment "too early" whereas a growth manager may be more likely to err on the side of selling it too late. This helps to shed light on some of the different risks faced by value and growth managers and their clients.

A close relative of the value style of investing is represented by wealth or fundamental weighted equity indices. Stockmarket indices are almost always constructed by giving different companies weights which reflect their comparative stockmarket valuation. These are the market capitalisation weighted indices such as the S&P 500 index for the US equity market. A criticism of these traditional indices from those who believe that the stockmarket is prone to overreaction caused by fads and fashions is that they overweight companies which are overpriced, but underweight companies which are underpriced. An alternative methodology has been suggested to reflect the contribution of each listed company to wealth creation, as indicated by their profit generation, cash flow and shareholders' equity (book value). If the underlying premise of this type of market overreaction is correct, these wealth-weighted indices should be expected to outperform the market capitalisation indices over time.

Value and growth managers

Value managers commonly have an investment process that starts with statistical screening of stockmarket databases for companies whose share price, earnings, dividend and balance-sheet data meet certain characteristics. A value stock will be one that has some combination of:

- higher than average dividend yield;
- lower than average ratio of the stock price to earnings per share or of the stock price to the book value of the company's assets per share;
- lower than average ratio of the company's valuation to sales or of valuation to cash flow.

These are some of the ratios that are used in constructing "value" indices of stockmarket performance. Individual managers will use different combinations of these and other indicators to screen for value in the stockmarket. Apart from purely quantitative managers, this screening process is best seen as a step towards reducing the potential universe of investable companies to a manageable number, which the investment manager can then research qualitatively in detail. This stage, involving management, product and industry research and ad hoc analysis, will often be the most important part of the investment process. But the screens are also important ingredients in describing a manager's investment style, and they will define the universe of stocks that the manager may then research further. As stock prices evolve, managers should be able to relate their actual portfolios back to those screens to demonstrate that the portfolios remain true to the managers' descriptions of their investment style.

Value managers divide into two camps:

■ "Deep" value managers invest in stocks that meet their qualitative and quantitative criteria irrespective of how unrepresentative the resulting portfolio may be of the market as a whole. In particular, they are happy to have a zero weighting in parts of the stockmarket where the value screens suggest that all stocks offer poor value.

■ "Relative" value managers manage the risks of their portfolios relative to the market as a whole, and so have disciplines that force the portfolio to hold some less expensive stocks in sectors that the screens suggest are absolutely expensive.

Money manager business leaders (who dislike the instability of assets under management that can be associated with deep value strategies) and investors who are particularly aware of "regret risk" generally feel more comfortable with relative value than with deep value management styles.

Growth managers are particularly concerned to exploit and profit from the relationship between earnings growth and stock price performance. Companies generally do not post unusually strong earnings growth results year after year. But as the market discounts the strong earnings of those companies that are growing rapidly, their stock prices can rise very, very strongly. This puts a premium on primary research into companies that may demonstrate unexpectedly rapid earnings growth in the future.

Many growth managers also use statistical screening of databases, but this is generally a less powerful tool than successful qualitative industry or thematic research. But such research is notoriously difficult to undertake successfully and consistently. The statistical screens used by the index compilers to define "growth" stocks are earnings per share growth, sales growth and the ratio of retained earnings to equity capital (the internal rate of growth).

Should cautious investors overweight value stocks?

Over the longest periods of time, by most measures, value stocks are shown to have outperformed growth stocks (see Figure 7.4). Despite this, by the traditional measure of risk, the volatility of returns, value stocks (in aggregate) have often appeared to be "safer" or at least "less risky" than growth stocks (see Figure 7.5), although noticeably this was not the case following 2008.

Investors who wish to tilt their investments to profit from the

FIG 7.4 **Cumulative total return performance of US growth and value equity indices**
Dec 1978–Sep 2013

FIG 7.5 **Volatility of US growth and value equity indices, 36-month rolling standard deviations of return**
% per year, Dec 1981–Sep 2013

FIG 7.6 **US value and growth equity indices, 5-year rolling performance**
% per year, Dec 1983–Sep 2013

potential for value investments (or high income producing stocks) to outperform need to be able to withstand prolonged periods of underperforming the market. During the late 1990s growth stocks outperformed value stocks by more than 60% in just over two years, a process that was reversed in the subsequent 18 months, but then repeated in 2007–09 when value stocks (influenced by bank stocks) underperformed growth stocks by a cumulative 25% (see Figure 7.6). Few investors have the confidence to withstand being entirely on the wrong side of such swings without making a mistaken reaction that would cost them dearly. As most equity investors now appreciate, maintaining balance is a prerequisite to sleeping easily.

Meanwhile, the possible risk explanations for the outperformance of both value as a style of equity investing and smaller company stocks cast doubt on the suitability of biasing cautious investors' portfolios in favour of value (or small cap stocks). This reinforces the case for a broad market approach to investing. To overweight value stocks or smaller company stocks then becomes appropriate for more aggressive investors.

Fashionable investment ideas: low volatility equity strategies

In recent years there has been an enormous number of research papers published by academics and investment managers into stockmarket "anomalies". The holy grail for investment managers is a strategy that offers the prospect of higher returns (and so high fees) at no higher or, even better, lower risk. Largely based on the finding that value stocks (which are often low volatility stocks) and also small cap stocks have delivered higher returns than would be expected by the original capital asset pricing model (CAPM), strategies have been designed to exploit these anomalies. This has led to a proliferation of minimum volatility equity strategies which select portfolios of stocks for their ability to deliver lower portfolio volatility than the equity market as whole.

It is a characteristic of these approaches that they tend to overweight low beta stocks. These strategies are often sold on the premise that it is an anomaly that low beta stocks perform better than would be expected by the simplified CAPM. However, as discussed above, there may be systematic sources of risk that are not reflected in the volatility or beta of a stock. If so, investors ought to be, and normally are, rewarded for taking such risk. "Bad beta" (see Stockmarket anomalies section above) would be one explanation.

A variation on this, proposed by Dan diBartolomeo, president of Northfield Information Services, an investment risk consultancy, is that the market may be reflecting the interaction of a company's share price volatility, its financial leverage, and so bankruptcy risk. If so, the market might rationally compensate investors for this termination risk (and implicit shorter corporate life expectancy) with a lower share price and higher return. This idea that the comparatively low volatility of a share price may be a misleading guide, when taken in isolation, to a company's investment risk has echoes of the lesson drawn from the completely different circumstances of the Madoff affair in Chapter 1: that investment risk is most obvious when an investment is volatile and is least obvious when a risky investment has not yet shown much volatility.

Equity dividends and cautious investors

Cautious investors should follow cautious strategies. In so far as their caution allows them a margin of equity investments, equity risk should not be magnified by following an undiversified approach to equity investing. A focus on dividend yield can easily result in amplified equity risk. The disadvantage of relying on a stock portfolio for essential income is that it will not provide the element of insurance that is available from government bonds as it provides a less certain source of income. High dividend-yielding equities are likely to be particularly vulnerable to company-specific and economy-wide disappointments in earnings growth and threats to the level of dividends.

In conclusion, treat sceptically any suggestion that investing in dividend-paying equities represents a sound investment strategy that is likely to deliver both dependable growing income and accumulating capital values. An aggressive investor who has a need for income might emphasise higher-yielding equities and fixed-income investments. For a cautious investor, any such tilt should be modest. Such a strategy is not a magic solution for constrained finances, especially in an era of unusually low yields on government bonds.

Home bias: how much international?

In recent years, investors around the world have allocated a growing proportion of their equity investments to international markets. Despite this, equity investors in almost all countries still have a strong bias towards domestic investment. The reasons for this have been debated widely. Any suggestion that domestic equities provide a better "match" for domestic currency obligations has little substance. The appropriate measure of "mismatch" is how well risk assets (such as domestic equities or foreign equities) correlate with the risk-free asset, which for a long-term investor is the domestic inflation-linked government bond. Although domestic equities may correlate better than international equities with domestic government bonds, they do not constitute any sort of "safe-haven" asset for long-term investment. But the reassurance of familiarity and habit, together with misunderstandings about the contribution of currency risk, largely explain the continuing home-country bias.

In most countries, this home-country bias is a significant risk management issue. However, the size and breadth of the US market, representing 48% of the world market in September 2013 according to MSCI, an index provider, means that well-diversified investors in US equities will have already achieved the bulk of the diversification gains that are offered by a global approach to investing. For investors in most countries international equity diversification matters a lot, but for US investors it matters less.

A recurring theme of this book is that investment strategy should be broadly appropriate for an investor's objectives, risk tolerances and preferences. Except for some cash flow matching bond portfolios, precision in identifying a suitable strategy is a pipedream. International investing is an area where strongly held differences of view on strategy are often indistinguishable within the range of broadly appropriate investment strategies. Despite this, when the performance numbers come in the differences can be large. This leaves a considerable margin of flexibility for an investor's gut preferences to influence policy legitimately. In international investing there is a range of appropriate diversified strategies and it would normally be inappropriate to suggest that a particular strategy is expected to be demonstrably superior to all others. For example, the diversification benefits of international investing are always subject to diminishing returns. Doing a little may get an investor a long way towards whatever is reckoned to be an "optimal" strategy.

Figure 7.7 shows (from a US perspective) the scale of the differences that can exist between US and international investing. After 1989, the United States substantially outperformed foreign markets, as much because of the prolonged weakness of the Japanese market after 1989 as the strength of the US market. This pattern was reversed after 2002. Figure 7.8 shows the UK has experienced fewer periods of marked outperformance or underperformance by international equities.

There are two reasons for investing internationally: opportunity and diversification. The natural starting point, from a textbook perspective, is the global market, with consideration being given to the possibility of hedging direct foreign currency risk. A global approach to investing should be appropriate for all equity investors. Other, domestically oriented approaches can also be appropriate; however, even for US investors there are demonstrable diversification benefits and increased opportunities to be gained from international equity investing.

FIG 7.7 **US and international equities, 5-year rolling equity performance**
% per year, $, Dec 1974–Sep 2013

Note: The MSCI EAFE™ Index is widely used in the United States to measure international equity market performance. It comprises the MSCI country indices that represent developed markets outside North America: Europe, Australasia and the Far East.
Source: MSCI

FIG 7.8 **UK and international equities, 5-year rolling performance**
% per year, £, Dec 1974–Sep 2013

Source: MSCI

FIG 7.9 **Volatility of domestic and global equities from alternative national perspectives**
Annualised % standard deviation of returns, Jan 1999–Sep 2013

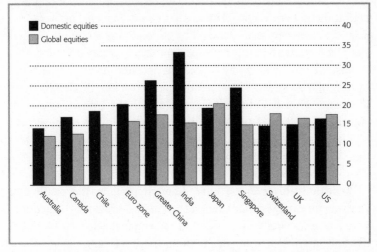

Source: All measurements in local currencies using MSCI All Countires World index. "Greater China" represented by MSCI Golden Dragon index, measured in US dollars, and includes China, Hong Kong and Taiwan

The easiest way to assess the benefits from international equity diversification is to examine how it affects the measured risk of equity investing, using the conventional measure of risk: the volatility or standard deviation of returns. This metric is also used as the guide to the expected gains from international investing, because the prudent (and consistent) assumption is that the same expected rate of return will apply to international and domestic equity investments. The outcome will not (except by chance) be the same, but in setting strategic allocations, it is safest to assume that we do not know in advance which equity market is more likely to do best.

This sidesteps the issue of whether there are any taxes or additional management costs that apply to international equity investing but not to domestic investors. If these are noticeable, they should be taken into account in determining international allocations. In what follows, this issue is ignored, and the focus is on volatility as the proxy for risk. Figure 7.9 shows for a number of countries the volatility of the MSCI World Index (shown unhedged for foreign exchange risk) and the volatility of the domestic equity market, both measured in each country's own currency.

The pattern varies with the period that is chosen, but for this 14-year period the pattern is clear. For smaller equity markets, more can be gained in reducing equity volatility by following a well-diversified global rather than a purely national approach to equity investing. This is illustrated in Figure 7.9 by comparing "greater China" (represented by the MSCI Golden Dragon index, which includes China, Hong Kong and Taiwan), India and Singapore with the United States. Not surprisingly, Figure 7.9 suggests that efficient equity management would require substantial international diversification by investors from these countries (among other countries), but this is much less clear for US investors.

Repeating this exercise over different periods, the result that consistently emerges is that the US stockmarket provides US investors with a level of equity diversification close to that achieved by global diversification. Other smaller national markets have not provided their domestic investors with comparable diversification, except over particular periods, which should not be extrapolated into the future.

Figure 7.10 shows the volatility trade-off between domestic and international equities for the United States, greater China and India in more detail. The difference in the lines shown for the three countries tells a story. From a US dollar perspective, there is little apparent benefit in terms of reduced volatility from international investing. For Indian investors in particular, the historical data show a clear pattern, with equity volatility potentially being almost halved for investors who invest 80% of their holdings in well-diversified holdings outside India. These exercises also illustrate the impact of diminishing returns on the process of diversification: the biggest contribution to diversification comes from the initial foray into (diversified) international equities.

The scale of the potential diversification gains from international investing depends on the volatility of the international equities and on how highly international prices correlate with those of domestic equities. The higher the correlation, the less well international equities will diversify domestic equities, and the less will be the scope for reducing overall equity volatility by adding international equities. It should be no surprise that the degree of correlation is unstable,

FIG 7.10 **Who needs international equity diversification? Volatility of equity investments from a US, Chinese and Indian perspective**

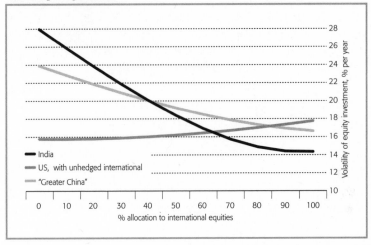

Source: Author's calculations using MSCI indices, January 1993–May 2013

as is the level of volatility. Critically, at times of crisis measures of correlation and volatility often "jump" upwards. But just because correlations increase, it does not necessarily follow that the benefits of international diversification are diminished if at the same time volatility increases. This will, however, mean that systematic or undiversifiable risk from equity investing has increased.

Figures 7.11 and 7.12 show movements in correlations of domestic and international equities from the perspective of US and UK investors. Having been unusually low in the mid-1990s, and having dipped again ahead of the credit crisis, correlations between US and international equities, whether with other developed markets or with emerging markets, have generally been high in the past ten years. Figure 7.12 shows a similar pattern for the UK. Despite the increase in correlations, international equities still provide valuable diversification benefits.

FIG 7.11 **Correlations between US equity market, international equities and emerging-market equities**
36-month rolling correlations, Dec 1990–Sep 2013

Source: Derived from MSCI index data

FIG 7.12 **Correlations between UK equity market, international equities and emerging-market equities**
36-month rolling correlations, Dec 1990–Sep 2013

Source: Derived from MSCI index data

Who should hedge international equities?

This discussion of international equity investing has ignored the impact of currency risk (which is discussed further in Chapter 8). The reliable rule of thumb is that currency exposure in international equities generally adds little to the risk of equity investing (this is in contrast to international bonds, where currency hedging almost always achieves a significant risk reduction – see Chapter 8). But recent research has shown that this generalisation needs qualifying to allow for the tendency for safe-haven currencies to move against equity markets, which is a particularly valuable characteristic at times of equity market stress. Research by John Campbell, Karine Serfaty-de Medeiros and Luis Viceira published in the *Journal of Finance* in 2010 has shown that between 1975 and 2005 holdings of the US dollar, the Swiss franc and the euro (and before that the Deutschmark) diversified global equity risk. This means that US, Swiss and German (and then euro) investors would have profited at times of global equity market weakness if they had hedged their international equity exposure for currency risk. Hedging international equities for currency exposure does not much affect the volatility of international equity investing but it does affect the pattern of equity returns. For investors from safe-haven currencies the research showed that it reduced losses (as compared with not hedging) at times of equity market weakness. An investor with a currency which tends to move with equity markets (for example, strengthening in bull markets and weakening when equities weaken) reduces risk by not hedging, and is likely to reduce losses in times of market stress. Historically, this has applied particularly to the Canadian and Australian currencies, and to a lesser extent sterling.

However, a currency can represent a safe haven in one period but not in another. The changing views of sterling, and also the euro, suggest that before drawing on this research to inform a decision to hedge or not to hedge international equities, a separate view needs to be taken on whether the investor's base currency is likely to have "safe-haven" status in the period ahead. Nevertheless, for investors with safe-haven base currencies (or whose currency is linked to a safe-haven currency), foreign currency hedging can provide an element of valuable (and inexpensive) insurance which is likely to provide a

FIG 7.13 **International equity volatility from the perspective of different countries, annualised standard deviation of returns**
%, Jan 1999–Sep 2013

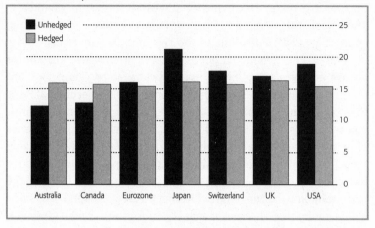

Source: MSCI World ex or All Countries World ex index data in local currencies.
For Canada and Switzerland international equities proxied by world equities

FIG 7.14 **US perspective on impact of hedging international equities, 36-month rolling standard deviation of returns**
% per year, Dec 1990–Sep 2012

Source: Derived from MSCI index data

FIG 7.15 **UK perspective on impact of hedging international equities, 36-month rolling standard deviation of returns**
% per year, Dec 1990–Sep 2013

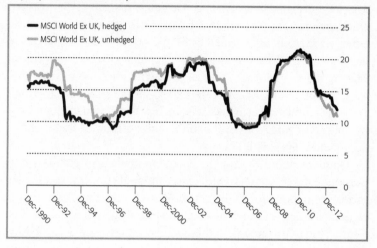

Source: Derived from MSCI index data

pay-off at times of crisis. Inexpensive insurance policies that are likely to pay out in "bad times" are particularly attractive to investors.

These different national perspectives on currency hedging are reflected in Figure 7.13, which shows the volatility of hedged and unhedged international equities (as measured by MSCI index data for the volatility of hedged and unhedged world equities excluding that country). Consistent with the findings of academic research, unhedged international equities were less volatile than hedged international equities for Australian and Canadian investors. For Japan, Switzerland and the United States, currency hedging noticeably reduced international equity volatility. For the UK and the euro zone the reduction in volatility was scarcely noticeable. This is also reflected in Figures 7.14 and 7.15 which show the volatility over time of unhedged and hedged international equities from a US and then a UK perspective.

How much in emerging markets?

Over the past 25 years "old world" developed markets have (in aggregate) declined in weight in global equity markets as the so-called emerging markets, particularly of Asia, have grown in importance. Emerging markets, as classified by MSCI, include such comparatively developed economies as the Czech Republic, Chile, South Korea, Taiwan, the United Arab Emirates and, with effect from November 2013, Greece. The MSCI emerging markets index represented less than 1% of the world market in 1988, a figure that had grown to around 13% by the end of 2012, with over half the index accounted for by China, South Korea, Brazil and Taiwan.

Opinions about the role of emerging markets in global equity portfolios differ. Some favour emerging markets because of their increasing importance in the global economy, their impressive track record, their diversification benefits and the prospect of higher rates of return. Faster GDP growth in these markets is often cited as a reason for expecting superior returns from emerging markets, but this is controversial, and history shows that the link between a country's economic growth and the domestic equity market can be more tenuous than is often supposed.

There are several reasons for this. First, much economic growth can reflect the activity of the government sector, the unlisted private sector, or of companies which are listed in other countries. In addition, even in emerging markets, domestic listed companies may earn much of their profits from abroad. Elroy Dimson, Paul Marsh and Mike Staunton of London Business School have examined the relationship between economic growth and stockmarket performance across 19 countries over more than 100 years and a further 40 countries with more than 25 years' stockmarket performance record and "find no evidence of economic growth being a predictor of stockmarket performance". However, they do think it is reasonable to expect higher performance from investing in emerging markets rather than developed markets, not because they are growing faster, but because they are riskier.

The figures below illustrate this. Figure 7.16 shows that emerging markets are more volatile than developed markets. In part this reflects

FIG 7.16 **Volatility of world and emerging-markets equities, 5-year rolling annualised standard deviations of returns**
% per year

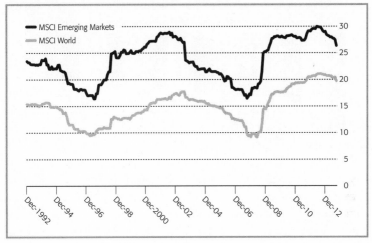

Source: MSCI World and MSCI Emerging Markets index data in US dollars

FIG 7.17 **Performance of emerging-market equities in best up months for world equities**
%, Jan 1990–Sep 2013

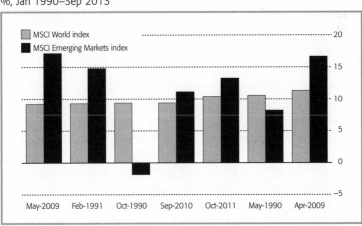

Source: MSCI

FIG 7.18 **Performance of emerging-market equities in worst down months for world equities**
%, Jan 1990–Sep 2013

Source: MSCI

inferior diversification in the emerging markets (which is not a risk that should systematically lead to higher returns) but also it reflects emerging markets behaving as if they provide a geared exposure to world markets (which leads to higher expected returns).

Figures 7.17 and 7.18 show that in the months when developed markets have performed best, emerging markets have tended to do even better, and that when developed markets have recorded their worst results, emerging markets tend to perform even worse. This high beta characteristic (see also Figure 7.19) is a reason to expect premium returns from emerging markets, but it is a reward for risk-taking and investors need to consider whether they will be sufficiently patient to weather the inevitable periods of disappointment to harvest that longer-term premium return.

Since the late 1990s, the emerging markets have consistently had a high beta with respect to world equities, averaging 1.3 between January 2000 and May 2013 (see Figure 7.19), suggesting it ought to be rewarded with an extra premium return of perhaps 1% per year, if markets operate efficiently and are fairly priced. But at the same time, the correlation of these markets with the world index has increased from

FIG 7.19 **5-year rolling beta^a between emerging-market and world equities**
Total return, %, Dec 1992–Sep 2013

a See Appendix1.
Source: Derived from MSCI world equity and MSCI emerging market equity indices

FIG 7.20 **10-year rolling returns from developed and emerging-market equities**
% per year, Dec 1997–Sep 2013

Source: MSCI world equity and emerging market equity gross return indices in US dollars around 0.4 in the ten years before the mid-1990s to around 0.9 in the five years to 2013. Even with these levels of correlation, an allocation to emerging markets provides useful diversification benefits in a more volatile environment. (Knowing the beta of emerging markets with world markets and also their correlation tells us about their volatility relative to world markets, as can be seen from Figure 7.17.)

Figure 7.20 shows that prolonged periods of disappointing performance are evident even in the short period covered by the MSCI Emerging Markets index. In the 15 years since the MSCI index started at the beginning of 1988, the rolling ten-year performance record has been equally divided between periods with developed markets outperforming emerging markets and periods when emerging markets outperformed. A predecessor index (covering years when emerging markets were much smaller as a share of global equity markets) shows emerging markets underperforming in the previous decade. Emerging markets may offer the prospect of superior performance to compensate for higher risk, but investors need to be able to withstand prolonged periods of underperformance.

For investors who are sure that they have the capacity and the inclination to act as risk-tolerant, long-term investors, Campbell Harvey, J. Paul Sticht professor in international business at Duke University's Fuqua School of Business, argues that the undiversifiable risk characteristics of investing in emerging markets goes wider than the observation that emerging markets provide a geared exposure to global markets. These wider systematic factors include illiquidity, the scope to exploit inefficiencies in pricing which are still reflected in segmentation of emerging equity markets, as well as a negative skew of returns, and the exposure to "tail risk" that is exacerbated by exposure of emerging markets to contagion and the risk of explosive volatility due to "regime changes". Harvey argues that these should be regarded as "known unknowns" of emerging-market investing. Emerging markets also benefit from the strong link between liberalisation of finance and subsequently lower discount rates and faster growth. A patient long-term investor should have the ability to "time diversify" these risks, but also needs to be aware that, often because of institutional failings, not all emerging markets can take advantage of their growth opportunities.

For a long-term investor with the appetite and capacity to stomach these risks, Harvey says that the allocation within global equities to emerging markets should take as a point of reference not just the weight of emerging markets in global equity markets (around 13% at the end of 2012) but also their weight in world GNP (around 37% in 2011, according to Goldman Sachs).

Fashionable investment ideas: frontier markets

In international investing, it is easy for investors to be drawn into the latest "fashionable" theme. What is fashionable is often potentially illiquid, with surprisingly low measured volatility and attractive diversification characteristics. Sometimes these characteristics will indicate inefficiencies and opportunities for active managers. They also indicate potential liquidity issues that could arise in a flight to quality. At such times, as investors learned in 2008, previously reassuring correlations between risk assets typically increase rapidly and investment vehicles whose diversification qualities were touted by eager

FIG 7.21 **World, emerging and frontier markets, 36-month rolling correlations**
Dec 2008–Sep 2013

Source: Derived from MSCI frontier emerging market, emerging market and world equity indices

salesmen suddenly detract from rather than add to portfolio balance. Frontier emerging markets are a likely candidate for such promotion.

Figure 7.21 shows rolling three-year correlations between emerging markets, frontier emerging markets and the MSCI World Equity market index. The Frontier emerging market index (whose largest country exposures at the end of May 2013 were Colombia, the Philippines, Kuwait, Nigeria and Qatar) shows a much lower correlation with world equity markets than does the mainstream emerging-markets equity index. But a more detailed examination of the returns series for frontier emerging markets shows a greater degree of stickiness of prices (serial correlation), negative skew and liability to extreme returns (excess kurtosis) than is the case with the broad emerging-markets index. As with emerging markets, an investment in frontier markets should be justified by a long time horizon, an appetite for taking risk and an expectation of long-term reward for taking risk. Any diversification story is most unlikely to be helpful when it is most needed.

8 Credit

THE CREDIT CRUNCH OF 2007–09 showed many bond portfolios to be less well diversified than their managers believed them to be. It also reminded all investors that creditworthy government bonds are usually by far the most reliable diversifiers of risk assets. Before the credit crunch most bond portfolios became increasingly complicated as managers embraced new ways of packaging, and they thought diversifying, credit risk. The bond managers who performed best in the "bad times" of 2008 included those who were previously dismissed as irredeemably old fashioned by some for not adopting what were widely seen as new and better ways of managing portfolio risk. Table 8.1 shows the performance of government bonds in the United States, Germany and the UK in 2008-09 and that of corporate credit and equities. It shows government bonds diversifying best when diversification is most needed, that is in "bad times".

A holding of government bonds should have been, and for many investors was, sufficient to mitigate materially the damaging impact on investor wealth of the collapse in risk asset prices in 2008. Most bond funds have always exploited the premium yield (in excess of government bonds) offered by exposure to credit and this undermined the diversification offered by bond holdings in 2008.

Many lessons have been learned, but the most important lesson is that bond portfolios do not need to be complicated, though they often are. This chapter provides an overview of credit and credit ratings and why investors may not receive the premium return seemingly promised by superior yields. It also introduces "securitisation", which is the process of turning pools of bank

TABLE 8.1 **Government bond and equity markets**
% annual total return, 2008 and 2009

	2008	2009
Barclays US Treasury index	13.7	−3.6
Barclays Municipal bond index	−2.5	12.9
Barclays US Corporate investment grade	−4.9	18.7
Barclays US Corporate High Yield	−26.2	58.2
MSCI USA All equity index gross return	−37.1	28.8
Barclays German Government bond index	11.2	2.9
Barclays Euro Aggregate Corporate investment grade	−3.8	15.7
Barclays Pan Euro High Yield	−34.2	76.1
MSCI EMU gross return equity index	−44.3	28.7
Barclays Sterling Government bond index	12.9	−1.0
Barclays Sterling Aggregate Corporate bond index	−10.0	14.7
MSCI UK gross return equity index	−28.5	27.7

Sources: Barclays; MSCI

loans (such as mortgages) into marketable securities, and gives a brief introduction to the world of credit derivatives, which are, and will continue to be, used extensively in the management of credit portfolios.

However, a useful starting point for thinking about credit is an elementary review written by John Maynard Keynes, an economist, in 1925 of a study of long-term returns from equities and bonds in the United States between 1866 and 1922. The study showed a substantial outperformance of equities over bonds in periods of both deflation and inflation. Keynes found this counter-intuitive, his expectation being that a period of deflation would be better for bonds than equities. He suggested a number of reasons for the inferior performance of bonds:

- The asymmetrical threat of changes in the price level. While bonds can be eroded by inflation without limit, the scope for the price level to fall (which would benefit bond holders, so long as bond issuers have the ability to repay these higher real values) is more constrained.

- Although a bond may default, no bond ever pays more than its coupon.

- Company management sides with equity investors rather than with bond holders and, "in particular, management can normally be relied on to repay bonds at dates most advantageous to the shareholders and most disadvantageous to the bondholders".

- Retained earnings provide an element of compound growth beyond the dividend yield, and this eventually accrues to shareholders in higher prices (while also making existing bond holders more secure in their entitlement to a fixed income).

This underlies the message of many advisers and of a number of academics that the natural habitat for genuinely long-term investors is the equity market. Nevertheless, almost all investors do, and should, seek diversification away from equity risk. In Part 1 this was argued from the perspective of investing in government bonds. This chapter provides the background to other types of credit instrument, which introduce new aspects of risk in return for the prospect of new sources of excess performance. An important element in this is the trade-off between credit quality and performance.

Credit quality and the role of credit-rating agencies

Credit-rating agencies originated early in the 20th century to assess the creditworthiness and publish ratings of securities. In practice, the two related risks that matter are default by a borrower and a deterioration in the assessment of creditworthiness of a borrower who nevertheless continues to meet contractual obligations. Investors routinely use the ratings of the leading agencies to measure the credit quality of their portfolios and also as thresholds to specify the minimum credit quality eligible for inclusion in particular portfolios.

TABLE 8.2 **Long-term rating bands of leading credit-rating agencies**

	Fitch	Moody's	Standard & Poor's
Investment grade			
Highest quality, extremely strong	AAA	Aaa	AAA
Very high quality	AA	Aa	AA
High quality	A	A	A
Moderate to good quality	BBB	Baa	BBB
Speculative grade			
Speculative, marginal or not well secured	BB	Ba	BB
Highly speculative or weak	B	B	B
Poor quality or very weak	CCC	Caa	CCC

Note: Precise definitions, which vary between rating agencies, are given on the websites of particular agencies.

In effect, this has enabled private investors and many institutional investors to outsource analysis of credit risk to these rating agencies. Furthermore, capital adequacy guidelines for international banks have incorporated a formal role for ratings assigned by the leading rating agencies. This development in the regulation of banks encouraged the process of securitising bank loans, which enabled banks to shift credit exposures to other investors on a large scale. It also promoted the development of new credit instruments and markets as well as what regulators quickly saw as an unhealthy reliance on the assessments of these rating agencies rather than research undertaken by banks and investment institutions themselves.

Historically, a rating from an agency has often been a precondition for marketing a new security and the credit-rating agencies have had a major role in promoting market liquidity. The late Peter Bernstein wrote in 2007:

> The rating agencies contribute (or at least have contributed) to market liquidity because they spare investors the trouble of carrying out their own credit research.

Acute problems with the rating of some structured products, particularly those focused on subprime mortgages, undermined confidence in the rating process. However, there has been no corresponding deterioration in the reliability of the ratings of corporate bonds. The long-term rating classifications used by the three main agencies – Fitch, Moody's and Standard & Poor's – are shown in Table 8.2.

An important break point in Table 8.2 is between investment grade securities and non-investment grade securities. The latter are commonly referred to as speculative or high yield. The ratings are intended to be objective assessments of the creditworthiness of borrowers or of instruments and are reflected in the spreads that borrowers must pay to compensate creditors for the risk of default (or of a deterioration in credit rating).

Table 8.3 shows average default rates for periods of up to ten years for corporate bonds of differing credit rating based on experience from Fitch over the period 1990–2012. The table demonstrates that the rating agencies perform at least reasonably well in assessing the likelihood of different corporate bond issues defaulting. It suggests,

TABLE 8.3 **Corporate bond average cumulative default rates**
%, 1990–2012

	Year 1	Year 2	Year 3	Year 4	Year 5	Year 10
AAA	0.0	0.0	0.0	0.0	0.0	0.0
AA	0.0	0.0	0.1	0.1	0.2	0.2
A	0.1	0.2	0.4	0.6	0.8	1.9
BBB	0.2	0.7	1.2	1.8	2.5	4.7
BB	1.1	2.8	4.5	6.0	6.9	11.6
B	2.0	4.8	7.2	9.5	10.5	11.6
CCC–C	24.9	31.9	35.6	38.5	36.8	43.8
Investment grade	0.1	0.4	0.6	0.9	1.2	2.3
High yield	3.0	5.5	7.3	9.5	10.3	14.1
All corporates	0.7	1.5	2.1	2.6	3.0	4.1

Source: Fitch Ratings Global Corporate Finance, 2012 Transition and Default Study

FIG 8.1 **Default rate of Fitch-rated issuers of corporate bonds**
% rated issuers

Source: Fitch Ratings Global Corporate Finance, 2012 Transition and Default Study

for example, that AAA bonds had no experience of default, while high-yield bonds rated CCC had a 25% risk of default over the next 12 months and a 37% risk of default over the next five years. These default rates are averages for Fitch-rated debt.

Figure 8.1 shows that the incidence of bond defaults is cyclical. It reflects the default experience of all issuers of Fitch-rated corporate bonds, whether they have been rated investment grade or speculative. Indeed, the overwhelming majority of defaults by rated companies were ascribed a speculative rating before they defaulted. For example, Fitch reports that all 18 of its rated bonds which defaulted in 2012 were bonds which Fitch had rated as speculative grade at the start of 2012.

The pattern shown in Figure 8.1 is consistent with the pattern over much longer time periods. A 2011 article by four financial economists, Kay Giesecke, Francis A. Longstaff, Stephen Schaefer and Ilya Strebulaev, "Corporate bond default risk: A 150-year perspective", found that default experience is highly clustered and that on average in the United States, 1.5% of corporate bonds defaulted each year between 1866 and 2008. However, the authors report, based on other research, that investors probably recovered on average around 40–50% of the amounts due, suggesting an annual loss rate to investors in all types of corporate bonds of around 0.75% per year. Over the long term, the authors found that "credit spreads are roughly twice as large as default losses, resulting in an average credit risk premium of about 80 basis points".

Table 8.4 shows how spreads over US Treasuries have varied with differences in credit rating. These spreads follow the ordering of formal credit-rating assessments, suggesting that the financial markets broadly share the assessments of the rating agencies as yields paid increase as ratings deteriorate. It also shows average performance of the corporate bonds with different ratings. Note that the premium returns earned (column 4) tend to be noticeably less than the average yield spread on which they will have been purchased (column 2). This discrepancy is discussed below.

TABLE 8.4 **US Corporate bond yields, spreads and performance**
Feb 1987–Sep 2013

	Average yield %	Average spread over Treasuries %	Geometric average total return % per year	Premium over US Treasuries % per year
	Column 1	Column 2	Column 3	Column 4
	Under 10-year maturity bonds			
US Treasury debt	4.7	0.0	6.0	0.0
Agency debt	5.0	0.3	6.1	0.1
AAA corporate debt	5.6	0.9	6.5	0.5
AA corporate debt	5.7	1.1	6.7	0.7
A corporate debt	6.1	1.4	6.8	0.8
BAA corporate debt	6.7	2.1	7.3	1.4
Corporate high yield bonds[a]	10.8	6.1	8.5	2.5

a All maturities.
Source: Barclays

FIG 8.2 **US corporate bond spreads**
% per year, Feb 1987–Sep 2013[a]

a Intermediate term bond yields relative to US Treasuries.
Source: Barclays

Figure 8.2 shows that credit spreads are, like the default rate, cyclical. However, the detailed research by Giesecke and her colleagues found that movements in credit spreads were a poor predictor of future default experience. Instead, they found that movements in credit spreads were best explained by movements in financial variables such as the stockmarket (spreads narrow as the market goes up), and of its volatility (spreads increase as stockmarket volatility increases), and by changes in the short-term Treasury bond rate (spreads generally increase as the risk-free rate falls). These results matter for investors, as they suggest that a generalised increase in spreads is more likely to reflect adverse changes in market liquidity, for example, which a long-term investor should be able to withstand, than to be a reliable forecast of the likelihood of default. This is consistent with the recovery of credit markets after the severe widening of spreads in 2008.

Although credit spreads have more than compensated for the default experience of corporate bonds, it does not follow that investors have necessarily been adequately rewarded for investing in

FIG 8.3 **Cumulative performance of US under 10-year Treasury and corporate bonds**
Jan 1987–Sep 2013, Jan 1987 = 100

a All maturities for high yield.
Source: Barclays

corporate bonds. Figure 8.3 shows the performance for the Barclays US Treasury bond index alongside that for single A-rated corporate bonds and also for high-yield corporate bonds. This shows the superior performance of single A bonds and also highlights the risks and volatile performance associated with high-yield bonds.

Table 8.5 shows how the performance of investment grade credit has persistently delivered a smaller premium return over Treasury bonds than would be suggested by the spreads offered by the index. In the table this is shown by the unexplained "performance gap".

Some performance gap should be expected from the impact of occasional defaults. But their impact has been too small to account for the performance gap in Table 8.5. Fitch, one of the three leading international rating agencies, reports that the average five-year cumulative default rate for Fitch-rated investment grade bond issuers averaged 1.2% between 1990 and 2012, or 0.25% per year. However, actual losses will have averaged less than this as a result of recoveries of, probably, around 40% of amounts due.

TABLE 8.5 **US investment grade credit spreads and excess returns**
% per year

	Jan 1973– Sep 2013	Jan 1973– Dec 1982	Jan 1983– Dec 1992	Jan 1993– Dec 2002	Jan 2003– Dec 2012
Average credit yield spread over Treasury bonds	1.32	0.98	1.34	1.22	1.74
Average credit index outperformance of Treasury bonds	0.77	0.01	0.74	0.73	1.44
"Performance gap"	0.55	0.97	0.60	0.49	0.30

Note: No allowance made for fees.
Source: Derived from Barclays intermediate indices for US Treasury bonds and US investment grade credit

Defaults of investment grade bonds therefore cannot explain the failure of the spreads at which investors buy such bonds to translate into corresponding premium performance. Other possible causes of performance difference include a movement of credit spreads between the start and end of a period of comparison and the likelihood that the corporate bonds and government bonds have different durations, and so respond differently to moves in government bond yields over a particular period. These can be important over short periods of time, but over the 40-year period covered by Table 8.5 this cannot be material (not least because the Barclays intermediate indices shown in the table comprise bonds with less than ten years' remaining maturity).

Instead the reason is institutional and related to index composition rules. Investors commonly have credit-quality guidelines for their portfolios or the funds in which they invest, and the managers of investment grade bond portfolios are typically obliged to sell when bonds get downgraded to a high-yield or speculative rating, and perhaps when the bonds have less than one year to maturity (and so are excluded from the index).

Antti Ilmanen, the author of *Expected Returns, An investor's guide to harvesting market rewards*, and Kwok-Yuen Ng and Bruce Phelps, authors of a 2011 *Financial Analysts' Journal* article, "Capturing the

Credit Spread Premium", have highlighted the asymmetry between a bond's underperformance before it is downgraded from investment grade and a bond's (possibly the same bond) outperformance before it gets promoted to investment grade from high yield. An investor with a credit-quality guideline which requires the sale of any speculative grade bond will lose out by suffering the underperformance before the downgrade and also by missing the outperformance of soon-to-be-upgraded bonds. The investor will also suffer from the much larger transaction costs that are paid when downgraded bonds are sold. A low-fee index tracking fund which is mirroring an investment grade bond index will suffer these performance penalties, while an actively managed bond fund which tries to exploit the phenomenon confronts a steep performance penalty from high fees. In their detailed analysis, Ng and Phelps estimated that a buy-and-hold approach to downgraded bonds would have improved investment performance on average by 0.38% per year between 1990 and 2009. The risk of default, which increases the longer the maturity of a bond, emphasises the need for any buy-and-hold approach to investing in corporate bonds to be well diversified.

Portfolio diversification and credit risk

The words that rating agencies use to describe sub-investment grade debt, such as "speculative", "highly speculative" or "poor quality", fairly describe the risk of individual issues when treated in isolation.

For a long time it has been evident to investors in well-diversified corporate debt that the performance of the market is much less volatile than the performance of an individual issue, and that when the market is performing well, good performance can be provided by a portfolio of well-diversified high-yield bonds. So, it is inappropriate to regard a portfolio of high-yield bonds as if it had the risk characteristics of an individual sub-investment grade bond. Equally, the strong language that rating agencies use to describe the risk of individual high-yield bonds should remind investors that the only sensible way to invest in such credit risk is through a well-diversified portfolio. Diversification among a portfolio of high-yield bonds will reduce the risk of an adverse event affecting a particular issue. However, while a fund will

TABLE 8.6 **Performance of selected debt markets in months of extreme US equity performance**
Jan 1994–Sep 2013

	MSCI US Large Cap 300 index	Barclays US Government bond index	Barclays US investment grade corporate bond index	Barclays US Corporate High Yield index	JP Morgan emerging market bond index plus
Worst months for US equities					
Oct 2008	−16.2	−0.3	−6.4	−15.9	−13.8
Aug 1998	−14.3	2.6	0.5	−5.5	−28.7
Sep 2002	−10.8	2.3	1.9	−1.3	−3.7
Best months for US equities					
Oct 2011	10.7	−0.7	1.8	6.0	4.4
Oct 2002	9.3	−0.8	−1.3	−0.9	7.7
Apr 2009	8.9	−1.3	3.5	12.1	5.1

Sources: Barclays; JPMorgan; MSCI

diversify the idiosyncratic risks associated with individual high-yield bonds, it does nothing to reduce the systemic risk that can drive all prices in the market.

Table 8.6 compares the performance of the US government bond and investment grade credit indices with that of the high-yield and emerging-market debt markets in the months of most extreme US equity market performance since 1994. Debt issued by sovereign (or corporate) borrowers of emerging markets offers an alternative source of debt-based risk-taking. This debt may be denominated in US dollars or in the currency of the issuer (but see Local currency emerging-market debt box below). Such debt performed well in the years after the liquidity crisis of August 1998. In that month, the JPMorgan emerging-market debt index fell by 29%, more than twice the amount it fell in October 2008 (see Table 8.6). The 1998 experience revealed the undiversifiable risk of contagion in the market for

TABLE 8.7 **US corporate high-yield and emerging debt markets summary statistics**
Jan 1994–Sep 2013

	Geometric return % per year	Standard deviation % per year	Skewness	Excess kurtosis	Serial correlation	Maximum decline %
MSCI US Large Cap 300 index	8.6	16.9	−0.7	0.9	0.1	−49.9
Barclays US Government bond index	5.5	4.5	−0.2	1.0	0.1	−5.4
Barclays US investment grade corporate bond index	6.4	6.0	−0.7	4.7	0.2	−15.4
Barclays US corporate high-yield index	7.7	9.8	−1.1	9.2	0.3	−33.3
JPMorgan emerging-market bond index plus	9.9	15.5	−2.1	12.5	0.0	−32.7

Data sources: Barclays; JPMorgan; MSCI

emerging-market debt. This risk may have lessened as more emerging markets have repaid debt, accumulated foreign exchange reserves, acquired investment grade credit ratings and evolved towards joining the group of developed financial markets. In the years leading to 2007, performance of the market relied heavily on spread compression. But the danger of systemic setbacks leaves emerging-market debt exposed to the risk of occasional extreme negative performance, which has historically been a characteristic of the marketplace.

Table 8.7 shows that emerging-market debt and US high-yield debt have a tendency towards extreme returns (as indicated by the measure "excess kurtosis"). Emerging-market debt has had a similar volatility to the US equity market, but it is more susceptible to sudden shocks. The high-yield market appears to have been less volatile, though it is also prone to extreme monthly results (and the score for "serial correlation" reflects a greater tendency for high yield prices to trend).

Local currency emerging-market debt

Early investors from developed markets who invested in emerging-market debt almost always invested in debt denominated in US dollars, or in other major currencies such as the yen or the euro. At the time there was little local currency debt available for international investors (which was a major structural weakness for debtor countries). This suited many investors because they did not wish to compound the credit risk of investing in emerging-market debt with the currency risk associated with emerging markets.

In the past 15 years a growing number of emerging-market governments have issued debt in their own local currency, which has been targeted at international investors. These steps are responding to a market opportunity that suits both investors and borrowers.

A well-diversified portfolio approach to investing in local currency emerging-market debt can be attractive to a range of investors because:

■ yields may be more attractive than comparable dollar debt (though this varies between countries);

■ it enables investors to position strategy to take advantage of a view of the relative performance of the US dollar and emerging-market currencies;

■ it may provide one source of efficient investment diversification for any investor (although the basis for any such calculation needs careful consideration).

Such investments may be particularly attractive to investors from emerging economies who have their investment accounts measured and reported in US dollars, and yet their base currency is to a degree ambiguous (see Chapter 1). The attitude to currency risk of these investors is less clearly defined than it is, for example, for a US resident. For some of these international investors, a portfolio of well-diversified emerging-market debt may offer an attractive way of mitigating some of their exposure to the US dollar.

The available benchmarks for emerging-market debt illustrate that these markets have been highly volatile in the past. Although diversification between countries is a major benefit, the impact of the 1997 Asian currency crisis shows how extreme the performance of individual markets can be, and even with a diversified approach, strong negative returns have been recorded at times of crisis. The JPMorgan local currency emerging-market liquidity index declined in US dollar terms by 15.7% between July 1997 and January 1998 and by 20% between July 2008 and February 2009. However, the 2008–09 decline owed much to movements in the US dollar and was just 2% when measured in euros and 9.5% in Singapore dollars (Singapore's currency floats with reference to a basket of trading partners).

Securitisation, modern ways to invest in bond markets and the credit crunch

In recent decades, innovations in securities markets have transformed investment markets and bank balance sheets. Securitisation was for a number of years welcomed as enabling banks to better manage their credit exposures by separating their lending decisions from their need to manage the risks of their balance sheets. This was possible because standardised arrangements evolved which enabled the banks to offload their risk exposures to other banks, to hedge funds or to long-term investors.

Securitisation was a major innovation and it is a process that can facilitate risk management in the financial sector. But it also lies at the heart of much that went wrong in the financial sector leading up to the credit crunch. With hindsight, it seems as though banks used the invention of a series of useful risk management devices as an excuse to take much more risk, rather than to manage better the risks that they were already taking. Behaviour and incentives lay at the root of this. Securitisation encouraged bank executives with sales targets to achieve to take less responsibility for the quality of their lending decisions, which they knew would no longer stay on their banks' balance sheets. Thus a mechanism that was heralded as a means of dispersing risk instead led to much greater and hidden concentrations of risk. Securitisation itself was a good idea, but it was applied in ways that encouraged, while providing no mechanism to rein in, much looser standards in banking.

Mortgage-backed securities

Securitisation started and developed in the United States. The major innovation came in 1970 with the introduction of a mortgage-backed security by the Government National Mortgage Association (Ginnie Mae), whose cash payments to investors represented a direct "pass-through" of the cash flows of the underlying household mortgages. Previously, mortgage-backed bonds had represented claims on the issuing bank, with a further claim on the underlying mortgages should the bank default. The principal investment feature of pass-through bonds is that they expose the investor to prepayment risk, because household mortgage holders in the United States can generally prepay fixed-rate mortgages without penalty. Prepayment risk is the main differentiator of mortgage-backed securities as investments. Individuals prepay for a number of different reasons, but the principal driver is the opportunity to refinance at a lower interest rate and cut monthly mortgage payments, after allowing for the fees involved. So prepayment risk is directly tied to changes in the level of interest rates. A defining feature of the US residential mortgage market is that interest and principal payment obligations of mortgage-backed securities issued by the three federally sponsored mortgage agencies are guaranteed by those agencies.

This differentiates mortgages that conform to the loan quality guidelines of the federal mortgage institutions from those that do not – for example, because of their size ("jumbo" mortgages), a high loan to house value ratio or the low credit score of the borrower, or because some other qualitative guideline is breached (these are known collectively as "subprime" mortgages). Mortgage-backed securities based on pools of conforming US mortgages did not have the dramatic spike in yields experienced by other credit securities during the credit crunch, but damage was inflicted on bank and investor portfolios by securities based on pools of commercial mortgage-backed securities (see Figures 8.4 and 8.5) as well as non-conforming home equity loans.

FIG 8.4 **Yields on US mortgage securities**
% per year, Jul 2000–Sep 2013

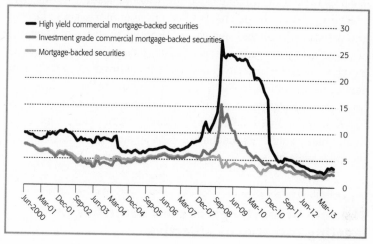

Source: Barclays

FIG 8.5 **Cumulative performance of agency mortgage-backed securities and commercial mortgages**
Jun 2000–Sep 2013, Jun 2000 = 100

Source: Barclays

By the mid-1980s the pass-through mortgage market led to the development of the collateralised mortgage obligation (CMO). The CMO arranges for the payments from a pool of mortgages to be split into a series of tranches, which are exposed to different elements of mortgage prepayment risk. These developments in the US mortgage market transformed the portfolios of investors in US dollar-denominated bonds. In the years before 2008, the repackaging of conforming mortgages provided the model for related but increasingly convoluted and often ill-fated innovations in other areas, where the credit-quality guidelines that have always applied to mortgage-backed securities were absent.

The role of mortgage-backed securities in meeting investment objectives

Mortgages that are subject to prepayment risk represent a peculiar investment which has become mainstream for many institutional investors. An investor, conscious of the need to meet particular objectives at dates in the future, is unlikely to have thought of an investment with the payout profile of a mortgage as a candidate for a core investment to meet those objectives. However, investors venture out of their safe-haven, minimum risk investment strategy in anticipation of a premium yield in return for accepting prepayment risk. The benefits of the mortgage market for issuers is clear. It provides liquidity and has increased access to additional capital, both of which have probably lowered costs to borrowers. The outstanding volume of US mortgage-backed securities was around $5.7 trillion at the end of 2012 compared with $11.6 trillion of outstanding US Treasury debt.

For an investor, replacing government bonds with mortgage bonds, which are subject to prepayment risk, introduces uncertainty to a previously low-risk investment strategy. When long-term interest rates fall, homeowners will refinance their mortgages. This will be reflected in prepayments on a mortgage bond, which will reduce the bond's ability to support a given level of income in the future because the prepaid income has to be reinvested at the lower rate of interest. In this environment, mortgages should be expected to underperform government bonds. By contrast, when long-term interest rates rise above expectations, homeowners will want to retain their current lower level of

FIG 8.6 **US government bond monthly returns compared with mortgage-backed securities**
Jan 1990–Sep 2013

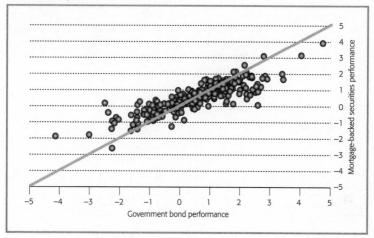

Source: Barclays

mortgage payment, and repayments are likely to be lower than expected. In other words, mortgage securities, which are subject to prepayment risk, prepay more when investors want less, and may prepay less when investors want more. They represent a source of dynamic mismatch risk in trying to meet long-term objectives.

In return for these undesirable features, investors in mortgage securities collect an insurance premium, which is the extra yield that mortgage-backed securities offer over conventional bonds (after making appropriate adjustments to ensure fair comparison). This represents the premium that borrowers must pay investors for the option to prepay their mortgages ahead of the maturity date of the loan. This insurance premium represents a source of performance for investors in mortgages.

The phenomenon just described is known as negative convexity and is in general an unattractive characteristic for an investor. However, for long-term investors whose future obligations are subject to uncertain timing (for example, an individual whose retirement date is unclear or a foundation whose expenditure profile is not fixed), introducing an element of negative convexity through investing in mortgages might not increase uncertainty about the

TABLE 8.8 **Performance and volatility of components of
Barclays US Aggregate bond index**
Jan 1990–Sep 2013

	% weight in Barclays Aggregate index Sep 2013	Geometric mean % per year	Standard deviation % per year	Maximum decline
Barclays US Aggregate bond index[a]	100.0	6.8	4.0	−5.1
Barclays Government bond index	40.5	6.3	4.5	−5.4
Barclays Mortgage-backed securities index	28.6	6.5	3.1	−4.0
Barclays Credit index	27.8	7.2	5.5	−13.5

a Components shown do not total to 100 as they exclude commercial mortgage-backed securities and asset-backed securities.
Source: Barclays

ability to meet future objectives, and might, thanks to the additional expected premium income, modestly reduce it.

The performance of mortgages in comparison with government bonds, as reflected in the Barclays Aggregate bond index, is shown in Figure 8.6. A line has been drawn across the chart to indicate equal performance of mortgages and government bonds. Observations above this line indicate mortgage outperfomance; observations below the line indicate months when government bonds outperformed mortgages.

Figure 8.6 indicates that in months of strong government bond performance, mortgage performance has lagged behind. It also indicates that when government bond prices have fallen, the mortgage index has often outperformed.

Table 8.8 compares the returns on the major components of the Barclays Aggregate Bond Index since 1990. It shows that over this 23-year period, on average, conforming mortgages did not reward investors with a premium return over other parts of the US bond market, though they did offer slightly lower volatility and lower drawdown when interest rates increased.

The position of mortgages in an investor's strategy should depend on analysis of the superior risk-adjusted return expected from mortgages (if any), its uncertainty and how it correlates with an investor's other sources of systematic return. Furthermore, since mortgages represent a source of systematic risk-taking and government bonds (of an appropriate maturity) provide a safe-haven investment, the appropriate balance between government bonds and prepayment mortgages (as one of a variety of risky assets) should be guided by the investor's tolerance for risk-taking rather than the composition of market indices.

International bonds and currency hedging

For all investors, foreign government bonds represent a way of diversifying yield curve risk and of seeking opportunities to add value beyond a domestic government bond benchmark. In Chapter 1, the ambiguity of the notion of a "home" currency for many international executives or families was discussed, and the importance was emphasised of carefully thinking through the currency composition of "safe-harbour" investments, such as cash or government bonds. Similar issues often apply to international investment funds, such as sovereign wealth funds. For textbook investors with a clear home currency, investing in foreign currency government bonds involves foreign exchange risk, which need not be a problem so long as that risk is properly managed. Otherwise the rationale for making a particular investment may be overwhelmed by the impact of currency fluctuations.

Currency risk is a manageable risk. It is also a big risk, which incorrectly handled can lead to windfall losses (or gains) of 20% or more over a 12-month period. Currency hedging is the way to manage this risk in international investments. The intuitive way of understanding currency hedging is to remember that it is equivalent to placing cash on deposit in the investor's home currency (for example, US dollars) and borrowing the equivalent amount in a foreign currency (for example, euros) to finance a foreign investment. In this way, fluctuations in the exchange rate will wash out, having an equal and opposite effect on the foreign investment and the foreign debt. The investor's investment return will be the performance of the foreign investment in foreign currency, plus the interest rate on the domestic currency deposit, less the interest rate on the foreign currency debt.

The more conventional way to describe this is to say that foreign currency risk can be neutralised through foreign exchange "hedging", where an investor contracts to sell foreign currency at a date in the future (or "forward") at the current exchange rate. The contract allows for differences in interest rates between the two countries. Typically, the contracts are for one or three months. They are then rolled forward and adjusted as needed to reflect any changes in value of the underlying investment, to make sure that it and any capital appreciation (or decline) remain fully hedged.

What does it achieve?

Currency hedging is interesting because it enables management of currency risk and, for many investments, it provides a marked reduction in the volatility of international investments. Figures 8.7, 8.8 and 8.9

FIG 8.7 **German government bond performance in euros**
%, Jan 1999–Sep 2013

FIG 8.8 **German government bond performance in US$, unhedged**
%, Jan 1999–Sep 2013

FIG 8.9 **German government bond performance hedged to US$**
%, Jan 1999–Sep 2013

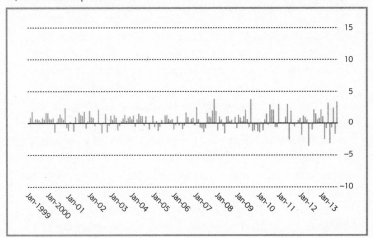

show this from the perspective of investors in German government bonds. Figure 8.7 shows the pattern of German government bond monthly performance in euros. Figure 8.8 shows the same investment performance translated into US dollars, with no attempt to hedge the foreign exchange risk. It is demonstrably much more volatile than the pattern of returns in euros. Figure 8.9 shows the same return series, again in US dollars, but this time hedged for foreign currency risk. The profile in Figure 8.9 is a close approximation to Figure 8.7. The same pattern of a marked reduction in volatility is evident for hedging highest quality investment grade bonds from whichever market over whichever period where there are liquid forward currency markets. For investments of moderate volatility, such as well-diversified high-yield bond funds or many hedge fund strategies, the arguments in favour of hedging currency risk remain strong. However, difficulties arise if the underlying investments are illiquid (see below). For more volatile markets, such as equities, currency hedging alters the profile of investment returns but has a much more modest effect on volatility (see Chapter 7).

What does it cost?

Three types of costs may be incurred in foreign currency hedging:

■ **Transaction costs.** Foreign exchange markets are among the most liquid markets in the world, and the transaction costs of putting in place and particularly of rolling forward hedges in the principal currencies are tiny – a small number of basis points each year. But it is important to check whether there are any supplementary transaction costs that over time could materially reduce the attractiveness of hedging. For currencies that are subject to occasional liquidity crises, the "spread" levied in the foreign exchange market between forward purchases and sales – which would be expected to reflect the difference in short-term interest rates – can widen sharply at times of market crisis. This will dramatically increase the cost of hedging in those currencies. For this reason, an investor should not normally hedge investments denominated in currencies that may, at a time of crisis, become illiquid.

- **Cash flow costs.** There are regular cash flows associated with currency hedging. These represent the currency gains and losses on the hedge that should be offset, perfectly with a perfect hedge, with currency losses and gains on the hedged investment. In an investment account, the gains and losses of the hedge will often be painfully evident, while the foreign exchange gains and losses on the foreign investment will be less obvious. Where the investment is illiquid – for example, if a US investor is hedging a European private equity investment back to dollars and the US dollar depreciates against the euro – the scale of the depreciation will be felt as a cash outflow associated with the hedge as the dollar depreciates. (See Chapter 11 for a discussion of foreign currency risk and illiquid investments.) Foreign currency hedging is best suited to highly liquid investments, such as government bonds. The cash flows associated with hedging can be both embarrassing and, for illiquid investments, painful.

- **Opportunity cost.** This is closely tied to regret risk, that is, the risk that the decision to hedge an international investment will be regretted because subsequent currency movements would have made it more profitable not to have hedged. In this case, the investor's accounts may show a negative cash flow impact of the hedge and encourage statements such as "this hedge has cost me …". Investors need to reflect on the reasons for the hedged investment when making these statements.

Sometimes, as with international equity investing, hedging decisions are finely balanced (see Chapter 7). Frequently, though, the appropriate rule of thumb is that certain types of international investment should not be made unless they are to be hedged. The obvious examples are investments in foreign bonds. Furthermore, many hedge fund strategies should be either managed or hedged to the investor's base currency. This is because exposing bond and hedge funds to unmanaged currency risk transforms the performance pattern that should be expected from the investment and this will often undermine the role that the investment is supposed to have in an investment strategy. If an investor likes the foreign bond market and likes the currency, a critic might ask: why hedge? The answer is that since currency volatility will contribute much more to the risk of losing money than bond market volatility, the position should be seen as a foreign currency view and not a bond market view.

How easy is foreign exchange forecasting?

Central banks, which ought to be well-informed about the nature of currency markets, sometimes admit that they do not know how to forecast exchange rates. With hindsight it may appear that a particular exchange rate was "bound" to trend in a particular direction. With foresight it is never that easy. One of the most dangerous things an investor can do is to take unstructured foreign currency bets. These almost always degenerate into "bet the ranch" gambles, which make nonsense of any considered risk-taking that might until then have characterised investment strategy. This is because foreign exchange is a source of significant volatility with, on average, no expected pay-off. Nevertheless, carefully managed foreign exchange risk can have a role in any strategy where an investor uses a team that has both insights and a track record, and where the risk management process reassures the investor that the downside risk for when things go wrong – which is inevitable from time to time – is acceptable.

IN THE DECADE BEFORE the global financial crisis there was an upsurge in money managed by hedge funds. In the early 1990s, they were fringe investment vehicles, managing money for some enterprising private investors as well as the hedge fund managers themselves. Then they became increasingly popular with endowments, innovative pension funds and insurance companies. They have since become mainstream assets for many institutional investors, while private client investment – though difficult to gauge – seems to have waned in comparison. But 2008 was a watershed year. Total assets managed reached a peak in late 2007 of $2.3 trillion (see Figure 9.1), according to BarclayHedge, a hedge fund industry research and database provider, before declining by over 30% by March 2009 through a combination of negative returns and investor redemptions. Private clients seem to have accounted for the bulk of these redemptions, leaving the hedge fund industry more evenly balanced between institutional and private client investors. In the years after early 2009, hedge fund assets increased steadily, and almost reached its earlier peak level of $2.3 trillion by June 2013.

The crisis year of 2008 was the hedge fund industry's bleakest. As leverage was withdrawn by banks, themselves under severe liquidity pressure, regulators changed rules on short selling, the signature hedge fund investment technique, and many hedge funds were confronted with a mismatch between the liquidity they had offered their investors and the illiquidity of many of their underlying investments. The result was a severe mark-down in the unit prices of hedge funds of almost all strategies, which in turn led to substantial investor requests to liquidate holdings. Performance losses were

FIG 9.1 **Hedge fund industry assets under management**
$bn, 1997–2013

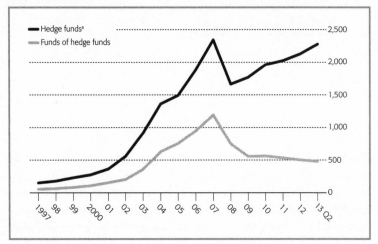

a Including managed futures funds (CTAs).
Source: BarclayHedge, www.barclayhedge.com

particularly acute in illiquid strategies. The year reached its nadir in November, when the previously low volatility Credit Suisse index of equity market neutral hedge funds recorded a decline for the month of 40.5%. Other index providers showed more modest declines, but the Credit Suisse index included three hedge funds that were revealed to be feeder funds for the enormous fraud associated with Madoff Investment Securities and were immediately written down to zero.

Since 2008 there have been important changes in the hedge fund industry. One has been a continuation of the earlier trend towards greater reliance by hedge funds on institutional clients. According to Preqin, a hedge fund consultancy, in 2008 institutional investors represented 45% of hedge fund assets. Following the crisis, institutions continued to increase allocations to hedge funds, while private clients pulled back, so that by the end of 2012 institutions accounted for 63% of hedge fund assets. A parallel trend has been a sustained decline in funds of hedge funds, which invest in a diversified selection of hedge funds. During the three years from 2005 to 2007, around 50% of the money invested in hedge funds (including managed futures funds) was channelled through funds of hedge funds. By mid-2013, this proportion had declined to around 25%. Initially, funds of funds were favoured as an efficient way of gaining access to hedge funds, especially by investors who did not feel confident to select hedge funds themselves. Several factors led to the decline of funds of hedge funds. One is that their rationale for undertaking due diligence on behalf of investors was undermined when it emerged that a number of funds of hedge funds (especially serving private clients) had incorporated so-called feeder funds which gave exposure to the Madoff fraud. Another is a growing determination among institutional investors to manage their hedge fund exposure cost effectively by replacing holdings in funds of hedge funds, with their extra level of fees, with less expensive and better tailored advice on individual hedge funds. Sometimes these portfolios of hedge funds are advised by the same teams of hedge fund experts as manage the funds of hedge funds. According to BarclayHedge, the assets invested in funds of hedge funds peaked at $1.2 trillion in 2007 and had declined to $480 billion by June 2013.

The hedge fund industry is dominated by US-based funds, which according to Preqin was home to 69% of global hedge fund assets in 2012, with the UK's 19% representing a distant second place. Five other countries accounted for 1–2% each. Switzerland is one of these, and its importance in hedge fund investing is increased by its being the home of a number of large funds of hedge funds.

What are hedge funds?

Hedge funds are best understood as private entrepreneurial investment companies that operate with few constraints. Their investment strategies can be sorted into generic types. They have historically been lightly regulated, though this position has changed in recent years with the introduction of the provisions of the Dodd Frank Act in the United States and the Alternative Investment Fund Managers' Directive in the EU. All hedge funds have in common remuneration structures that are exceptionally favourable to the hedge fund managers when their fund performance is good. However, when performance is poor, management stability may be undermined by the improbability of employees being able in the near future to earn substantial remuneration at that hedge fund. Three other characteristics are the investment of a substantial part of the managers' net worth in their own fund; their ability to have short positions in investment portfolios; and the secrecy that has often surrounded their underlying investment positions. They are also distinguished in being designed to generate positive returns, rather than to beat or match a stock or bond market index. The illiquidity of the underlying investments of a number of hedge fund strategies has always meant that those strategies are not suitable for short-term investors – something that investors were reminded of in 2008 when many funds delayed withdrawals to protect the interests of other investors.

Alternative sources of systematic return and risk

Hedge funds offer a range of sources of risk and return. Some of these have direct parallels with long-only stock and bond portfolios. Hedge funds typically attempt to isolate manager skill by reducing the influence of market returns on the portfolio, although funds still have a significant exposure to market risk. The origins of hedge fund investing in the late 1940s were represented by such funds, which today would be known as long-short equity funds.

But other funds offer completely new opportunities, for example the ability to treat market volatility as an investment to be bought and sold and to exploit trends in its pricing. Others include a number of market efficiency raising arbitrage strategies, including merger arbitrage, statistical arbitrage (exploiting short-term momentum in markets), fixed-income and convertible arbitrage. There is no long-only equivalent to the technical skill and market timing involved in such strategies, which are sometimes called "alternative beta" strategies. Each of these represents a potential source of systematic return, although the hedge fund industry's casual use of the word "arbitrage" must not be taken to mean that these strategies are low risk (see below). Correspondingly, macro and commodity trading advisers (CTAs, also known as managed futures funds) are other strategies that have no long-only parallel, and in the case of CTA strategies represent an indirect way of profiting from the systematic return that appears to be offered to long-term investors who supply liquidity to the commodity markets.

In these and other areas, hedge funds provide a risk transfer and liquidity service which in previous times either was not systematically provided or was provided by commercial banks. Hedge funds need considerable skill in providing these services, but the return that investors might expect from these services derives primarily from the market return to such risk-taking. It became clear in 2008 that many of these rely on ready access to liquid markets as well as a stable regulatory regime.

"Do hedge funds hedge?"

Figure 9.2 shows that the index of hedge fund industry performance (net of fees) has outperformed the US and global stockmarket indices (before fees) since the early 1990s and with evidently less volatility. The prospect of being able to earn superior risk-adjusted returns from diversified investing in hedge funds has always been one of the principal attractions of such funds.

This argument was cemented in the minds of many investors during the equity bear market of 2000–02, when hedge fund indices comfortably outperformed equity market indices. This helped to lay the foundations for the enormous growth of the hedge fund industry in the following five years. In 2008 the modest margins by which hedge funds in aggregate outperformed collapsing equity indices will have satisfied few investors. Although around one in five hedge funds did report positive returns for 2008, the experience of that year will be etched on investors' collective memory: hedge funds may help to diversify equity market risk, but they are risk assets and they provide no safe haven. This is not a new revelation. Best practice among private client and institutional advisers has for years been that hedge funds represented an interesting way of diversifying, but not of avoiding, equity risk. For investors who accepted that hedge funds were risk assets, the role of hedge funds in diluting equity market risk, while offering the prospect of additional sources of return, may even be confirmed by the experience of 2008.

FIG 9.2 **Cumulative performance of hedge fund index and equities**
$, Jan 1993–Sep 2013, December 1993 = 100

Sources: © 2013 Credit Suisse, all rights reserved; MSCI

Many equity hedge fund managers adjust their exposure to what they see as trends in markets, raising exposure after market rises and cutting after market falls. The 2000–02 equity bear market was unusual in being long and drawn out. That experience probably

TABLE 9.1 **Hedge fund performance during calendar quarters of equity market crisis**
1994 Q1–2013 Q3, % total return in $

	MSCI World gross return	**Barclays US Treasury total return**	**Credit Suisse Hedge Fund Index**
2008 Q4	−21.7	8.8	−10.2
2002 Q3	−18.3	7.4	−0.4
2011 Q3	−16.5	6.5	−4.8
2008 Q3	−15.2	2.3	−10.3
2001 Q3	−14.3	5.5	0.1

Sources: Barclays; Credit Suisse; MSCI

misled investors to expect hedge funds to be able to hedge in the event of sharp equity market reversals. During 2007–09, the credit crunch forced deleveraging and asset sales, whether or not hedge fund managers would have preferred to act differently. Table 9.1 shows the performance of an aggregate hedge fund index during the most disappointing equity market calendar quarters since the index started in 1994. These figures emphasise that investing in hedge funds may mitigate market risk, but it does not avoid it.

The quality of hedge fund performance data

The quality of hedge fund performance data is a subject that arouses considerable debate. This was brought to the forefront again by the Madoff scandal. The Credit Suisse indices are asset weighted to show the performance of the average dollar invested in the Credit Suisse sample for that strategy. Other index providers use a simple average of the returns of each fund (of whatever size) that qualifies for their index.

The focus of much commentary on hedge fund performance is that published indices overstate the actual experience of investors. One historic example was the 1998 failure of Long-Term Capital Management (LTCM), the largest hedge fund that would then be described as following a fixed-income arbitrage strategy. However, its failure is not reflected in the hedge fund industry performance numbers because from the outset LTCM, a highly secretive organisation, did not wish to share its performance numbers with anyone apart from its investors. Participation in databases of hedge fund performance is in part voluntary and the indices are not comprehensive.

The LTCM example is an illustration of incomplete reporting distorting the performance of hedge fund indices. However, consistent non-reporting by individual funds is not an obvious reason for the index numbers to overstate performance. Some have argued that the opposite may be true as consistent non-reporters may be among the group of successful, historically well-performing funds. Other data issues might bias the numbers. One is that new hedge funds are able to "backfill" their performance numbers in databases of hedge fund performance after they decide to start reporting performance (the disappointing "incubator" results may not get reported at all). However, reporting data to a database says nothing about the rules for eligibility for inclusion in an index; these are generally designed to exclude backfill bias by ignoring data for months before the date the data are first reported.

The consensus is that hedge fund indices do suffer from some element of survivor bias, which causes reported performance to be higher than the average experience of hedge fund investors. Furthermore, the track records that investors are shown ahead of new investment decisions are almost always subject to bias – investors do not invite the poor performers to make new business presentations. However, investors should not take investment decisions based on past performance alone. The key is always the expected future performance (and its source), how a fund might perform in "bad times", how this relates to the pattern of performance expected from the investor's other assets, and whether the investor can access that source of performance and risk from anywhere else. An understanding of these issues should be much more important than historical reported performance numbers in informing investors' decisions.

What motivates hedge fund managers?

The remuneration of hedge fund managers is important in understanding what to expect, and what to demand, from hedge fund arrangements and for judging whether enough value is likely to be left over for external investors.

The skill of any fund manager is subject to uncertainty. It is investors' money that is used to discover the difference between skill and luck, even though in some instances skill will be obscured by bad luck, and in others lack of skill will continue to be obscured by extended good luck.

This highlights a disconnection between the interests of investors and the interests of hedge fund managers and is another aspect of the "principal–agent" problem which complicates relationships between investors and their advisers in many investment relationships (see Appendix 3). In hedge fund investing, the extent to which investor and hedge fund manager interests are aligned can change if and when a particular fund starts to prosper and the manager starts to accumulate wealth. In this case, hedge fund managers are likely to be much more concerned to preserve and grow rather than put at risk their own wealth, which is invested in the fund. This can lead to a subtle shift in hedge fund business strategy from the pursuit of performance to a greater focus on asset gathering, on the basis of the past performance record. At this stage, some hedge funds diversify their business and wealth risk by adding new strategies; others, which continue to manage a single strategy, may respond by reducing risk-taking.

Are hedge fund fees too high?

Hedge fund fees need to be kept at the forefront of investors' minds. The headline fee payable on an individual hedge fund has been "2 and 20". In other words, 2% a year of the value invested is levied as a base fee and 20% of the return earned each year is retained as a performance fee, so long as the return is positive and exceeds the previous "high watermark" or maximum level of performance. In recent years, base fees have been under some pressure, and in 2012 are estimated by Preqin to have averaged 1.6%, but it seems that typical performance fees have remained close to 20%. It is notable that there has normally been no hurdle rate of return before performance fees are paid, other than the high watermark. In other words, a "2 and 20" fee can be payable on a performance no higher than a Treasury bill return. Although it is bizarre to offer to pay a performance fee on a return that might be less than that guaranteed to be paid by the government, such an agreement is made in expectation that a premium return will be earned. Anecdotal evidence from the boom years before 2008 indicates that some hedge funds that were normally closed to new business did selectively accept new business for a performance fee as high as 50% of future positive returns.

The fee structure places great pressure on hedge fund managers to generate positive returns. Even before 2008, there were examples of hedge funds that incurred significant negative returns closing, not just because existing investors lost confidence and withdrew funds, but also because the managers had difficulty motivating staff (and themselves) when there was little immediate prospect of a performance fee being earned. In these circumstances, they would rather start a new fund than have to wait to recoup past performance losses before earning a performance fee. This becomes a self-fulfilling prophecy as investors come to expect managers to respond to poor performance in this way.

The existing fee structure is already sufficiently rich to weaken (but not remove) the case for investing in hedge funds. As stated in Chapter 5, a reasonable magnitude for the equity risk premium is 4% a year over ten-year Treasury bonds, and a normal relationship might be for Treasury bonds to offer a yield premium of around 0.5% a year over cash. A "2 and 20" fee schedule means that if investors expect to receive an after-fee return from hedge funds that is comparable to the after-fee return from a passive equity strategy, they need to be willing to pay to hedge fund managers around 50% of the pre-fee excess return over Treasury bills. For a fund of hedge funds arrangement, which involves an extra fee, the comparable figures would be even higher. These are generous takes by any reckoning.

The importance of skill in hedge fund returns

By far the longest chapter in Charles Mackay's book *Extraordinary Popular Delusions and the Madness of Crowds* is devoted to "the alchymists". For centuries they gripped the popular imagination of Europeans in their search for and false claims to have discovered the secrets of the philosopher's stone, which was to create an abundance of wealth by turning base metals into gold. Hope springs eternal, and the alchemists' claims would stand comparison with some hedge fund marketing material.

There is an abundance of research and practical experience that testifies to the scarcity of unusual skill in managing traditional investment portfolios. This is demonstrated by the difficulty of identifying managers who are likely to outperform in the future.

However, hedge funds give skilled managers greater scope to implement their skills, although they will also need to find new competencies. The extra latitude offered by hedge funds arises from the fewer constraints they face (compared with long-only investing). The first is the ability to establish leveraged positions through borrowing. The second is the ability to establish short positions, and to make money from their negative investment views (long-only managers have to pass up such opportunities). Long-only managers who become hedge fund managers are quickly struck by the contrast between the way in which a large investment position in a traditional portfolio that underperforms because its price falls becomes a smaller, less risky position, and a short position in a hedge fund that underperforms because its price increases becomes a larger, more risky position. These extra flexibilities require additional investment risk management and back-office operational skills. However, they do not make it easier to assess the skill of a hedge fund manager than that of a long-only manager. This is probably more difficult because hedge fund strategies are less transparent.

It is a mistake to think that unusual manager skill is the only element of performance that should attract investors to hedge funds. Hedge fund performance is a reflection of manager skill, leverage and market returns. Sometimes the exposure to market returns generated by hedge funds represents exposure to equity or credit market returns that can be obtained at much lower cost by investing passively in equity or credit markets. There is no need to pay hedge fund fees to access such returns. However, there are other types of market returns that cannot be accessed efficiently through traditional investment manager mandates and which represent investment performance paid for providing valuable services. These liquidity and risk transfer services are offered by a number of hedge fund strategies, which came badly unstuck in 2008.

The shape of the hedge fund market

Figure 9.3 shows how allocations to broad categories of hedge funds have evolved, particularly since 2007. Equity and emerging-market hedge funds accounted for the bulk of the decline in assets under management after 2007, with these types of hedge funds managing in early 2013 around one-third less money than in 2007. By contrast, all other types of hedge funds, including fixed-income and arbitrage hedge funds, in aggregate had experienced an increase in assets over this period in excess of 25%.

FIG 9.3 **Hedge fund assets under management by type of strategy**
$bn

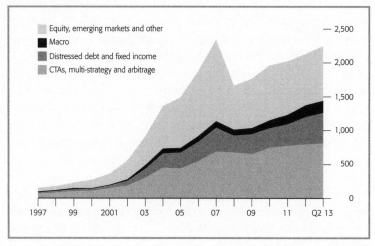

Source: BarclayHedge, www.barclayhedge.com

Table 9.2 shows the weight of money directly invested in the different types of hedge funds, according to BarclayHedge. One-quarter of the $1.9 trillion estimated to have been invested in hedge funds in June 2013 was invested through fund of hedge fund arrangements, where fund of fund managers are responsible for selecting individual hedge fund managers and for the risk management of the hedge fund arrangement. Also in June 2013 a further $330 billion was invested in managed futures programmes with CTAs, which are not generally classified as hedge funds but are directly comparable (see Commodity trading advisers section).

Table 9.2 shows that, according to data from BarclayHedge, of the total amount allocated directly by investors to different hedge funds in June 2013, 22% was placed with equity hedge funds; 13% with emerging-market funds; 16% with fixed-income and distressed-debt funds; 12% with multi-strategy funds; and 10% with event-driven funds.

TABLE 9.2 **Hedge fund industry: assets under management**
June 2013

	$bn	% of total
Hedge fund industry[a]	1,946	–
Fund of funds industry	480	–
Sectors		
Convertible arbitrage	38	2.0
Distressed securities	147	7.6
Emerging markets	261	13.4
Equity long bias	168	8.6
Equity long/short	170	8.7
Equity long-only	74	3.8
Equity market neutral	21	1.1
Event driven	188	9.7
Fixed income	308	15.8
Macro	176	9.0
Merger arbitrage	24	1.2
Multi-strategy	230	11.8
Other[b]	35	1.8
Sector specific[c]	107	5.5
Total	1,946	

a Excludes fund of funds assets and managed futures funds (CTAs).
b Includes funds categorised as regulation D, equity short bias, mutual fund timing, statistical arbitrage, closed-end funds and without a category.
c Includes sector funds categorised as technology, finance, real estate, metals and mining, and miscellaneous oriented.
Source: BarclayHedge, www.barclayhedge.com

Hedge fund replication and "alternative betas"

The enormous growth of the hedge fund industry in the past few decades and the combination of high fees and the apparent competitive performance of hedge fund indices have attracted much academic analysis. Two strands of this research stand out for investors. One is the analysis of what can be deduced about the risks of hedge fund investing from the patterns of monthly returns for different types of hedge fund (see later in this chapter). The other related area of research has been to estimate the extent to which the performance of hedge funds can be explained by different market risk exposures (which may take significant expertise to access) rather than pure manager skill. If the performance of hedge funds can be replicated, so the argument goes, by combinations of inexpensive, easy-to-access market returns, it should be possible to obtain the benefit of hedge fund investing less expensively, with more liquidity and transparency, than by investing in hedge funds. Harry Kat and Helder Palaro, working at Cass Business School, London, in 2005, and then Jasmina Hasanhodzic and Andrew Lo, both academics at MIT (Kat and Lo are also investment managers), were among the first to suggest such a liquid alternative to hedge fund investing. So-called hedge fund replicators have since been marketed by a number of banks and asset managers. They have, however, been subject to criticism, not least because the lacklustre performance of hedge fund indices in the years up to 2013 (when risk asset markets were generally strong) meant that the replicators also suffered dull performance. Furthermore, a number of the replication strategies, though offering liquidity and transparency, nevertheless levied fees in excess of the charges that might be expected for such a commoditised (though technically sophisticated) product.

The analysis of hedge fund performance highlighted that investing in hedge funds often includes a large degree of exposure to equity, credit and interest-rate risk, as well as other easy-to-access exposures such as smaller companies and foreign exchange risk. Investors do not need sophisticated products to access these risks. However, hedge fund investing has two principal attractions. One is to access the performance benefits of unusual and exceptional investment management skills, which are rare, difficult to find and command a premium price. Another is to access alternative sources of market returns, so as to better diversify investment portfolios which are otherwise dominated by equity, credit and interest-rate risk, each of which can be accessed inexpensively using passive investments. Some of these alternative sources of return, also called "alternative betas", include collecting insurance premiums (and so risk suffering occasional large losses), which are represented, for example, in volatility and event-driven hedge fund strategies. (Volatility strategies may collect premiums in effect for providing insurance against stockmarket crashes.) Other strategies seek to capture systematic returns offered by momentum strategies. These sources of risk and return are recognised to be underrepresented in most investment portfolios and the techniques of hedge fund replication offer the prospect of being able to access them inexpensively. This is different from an attempt to replicate the performance of broad hedge fund indices (which research has shown to be dominated by equity, credit and interest-rate risks). Suitably tailored to offset the risk exposures already present in an investment portfolio, this offers the prospect of helping investors to diversify, a bit, the risks in their strategies to achieve a better overall balance between risk and return.

Directional strategies

Global macro

In the early 1990s macro funds were the dominant type of hedge fund. Their importance has diminished in the past two decades as the range of other hedge fund strategies grew.

A macro fund may use leverage to exploit a diverse range of opportunities, investing in individual companies, equity or bond markets, commodities or currencies. The instruments a macro fund uses range from long and short positions in highly liquid (and potentially highly leveraged) currency or futures markets through quoted securities to illiquid investments in private equity or direct loans to companies. Historically, investment banks were able to replicate this range of opportunistic investing, but few other investment vehicles can come close to a macro hedge fund for the diversity of its entrepreneurial risk-taking. Performance comes from manager decisions: the changes in their market exposures mean that there may be no persistence of such exposures, and that little comfort should be taken from the low average correlation between macro funds and the equity market shown in Table 9.4. The flexibility of a macro fund's strategy means that sometimes it will diversify equity market risk and sometimes it will amplify it. The macro fund's investors probably will not know until after the event how the fund was positioned during turbulent market conditions.

Equity hedge, equity long/short and equity market neutral

The hedge fund business is traditionally considered to have started with the partnership set up by Alfred Jones in the late 1940s (though

TABLE 9.3 **Hedge fund performance during calendar quarters of equity market crisis**
1994 Q1–2013 Q3, % total return in $

	MSCI World gross return	Barclays US Treasury total return	Credit Suisse Global Macro
2008 Q4	−21.7	8.8	−2.6
2002 Q3	−18.3	7.4	4.2
2011 Q3	−16.5	6.5	4.4
2008 Q3	−15.2	2.3	−10.3
2001 Q3	−14.3	5.5	2.9

Sources: Barclays; Credit Suisse; MSCI

there are other claims for earlier antecedents). It would be recognised today as an "equity long/short" or "equity hedge" fund. It incorporated short selling of overvalued stocks alongside holdings of undervalued stocks. In this way its exposure to market movements was reduced and its exposure to manager skills was emphasised.

Equity long/short funds normally have some positive exposure to equity markets and are considered to be directional funds. This is confirmed in Table 9.4, which shows that between 1994 and 2013

TABLE 9.4 **Selected hedge fund strategies: correlations with global equity market**
Jan 1994–Sep 2013, % total return in $

	MSCI World
Equity long/short	0.71
Global macro	0.23
Managed futures	−0.03
Short bias	−0.74

	MSCI Emerging market equity index
Emerging markets	0.80

Sources: Credit Suisse; MSCI

the correlation between the index of equity long/short hedge fund manager performance and that of the world stockmarket was 0.71. Furthermore, the pattern of returns generated by these funds often indicates that the stocks that they "short", or sell, tend to be easy-to-borrow liquid large cap stocks or even index futures contracts, whereas the stocks that they purchase (or go long) tend to be less liquid, smaller company stocks. This pattern introduces a distinctive element of systematic risk into many of these hedge funds, which may have a leveraged exposure to the performance of small companies relative to large companies.

Equity long/short hedge funds typically have much less diversified portfolios than conventional long-only portfolios. Some of these equity hedge funds seek to neutralise market risk exposures and to offer an investment return that, as near as possible, reflects only the investment manager's stock-picking skills. These, called equity market neutral, form a minority of the equity hedge funds.

Short-selling or short-biased managers

Short-selling managers sell stocks that they expect to decline in value in the expectation of being able to buy them back at a later date at a lower price. These directional funds should perform particularly well when the stockmarket declines. How well a short-selling fund provides this insurance will depend upon how well it is diversified. In practice, the average performance of the short-selling strategy in calendar quarters of equity setback has been strongly positive (see Table 9.5).

Table 9.4 indicates that the correlation between short-biased hedge funds and the US stockmarket has been around −0.74. Short-selling funds are particularly used by fund of hedge fund managers to reduce the overall equity market exposure of their portfolios of hedge funds. In practice, the money managed by short-selling funds is normally modest.

Long-only equity hedge funds

These exist. They do not hedge, but they call themselves hedge funds and during the bull market before 2007, they represented a

TABLE 9.5 **Equity hedge fund performance during calendar quarters of equity market crisis**
1994 Q1–2013 Q3, % total return in $

	MSCI World index	Barclays US Treasury index	Credit Suisse Dedicated short bias	Credit Suisse Long Short Equity strategy	Credit Suisse Equity market neutral strategy[a]
2008 Q4	−21.7	8.8	11.1	−7.5	−41.3
2002 Q3	−18.3	7.4	11.1	−2.4	2.4
2011 Q3	−16.5	6.5	19.0	−9.8	−3.3
2008 Q3	−15.2	2.3	−7.6	−12.9	−2.0
2001 Q3	−14.3	5.5	11.1	−1.8	1.2

a See text for comments on 2008 Q4 equity market neutral performance.
Sources: Barclays; Credit Suisse; MSCI

way for hedge funds to diversify their business. The principals own a significant equity stake and typically they invest opportunistically in smaller quoted and perhaps some unquoted private companies. The fee arrangements are much more attractive to the managers of these funds than those for their close relative, the small cap mutual fund. Furthermore, they are given a greater degree of investment flexibility by being in a stronger position (than a mutual fund) to manage the terms on which clients can exit from the fund.

Emerging-market hedge funds

As the name suggests, these funds exploit opportunities in emerging markets. They are directional funds which invest in both equities and bonds. It can be difficult to borrow stock in these markets and one means of altering market exposure is by leveraging the entire portfolio through borrowing, or by scaling back exposure through building up holdings of cash. Their performance is often highly correlated with emerging-market equities (see Tables 9.4 and 9.6).

TABLE 9.6 **Emerging-market hedge fund performance during calendar quarters of equity market crisis**
1994 Q1–2013 Q3, % total return in $

	MSCI World index	Barclays US Treasury index	MSCI Emerging Markets index	JPMorgan Emerging Markets bond index plus	Credit Suisse Emerging markets index
2008 Q4	−21.7	8.8	−27.6	−4.8	−15.1
2002 Q3	−18.3	7.4	−16.3	−1.1	−1.9
2011 Q3	−16.5	6.5	−22.5	−1.2	−8.9
2008 Q3	−15.2	2.3	−26.9	−4.6	−15.1
2001 Q3	−14.3	5.5	−21.6	−5.2	−8.2

Sources: Barclays; Credit Suisse; JPMorgan; MSCI

Fixed-income hedge funds: distressed debt

"Distressed debt" conjures up images of the obligations of companies that are close to bankruptcy. This is the traditional fishing pond for hedge funds specialising in distressed debt. This group of hedge funds also includes some significant hedge funds which can resemble "private debt funds". The risk for investors is a function of the underlying investments, of the leverage and of the illiquidity of the fund. The largest of these have much in common with large private equity funds (see Chapter 10). For an investor, there is likely to be an overlap in terms of the underlying investments with the much less expensive, well-diversified, high-yield corporate debt fund. A distressed-debt fund, however, may be more leveraged.

Nevertheless, a distressed-debt fund is quite distinct from a high-yield mutual fund. First, the hedge fund managers may be the bankers extending loans to their investee companies. They will have a much more direct sense of ownership for their holdings, and greater scope to influence corporate management, than the best-informed high-yield manager. Second, the hedge fund can impose lock-up periods on investors and so can gain the advantage of time and be in better control of flows of liquidity into and out of the fund. This can provide

an investment advantage to a distressed-debt hedge fund compared
with a high-yield bond mutual fund.

TABLE 9.7 **Fixed-income hedge fund performance during
calendar quarters of equity market crisis**
1994 Q1–2013 Q3, % total return in $

	MSCI World index	Barclays US Treasury index	Credit Suisse Fixed income arbitrage index	Credit Suisse Event driven distressed debt hedge fund index
2008 Q4	−21.7	8.8	−19.5	−12.7
2002 Q3	−18.3	7.4	1.2	−4.2
2011 Q3	−16.5	6.5	0.1	−7.8
2008 Q3	−15.2	2.3	−7.8	−7.7
2001 Q3	−14.3	5.5	1.7	1.5

Note: See text comments for discussion of August 1998 fixed-income arbitrage reported performance.
Sources: Barclays; Credit Suisse; MSCI

Arbitrage strategies

Before the credit crisis, arbitrage hedge fund strategies commonly
used significant leverage and often had illiquid holdings. The crisis
put such funds under severe pressure. A number of them closed, but
those that survived adjusted to operating with the lower levels of
leverage and often higher levels of margin payments requested from
the banks.

Fixed-income arbitrage

Fixed-income arbitrage strategies exploit pricing anomalies in fixed-
income instruments while managing exposure to interest-rate risk.
Fixed-income arbitrage funds establish long and short positions in
closely related fixed-income markets or securities. Where the offsetting
positions are close substitutes, leverage may be used, though the
degree of leverage was curtailed by the credit crisis. Short positions
are generally highly liquid and long positions may be less liquid.

These strategies will often be positively affected by a narrowing of credit spreads and vice versa, although the hedge funds can equally easily bet on credit spreads widening as narrowing.

Merger arbitrage

Merger arbitrage (sometimes simply called "risk arbitrage") funds provide an insurance which previously was left as unsought risk by long-only equity managers. When an intended merger or takeover is announced, the share price of the target company moves close to the announced takeover terms. Its new share price is normally (unless a higher bid is anticipated) less than a cash bid price. The amount of the discount will reflect the probability that the bid will succeed, as well as the intervening rate of interest. Merger arbitrage funds provide insurance against the risk that the announced merger might fail by acquiring the target company and hedging that by selling the acquiring company. As well as potential restrictions on fund leverage or short selling, this strategy is vulnerable to two risks that can undermine positions: company-specific issues could cause the merger to fail; or a severe equity market decline could cause a renegotiation of the terms of the deal. In common with other difficult-to-diversify insurance arrangements, merger arbitrage provides a steady flow of income with the risk of occasional large losses.

TABLE 9.8 **Arbitrage hedge fund performance during calendar quarters of global equity market weakness**
1994 Q1–2013 Q3, % total return in $

	MSCI World index	Barclays US Treasury index	Credit Suisse Convertible arbitrage index	Credit Suisse Fixed income arbitrage index	Credit Suisse Event driven index
2008 Q4	−21.7	8.8	−15.1	−19.5	−9.3
2002 Q3	−18.3	7.4	0.4	1.2	−3.0
2011 Q3	−16.5	6.5	−3.6	0.1	−10.9
2008 Q3	−15.2	2.3	−14.7	−7.8	−8.3
2001 Q3	−14.3	5.5	3.4	1.7	0.5

Sources: Credit Suisse; MSCI

Convertible arbitrage

Hedge funds were said in early 2005 to hold around three-quarters of outstanding convertible bonds, such was the popularity at that time of convertible arbitrage strategies. Convertible bonds pay a low coupon (or low yield) because they have the added benefit that they can, at the discretion of the investor, be converted into equity. They provide the upside potential of equities and the downside protection of a bond. They offer a natural opportunity for hedge funds seeking to exploit any technical anomalies in the pricing of the debt, convertible bonds, warrants (that is, options on equity) and equity of a particular issuer.

In principle, these strategies should be able to deliver steady profits. However, illiquidity can cause anomalies to become more exaggerated before the date at which the arbitrage profit should be crystallised. If the fund is subject to severe redemptions as investors respond to disappointing performance, forced sales can easily have a cumulatively negative impact on performance. In 2008, the impact of this was compounded by the need to cut positions as margin requirements were raised, and by the impact of bans on short selling. These contributed to an unprecedented negative return for this strategy. Nevertheless, in principle there can be clear arbitrage profits for patient long-term investors, and hedge funds provide the obvious vehicle to exploit such anomalies.

Statistical arbitrage

There are a number of arbitrage strategies that may be used by relative value hedge fund managers and that may be found within multi-strategy funds. These include liquidity arbitrage trades to exploit (and correct) the short-term impact on market prices of securities of large market trades. Historically, another type of trade was the observed positive or negative impact on stock prices of companies joining or leaving an index that is widely used as an investment benchmark. This declined in profitability as new money chased the unusual profits that had previously been earned by exploiting these phenomena. Both these types of statistical arbitrage trades show how hedge funds can improve the efficient functioning of markets by reducing the scale of these short-term anomalies. But they also illustrate how anomalies can be eroded by a weight of money, leaving few if any profits for latecomers.

Multi-strategy funds

From the beginning of the hedge fund industry, larger funds have often managed their own risks and their investors' risks by having more than one team of portfolio managers, each dedicated to a different investment strategy. This enables the hedge fund's management to take responsibility for allocating resources as opportunities in the different strategies change. Multi-strategy funds provide increasing competition with fund of hedge fund arrangements because of the central ownership of risk management and decision-making, and, critically, lower fees, as performance fees are payable on the combination of strategies, rather than on each strategy individually.

Multi-strategy funds include some of the largest hedge funds. Some multi-strategy funds have developed expertise in corporate finance, to facilitate involvement in corporate takeovers and management buy-outs.

TABLE 9.9 **Multi-strategy hedge fund performance during calendar quarters of equity market crisis**
1994 Q1–2013 Q3, % total return in $

	MSCI World index	Barclays US Treasury index	Credit Suisse Multi-strategy index
2008 Q4	−21.7	8.8	−12.6
2002 Q3	−18.3	7.4	0.7
2011 Q3	−16.5	6.5	−3.7
2008 Q3	−15.2	2.3	−10.8
2001 Q3	−14.3	5.5	1.0

Sources: Barclays; Credit Suisse; MSCI

Commodity trading advisers (or managed futures funds)

Commodity trading advisers (CTAs) provide one of the most interesting absolute return strategies. Their investable universe is provided by the world's futures, options and foreign exchange markets. The dominant group of CTAs is systematic traders who are highly quantitative followers of trends ranging from a few days to several months in the futures markets covering agricultural commodities, industrial and precious metals, currencies, government bonds and equity indices. These are generally highly liquid and easy to value. Some investors are nervous of the opaque, model-driven (black-box) approach to investing in systematic CTAs. One concern is that the highly qualified quantitative analysts building the models in the different firms may unwittingly identify the same trends and lead to hidden concentrations of positions held by CTA funds in individual futures contracts. Discretionary CTAs, which rely on manager judgments of when to trade, accounted for just 7% of CTA assets in mid-2013.

CTA strategies have been subject to extensive statistical analysis, which shows that, on average, they have demonstrated strong diversifying characteristics and a tendency to perform well at times of equity market crisis when other hedge fund strategies often underperform. The pattern of returns shown by indices of CTA manager performance during calendar quarters of equity market weakness (see Table 9.10) is immediately different from the corresponding figures for hedge fund performance. With the exception of dedicated short strategies, the overriding message from hedge fund data is that hedge funds do not provide short-term insurance against poor equity market performance. On average, CTAs have provided some such hedge. This continued in 2008 when the Credit Suisse Managed Futures index returned 18.3%, compared with a negative return of 19.1% for the broad index. There is no assurance that this pattern will continue, and the performance of individual CTAs can be very different.

The role of CTA funds in providing readily marketable portfolio diversification can be compared with the role of commodity index exposure, which became popular for institutional investors in the years before the credit crunch, when commodity indices rose strongly.

TABLE 9.10 **Managed futures fund (CTA) and commodity index performance during calendar quarters of equity market crisis** 1994 Q1–2013 Q3, % total return in $

	MSCI World index	Barclays US Treasury index	Credit Suisse Managed Futures index	Dow Jones–UBS Commodity index
2008 Q4	−21.7	8.8	10.9	−30.0
2002 Q3	−18.3	7.4	14.2	7.3
2011 Q3	−16.5	6.5	3.5	−11.3
2008 Q3	−15.2	2.3	−7.1	−27.7
2001 Q3	−14.3	5.5	6.4	−5.6

Sources: Barclays; Credit Suisse; MSCI; S&P Dow Jones Indices

Table 9.10 shows that on average CTAs have performed better during months of equity market weakness than the Dow Jones-UBS Commodity index. However, while investors in commodity indices should receive the index performance, the dispersion of manager performance means that it is much more likely that an individual CTA manager will differ strongly from the results for the index of CTA managers.

There are various possible explanations for the apparent insurance against equity market setbacks that CTA strategies have provided. It may be down to luck that in the relatively small number of quarters (or months) with large negative equity returns the average CTA manager has delivered a somewhat surprisingly strong performance. Or, more likely, CTAs have provided insurance against equity market setbacks when their models have been able to identify a change in market direction, which has subsequently proved to represent a change of trend that the CTAs have successfully exploited. Sometimes this will work and sometimes, when markets are affected by a sudden setback, it will not. Nevertheless, an investment that offers the prospect of good performance during bad times is rare and valuable to investors.

Hedge fund risk
Madoff, hedge fund due diligence and regulation

Hedge fund risk should feature prominently in any assessment of hedge fund investing. There have been well-publicised examples of hedge fund fraud and apparent fraud, and it is likely that the entrepreneurial, cottage-industry nature of some parts of the hedge fund industry make it more prone to elementary process weaknesses. The scale of the multibillion-dollar fraud at Bernard L. Madoff Investment Securities, which was revealed in late 2008, was particularly shocking as it was far removed from any idea of a cottage industry. It exposed the shallowness of ways in which many private clients appeared to have chosen hedge funds – often being led by personal recommendations and a review of historic performance data, together with a confirmation of the evident esteem and reputation of the principals.

Rigorous due diligence is different. Many investment firms avoided dealing with Madoff, and since the event there have been several reports highlighting concerns that a thorough due diligence process should have picked up. These are summarised in "Madoff: a riot of red flags", a report by Greg Gregoriou, professor of finance at Plattsburgh State University of New York, and François-Serge Lhabitant, professor of finance at EDHEC Business School in France, published in January 2009. These reports provide useful training material for hedge fund researchers.

Operational risks

The hedge fund industry is rapidly evolving and the flurry of industry reports in recent years on hedge fund risks and best practice are indications of both shortcomings and the emergence of an understanding of best practice. Nevertheless, investors cannot take for granted that their hedge funds are managed to a high standard. Operational risk should be a particular focus of a hedge fund due diligence process since it has been highlighted as a prime reason for sudden catastrophic closures of hedge funds. One issue that investors need to consider arises from the difficulties that hedge funds have in developing an enduring franchise, partly because of the incentive effects of hedge fund performance fees, which lead to a high rate of fund closures. For example, according to HFR, a hedge fund consultancy, 15% of hedge funds closed during 2008, and almost 9% closed in each of the three years to 2012. This rate of closure, as well as the potential incentive for hedge funds to close after a period of poor performance, suggests that investors in hedge funds or their advisers should always be searching for replacement hedge fund managers – which adds to the cost, at least in time and effort, of hedge fund investing.

Illiquid hedge fund investments and long notice periods

Many hedge funds find promising opportunities in unquoted and illiquid investments. Typical examples include private loans to corporations, which may be investment grade or distressed debt, and unquoted or illiquid equity opportunities. These are precisely the sort of opportunities that an entrepreneurial investment company would be expected to exploit.

However, 2008 exposed the long-established weakness of the hedge fund industry, which is a mismatch between the illiquidity of underlying investments and the frequent opportunities to redeem. This has always been a concern because errors in valuing illiquid investments when hedge funds are bought and sold give rise to windfall transfers of wealth among fund participants. In 2008 these issues led to the widespread imposition of restrictions on redemptions of hedge fund holdings by funds that were unable, or unwilling, to meet their regular schedules of dealing dates. In March 2009, Credit Suisse estimated that 17% of hedge funds (by assets) were "impaired" by having put restrictions on, or suspended, redemptions or had frozen investors' share of hard-to-value investments in a separate portfolio. This illustrates that investors in illiquid hedge fund strategies should not object, indeed should demand, that fellow investors are subject to early redemption penalties (to accrue to the fund) that properly reflect the underlying illiquidity of the hedge fund. Long lock-up periods, seemingly inflexible redemption arrangements or wide bid-offer spreads for hedge funds with illiquid underlying investments can be in the best interests of all investors in those funds.

Lies, damn lies and some hedge fund risk statistics

There are other problems that arise with illiquid hedge fund investments. Any price for an unquoted investment will be an appraisal price. Appraisal prices unavoidably smooth and lag changes in underlying market prices. This means that if investors have the opportunity to transact at an appraisal price for a fund, trends may be evident that enable them to buy or sell when they reasonably assess that the appraisal price is higher or lower than where the market actually appears to be.

Furthermore, appraisal prices are less volatile than market prices. This means that the volatility of monthly appraisal prices should not be used as a guide to the risk of a strategy that involves a significant element of appraisal prices in its valuations. Where the price data are smoothed, calculations for volatility and for risk-adjusted returns (such as Sharpe ratios, see Appendix 1) will be distorted, with risk looking lower than it is and risk-adjusted performance better. Appraisal prices can provide useful management information, but they must be used with care.

There has been extensive research into the issue of illiquidity and the unavoidable smoothing of hedge fund returns, and the implications of this for measures of hedge fund risk. The results tend to be uniform in establishing the importance of the issue and the way that it is focused on illiquid hedge fund strategies. The affected categories include distressed debt, convertible arbitrage, event-driven and emerging-market strategies. The strategies that are not normally affected by this valuation-smoothing phenomenon are the generally liquid strategies: equity long/short, macro, short-biased and especially CTA or managed futures funds.

Compiling prices for funds that include large proportions of illiquid and private investments runs the risk of accurately following a procedure to compute valuations, but then using the data to construct performance and especially risk statistics that are more likely to misinform than to inform. In private equity, where the same issues arise, appraisal valuations of underlying investments provide management information, but not normally dealing prices, and it is understood that the only performance that matters is the internal rate of return calculated from the amount of cash originally invested, the cash subsequently paid back to investors and the passage of time in between (see Chapter 10).

Subscriptions to private equity funds are designed to be held until realisation, and in so far as there is a secondary market for holdings in private equity funds, these do not set the terms for wholesale exits from a fund. For example, investors in a private equity fund would be surprised if they were shown a pattern of monthly statistics of returns for a venture capital or private equity portfolio from which "risk" statistics, such as standard deviations or Sharpe ratios, were calculated. But in the hedge fund world this sort of thing happens routinely, even for portfolios that include a large element of illiquid investments. More useful as performance indicators that may shed light on risk can be measures such as maximum drawdown, which measure the experience of negative returns in the fund and generally mitigate the problem of smoothed valuations.

Another danger that investors should look for is where there is a combination of price smoothing and the pursuit of an investment strategy involving the collection of option or insurance premiums which happen not to have been reflected in periodic poor performance, so far. Clifford Asness, co-founder of AQR Capital Management, wrote in 2004:

> Combining some lags in marking to market with invisible option writing can produce one heck of a historical Sharpe ratio, but with a potentially toxic combination going forward.

These weaknesses of widely used hedge fund risk indicators have been known for a considerable time, but they have made less impression on hedge fund practice than would be hoped. A survey of hedge fund performance and risk reporting standards by EDHEC, a French business school, in 2008 found that only 5% of hedge funds adjust their results for the smoothed pattern of many hedge fund returns, and that most hedge funds did not know how to allow for a "non-normal" pattern of hedge fund performance in calculating risk statistics. Instead hedge funds have found it convenient to rely on the flattering and easy-to-calculate Sharpe ratio, whose use is valid only under conditions which often do not apply to hedge funds.

"Perfect storms" and hedge fund risk

Money managers often attribute unusual poor performance to a highly improbable confluence of events. Nowhere is this more true than in hedge fund investing. Events that are described by hedge fund managers as "being expected" to occur only "once in a million years" seem to be so common as to be unremarkable. In 2008 the combination of the evaporation of market liquidity and restrictions on short selling made it seem as if no matter how insightful was a fund's investment process, events were conspiring to undermine its endeavours. But an apparently unusual frequency of extreme events always has accompanied hedge fund investing.

This can be illustrated with the historical anecdote from the car industry described in Chapter 6. On that occasion groups of hedge funds found themselves on the wrong side of offsetting positions in GM securities that they thought were good hedges for each other. A similar example arose in 2008, when Volkswagen shares were squeezed when it became known that Porsche owned much more of VW than had previously been believed. The GM episode was described by one hedge fund (which was caught short) as an "eight standard deviation event", which should almost never happen if markets behaved as simple models would suggest they should. However, the apparent frequent occurrence of "bad news" in hedge fund performance reflects a particular characteristic of many hedge fund strategies that investors must understand. Since they are often comparable to investment insurance-type arrangements, they provide steady returns most of the time, as the insurance premiums are collected, while being exposed to the risk of occasional large losses, when the insurance policy must pay up.

This is illustrated in Figure 9.4, which combines the monthly performance for the multi-strategy and arbitrage strategy indices as reported by Credit Suisse. It vividly reflects this combination of modest positive returns most of the time, with occasional large negative returns.

As Bill Sharpe, the Nobel Prize-winning originator of the standard measure of risk-adjusted returns, said in an article in August 2005 in *Wall Street Journal*: "Past average performance may be a terrible

FIG 9.4 **Monthly performance of arbitrage and multi-strategy hedge fund indices**
1994–2013

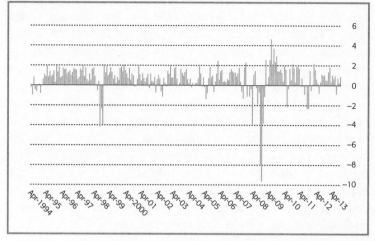

Note: Shows equally weighted performance of Credit Suisse convertible arbitrage, event-driven, fixed-income arbitrage and multi-strategy hedge fund indices.
Source: Credit Suisse

predictor of future performance." This pattern of returns is particularly common in some hedge fund strategies that offer investors the prospect of systematic market returns for bearing this insurance risk.

Managing investor risk: the role of funds of hedge funds

Investors should accept the risk of an occasional extreme negative return only if it is judged to be more than outweighed by the prospect of compensating performance over time. Even then the risk will need to be offset as far as possible within an overall asset allocation. Most commonly this means combining different hedge fund strategies in a way which tries to manage these risks, and then making sure that the allocation to hedge funds fits in with the overall risk appetite, or at least comfort level, of the investor.

The portfolio construction role may be undertaken by fund of hedge fund managers, who manage portfolios of hedge funds. Fund of hedge fund managers perform two critical roles: one is portfolio construction and overall investment risk management; the other is hedge fund manager due diligence. At the end of this chapter there is a list of some of the issues that need to be covered in a hedge fund due diligence process. Given the high level of operational and reputational risk involved in hedge fund investing, a fund of hedge funds arrangement is often the most appropriate way for novice hedge fund investors to proceed. Following the work of the fund of hedge funds manager is also an effective way for investors to see professional hedge fund risk management in action.

Investors need to try to satisfy themselves that the due diligence process they are using is thorough. But there will always be a risk of a surprising investment performance or operational mishap and of investors saying to their due diligence team: "I thought you were supposed to check on that." These risks should be mitigated by a fund of hedge funds approach. However, it does come at a price. In particular, it has to overcome the hurdle of imposing an additional level of fees on top of an already expensive structure.

How much should you allocate to hedge funds?

You do not need to allocate anything to hedge funds, and you should not unless you think that you can access a hedge fund arrangement which complements your other investments. Paying higher fees for a diluted version of your equity investments is wasteful. There should be an element of extra skill or access to rewards that are not available elsewhere to justify a decision to invest in hedge funds.

A common weakness with a fund of funds approach to hedge fund investing is that it is typically structured in ignorance of the investment risks that are present elsewhere in an investor's strategy. With some aspects of hedge fund performance and risk being close substitutes for those available elsewhere and others being unique, asking how much to allocate to hedge funds ceases to be a sensible question. Instead, the investment issue is how much should investors wish to allocate to different types of systematic risk? Thus there is a strong argument in favour of the approach of some funds of hedge funds managers, which is to offer combinations of funds segregated into different categories or "buckets" of risk-taking. For example, some hedge fund strategies (such as equity hedge funds) offer combinations of equity market risk and manager skill exposures which are obvious alternatives to, or competitors with, the risks and opportunities that investors expose themselves to when they select conventional equity managers. The same principles apply to hedge funds that specialise in, for example, emerging markets or some credit market strategies: the allocation to such managers should be considered at the same time as decisions are made to allocate to emerging-market debt or equity or, for example, sub-investment grade corporate debt (allowing for the different elements of diversification provided by each).

This much is clear, and it is a process that is followed by increasing numbers of institutional investors. More interesting is how to decide what to allocate to hedge funds which offer sources of investment performance and risk that are different from those found in equity and bond markets. This is the reward offered to hedge fund investors for providing a variety of insurance services, most commonly through the provision of liquidity and intermediation services in different markets. These include the range of "alternative market beta" strategies, loosely described as arbitrage strategies, each of which also has a strong component of manager skill. The process of determining how much to allocate to these strategies should be driven by a view of the risk associated with them and how well it is diversified by other investments, and by an informed opinion on how much reward is expected to be earned from allocating capital to them.

From an investor's perspective this is where difficulties arise, because this is still relatively uncharted territory, particularly in respect of return expectations. Nevertheless, several conclusions would be broadly agreed:

■ The diversification benefits of a number of these strategies appear well established (although they are not robust in all periods).

■ It is reasonable to assume that the market should reward these services since other market participants are demonstrably willing to pay for them.

■ The diversification benefits are such that the required premium return (above the return on safe-haven investments) needed to justify an allocation to these alternative hedge fund strategies is modest.

This leads to the two final conclusions:

■ The uncertainties involved mean that an allocation to these alternative betas should err on the side of caution by not dominating an investor's strategy.

■ For most investors, some such allocation can normally be justified.

Questions to ask
Your hedge fund manager

A good starting point is Gregoriou and Lhabitant's report "Madoff: a riot of red flags". Investors should be able to confirm the presence of green rather than red flags in whichever arrangements they are considering.

Some general guidance for investors can be found on the Securities and Exchange Commission (SEC) website. The background of some individual hedge fund managers licensed by the SEC or National Association of Securities Dealers (NASD) can be checked on their respective websites. The questions that follow are too detailed for most hedge fund clients to ask a representative of a hedge fund or even a financial adviser who is recommending hedge fund investments to answer. However, they are the sorts of questions that an investor should want to know someone at some stage has asked a hedge fund manager on behalf of investors, and received satisfactory responses.

Performance and investment

■ Please provide a monthly track record of the performance of the fund.

■ Please summarise the strategy of the fund and the major determinants of fund performance. Please relate this to the pattern of monthly returns.

■ What was the size of assets of the fund at the start of this track record, and what is the most recent size of the fund?

- How has the strategy of the fund changed since the start of the track record?
- Do you manage or have you managed a fund with comparable objectives? If so, what was its performance track record?
- How do you judge the investment success of the fund?
- Please describe how the management of your fund responded to the market and regulatory challenges of 2008.
- Please describe the investment decisions that led to your most disappointing monthly performance results and, separately, the best monthly performance results.
- What conclusions did you draw for the future management of the fund?
- How do you expect performance to correlate with equity and fixed-income markets?
- Is there any investment strategy reason to expect performance to be particularly correlated with extreme equity market performance?
- How do you manage the possibility of extreme negative performance results?
- How large could the fund grow and still have the same prospect for success?
- Has your (and your fund's) past success led you to scale back the risk-taking in the fund?
- How do you conduct research?
- How does research affect portfolio construction?

Business, operations and valuation

- Who, if anyone, is the fund manager's regulator? If it is the SEC, request a copy of the most recent form ADV.
- What proportion of the fund is valued at month end using third-party pricing sources?
- What proportion of the fund is represented by quoted securities?
- Are any investments valued at book cost?

- Has this proportion changed over time?

- Please describe the unquoted investments and explain how they are valued.

- Do these investments smooth the reported performance of the fund?

- Do you monitor net asset value each day? How do you price unquoted investments for this?

- How frequent are the fund dealing dates, and are there any lock-up periods for new investments?

- What provisions exist for delaying redemptions?

- Did your fund impose restrictions on redemptions during 2008–09?

- How quickly can I withdraw my funds?

- What exit penalties apply?

- What discretion does the manager have to alter these terms, and with what notice to investors?

- What were capital outflows and inflows in the last 12 months?

- To whom does the back-office report?

- How often are reports produced for investors?

- How do you manage inflows and redemptions?

- How do you monitor the fund's counterparty exposure?

- Who is your fund administrator? Please describe their role for you.

- Do you have one, or more than one, prime broker? Please explain why.

- Who is your prime broker? Please describe their role for you.

- What credit risks do your clients face vis-à-vis your prime broker?

- Do you allow your prime broker to make any use of the fund's assets for their own purposes (ie, "rehypothecation")?

- Is the custody of the hedge fund's assets independent from the prime broker?

- Please explain the extent of use of over-the-counter derivatives and the collateral requirements which accompany these positions.
- What problems do you encounter in short selling?
- How was your fund affected by the restrictions on short selling in 2008?
- Do short-selling difficulties limit your ability to implement investment policy?
- How many failed trades do you have outstanding at present?
- Is this number of failed trades usual or unusual?
- How do you monitor failed trades?
- Is pricing done in-house or by a third party?
- Who are your external auditors? When did you last change auditors?
- Please provide a time line for payments on redemption of units in the fund.
- How do you ensure fairness in pricing illiquid or unquoted investments when making redemption payments?
- How is your personal financial interest aligned with that of your clients?
- Who are the founders or principals of the fund? When are they expected to retire? What succession plan is there?
- Please provide references.

Risk

- How do you monitor investment risk?
- Who does this work and to whom do they report?
- How reliable are the risk measurement tools? Please illustrate.
- How do you allow for the weaknesses that are inherent in risk models?
- How do you manage the credit risk of your investments?
- How do you manage the credit risk of your counterparties?

- Have you stress tested your strategy against the market developments of extreme market conditions, such as October 1987, August–September 1998, or the last four months of 2008? Has this affected investment policy?
- What is the worst historical drawdown the fund has experienced?
- Has investment policy been altered to reduce the risk of this happening again?
- Are there any elements of investment strategy that expose the fund to the low risk of an extreme negative return?
- How does this relate to your investment policy, redemption terms and assessment of extreme events in markets?
- Do you have formal parameters that limit your risk-taking? Please describe.
- What is your leverage policy? Has this changed since 2007–08?
- How do you define leverage? Please contrast this with other definitions used in the hedge fund industry.
- Is it intended that the risk profile of the fund should be predictable or opportunistic? If predictable, please provide a proof statement of practice.
- Do you have a formal set of permissible investments?
- What is the best or worst monthly performance that I should expect to experience?
- How do you allocate risk in constructing the portfolio?
- How do you report investment risk to investors?

Liquidity

- How do you manage liquidity risk in your investments?
- How do you manage the liquidity of your funding or client redemptions?
- How do you monitor the adequacy of your fund's access to liquidity? How do you monitor the liquidity of the investments of the fund?

- How do you ensure that you always have enough liquidity to meet collateral requirements?
- How do liquidity considerations alter your approach to portfolio construction?
- Do you monitor any liquidity risk measures?
- Does illiquidity of your investments cause the measures of risk that you show to investors to be understated?

Your hedge fund adviser

- Who regulates you?
- Do you research and recommend products from the whole market, or only selected providers?
- How do you get compensated?
- Do you get an introduction fee or any other form of remuneration from the hedge fund if I invest?
- If yes, how much and how does it influence your recommendations?
- Is the proposal to invest in the hedge fund, or in a vehicle that invests in the hedge fund?

Your fund of hedge funds manager

- How do you manage the investment risk for your recommended or chosen combinations of funds?
- Do you receive a fee from funds that you select for your fund of funds?
- Do you include any funds which do not pay you fees?
- Do you use leverage? If so, why?
- How many of the underlying funds in which you invest have imposed restrictions on redemptions by investors?
- What is your biggest administrative headache?
- How do you manage cash inflows and outflows?
- Can client cash flows alter the investment allocation for all your clients?

10 Private equity: information-based investment returns

THE PAST AND PROSPECTIVE investment performance of the private equity market has been analysed in numerous studies. But even if the estimates produced by those studies are reliable, investors cannot take for granted that they will be able to earn them.

Investors should avoid private equity investing unless they believe that they have access to skilled investment managers. The key to unlocking returns in private equity is information, and investors have to believe that their managers have an edge that enables them to deliver at least market returns. Investing in an arrangement that lacks this edge will condemn the strategy to inferior performance.

The appropriate place for private equity in investment strategy is straightforward. Private equity is what it says. It is equity, and so if included in strategy it should form part of an investor's allocation to equity. It is also private, and so unquoted and illiquid and not suitable for short-term investors, and its illiquidity will add inflexibilities and opportunity costs into any investment portfolio. Investors need to satisfy themselves that they can expect a premium return to compensate for these costs. All the comments about diversification by style, by size and by geography for investing in quoted equities (see Chapter 7) can be applied to private equity. However, since private equity is only part of an investor's allocation to equity, there is no requirement to include in a private equity portfolio all the diversification that can be obtained from the private equity market, when it can also be obtained inexpensively and with confidence from the quoted equity market. The key for investors is to be driven by a dispassionate assessment of their ability to gain access to skilled managers. The investor has to attempt to separate the impact of skill from that of leverage on the manager's track record. Having done this and become comfortable with the manager's approach to gearing the investments, the investor can then decide whether to make an allocation. The next step is to ensure that the total equity allocation (public as well as private) has the degree of diversification with which the investor is comfortable.

What is private equity?

It is useful to think of the market in two distinct parts. The first is start-up venture capital. The second is the market for leveraged buy-outs of existing businesses. The market is commonly divided further, with venture capital differentiated between seed capital and early-stage venture capital, while the later stages of investing differentiate between buy-outs and expansion capital.

Expansion capital may take the form of "mezzanine" financing, which is the riskiest form of debt obligations. It will often have options to convert into equity if the firm fails to meet the terms of its debt, which will be priced to deliver a high rate of return. Mezzanine finance is expensive for companies. Management buy-outs occur when an existing management team is supported with external private equity, for example when a family business is sold, or a larger firm decides that an existing division is no longer a core business for the parent company.

The word "leverage" in a leveraged buy-out (LBO) refers to the financing of the deal, when the new private equity owners will have leveraged their equity ownership. This may occur, for example, through the issue of asset-backed loans or the sale of high-yield bonds, or, where bond or loan covenants are weak, by restructuring the company's balance sheet such that existing debt becomes devalued, and so higher yielding. This focus on the use of leverage is the principal reason private equity should, in general, be regarded as more risky than quoted equity.

Private equity firms transform the businesses they acquire through financial engineering, through changing the incentives facing managers, through more direct management of the governance of firms (than, for example, is possible with a shareholding in a listed company) and by deploying industry expertise to transform the operational management of the business. Buy-outs are also often associated with restructuring, which includes the divestment of non-core activities and also the acquisition of related businesses.

Private equity market risk

In all countries there is a wide variety of private companies, of which most are small but some are large enterprises. In the years before the credit crunch, the development of private equity groups controlling large amounts of investor money led to the emergence of substantial private industrial and commercial conglomerates controlling private companies across different sectors of the economy throughout the world. These have branched out into new areas of investing, which have caused the boundaries between private equity, hedge funds and real estate funds to become blurred.

Private companies often look similar to the quoted companies with which they compete. However, this does not mean that the risks for investors are comparable with those of the stockmarket. Alongside leverage, a principal risk is illiquidity, and the great difficulty of selling a part ownership in a private company and the impossibility, other than at infrequent intervals, of rebalancing the allocation to private equity. Another risk is that there are systematic biases in the characteristics of private companies compared with quoted companies (for example, private companies will have a bias towards small and medium-sized companies). Nevertheless, it might be thought that the inherent risk or volatility of their aggregate value should be broadly comparable to that of quoted companies. Leverage normally means that this is not true. Furthermore, even if this was the case, illiquidity would mean that it was not an adequate measure of risk.

One perspective on the intrinsic volatility of the private equity market is given by the volatility of diversified listed private equity firms. An example is provided by the 3i Group, which has been listed on the UK stockmarket since 1994, and was for a number of years the world's largest quoted company whose core business is the management of a diversified private equity portfolio. The evolution of the volatility of the 3i share price and that of the UK stockmarket

FIG 10.1 **Volatility of public and private equity, proxied by 3i share price and FTSE 100 index**
% per year, Oct 1994–Oct 2013

Source: Bloomberg

FIG 10.2 **Volatility of private and public equity, proxied by 60-day volatility of 3i relative to UK stockmarket**
%, Oct 1994–Oct 2013, UK stockmarket volatility = 100

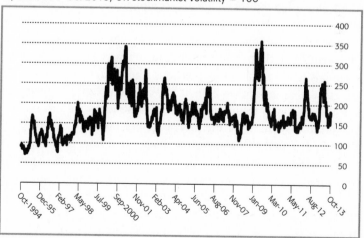

Source: Bloomberg

is shown in Figures 10.1 and 10.2. Since the late 1990s, 3i has always had a volatility significantly higher than that of the UK stockmarket; between June 1995 and August 2013 this was on average 80% higher (see Figure 10.2). This would not be the case for a diversified portfolio of listed UK stocks.

Some systematic differences apart from smaller size should be expected between the types of firms that are included in buy-out and venture capital funds and those that dominate the stockmarket. These biases will vary over time. For example, a focus on technology companies was a feature of many private equity funds, especially venture capital funds, in the late 1990s. That this occurred is unsurprising, as a bias towards whatever is the latest "new, new thing" will always be a characteristic feature and risk of early-stage venture capital investing. But if it was inevitable that venture funds should find themselves heavily exposed to technology companies in the late 1990s, it was also unsurprising that private equity funds should become more heavily leveraged during the run-up to the credit crunch, when liquidity and the ability to leverage portfolios were readily available.

Researchers have used a variety of other more or less satisfactory ways of getting a handle on private equity market volatility. These include examining the volatility of returns earned from private equity funds and using indices of smaller company stocks as a proxy for private equity.

Individual venture investments will always be subject to considerable stock-specific risk and, to diversify this risk, venture portfolios tend to hold more positions (though they may focus on a particular sector or theme) than buy-out portfolios. The financing structure is critical to the risk of LBO investments. For this reason, the intrinsic volatility of the private equity market, however well diversified, is probably significantly higher than that of the quoted equity market. Investors should not be satisfied with an expected return that does not compensate them for this leverage. Moreover, it makes no sense to pay performance fees simply to leverage an investment portfolio. Any investor can achieve this at minimal cost by buying equity index futures or a levered equity tracker fund. Few seem to choose to do so.

The process of allocating investment capital requires some rules of thumb for the risk of private equity. Here are some suggested guidelines:

- A major risk for both investors and managers of private equity portfolios is to act on inferior information. Do nothing in private equity unless you can access a credible information advantage.

- A broad-brush fund of funds approach that combines exposure to buy-outs and venture capital can be severely undermined in adverse markets by a combination of leverage and rising risk premiums, even if great skill has been applied in selecting the underlying companies in which the funds are invested.

- Investors need to ask what information advantage a well-diversified fund of funds arrangement is likely to have.

- An assumption that a well-diversified fund of funds has a volatility approximately twice that of the quoted market is probably reasonable. For a more concentrated approach, an assumption of a volatility three times that of the market might be used, but this might exaggerate the intrinsic volatility unless leverage was particularly high.

- In so far as private equity represents a leveraged version of quoted equity, investors should require a premium return for incurring the additional risk introduced by that leverage, and should benchmark their private equity against a leveraged quoted equity index. However, investors should be aware that the level of leverage, and so the level of risk-taking, in buy-outs is cyclical.

These magnitudes matter because investors need to have a feel for how an allocation to private equity is changing the risk that is already present in their allocation to quoted equity. Figure 10.3 gives an indication of how an allocation to well-diversified private equity, alongside an allocation to the quoted equity market, may affect the volatility of the combined equity portfolio. The important message is that a diversified allocation to private equity of, say, 10% of an investor's equity allocation will, with the assumptions used here, have a noticeable but not transforming effect on the volatility of the overall equity portfolio.

FIG 10.3 **Volatility of total equity as private equity increases**

- Private equity 3x public equity volatility
- Private equity 2x public equity volatility
- Private equity 1.5x public equity volatility

Private equity allocation, % of total equity

Total equity volatility, %

Source: Author's illustration

Listed private equity

The traditional way for institutions to invest in private equity or venture capital is through buy-out or venture capital funds, or through funds of funds that invest in these funds. Typically, they have a high minimum subscription. Wealthy individuals often obtain exposure to ventures through less formal business angel (see Appendix 1) arrangements, as only the wealthiest have been able to subscribe to partnerships or to funds. The emergence of the listed private equity sector within mainstream equity markets offers an additional route to obtain private equity exposure. In the years before the credit crunch, this sector of the market expanded rapidly as private equity firms including Blackstone, KKR and Brookfield, a Canadian firm, obtained stockmarket listings for parts of their private equity investment businesses. In the UK, the globally diversified private equity business 3i has been included in the FTSE All-Share index since 1994, and in Japan, Jafco has been listed in the first section of the Tokyo Stock Exchange since 2001.

TABLE 10.1 **Geographical spread of Standard & Poor's Listed Private Equity index**
Oct 2013

	%
US	58.7
UK	12.0
Canada	11.6
France	6.8
Switzerland	3.5
Japan	3.0
Sweden	2.2
Germany	0.9
Other	1.2

Note: Index covers largest listed private companies that meet liquidity, free float and other eligibility criteria.
Source: S&P Dow Jones indices

There are now estimated to be over 100 listed private equity companies spread around the world. The geographical breakdown of the Standard and Poor's index is given in Table 10.1 and Figure 10.4 shows the cumulative performance of this global index of listed private equity companies since 2003. The correlation between the broad equity market and the listed private equity sector is apparent, as is a leveraged relationship between private equity and global equities.

The listed private equity sector enables private investors with modest resources to establish exposure to private equity through the quoted market. It also provides a market price that shows either a premium or a discount to the appraisal values at which private equity funds are otherwise valued. This premium or discount to appraisal net asset values "marks-to-market" those valuations and so gives a benchmark that could be used as a check against appraisal values.

However, the premium or discount of listed private equity combines several factors. One is the valuation of business prospects of underlying companies. A second is the assessment of the management of the private equity firm (for example, whether it will

FIG 10.4 **Cumulative performance of global listed private equity companies and global equities**
Nov 2003–Sep 2013

Source: S&P Dow Jones Indices

successfully manage the cash flow needs of its underlying firms during a recession). The share prices of the listed private equity companies will incorporate more up-to-date information about these factors than are reflected in appraisal values.

A third, most important, influence on the premium or discount is liquidity. It reflects the price that buyers and sellers of a listed private equity firm pay for the ability to trade immediately (at least for small amounts) while investors in funds (which may have the same or similar underlying investments) normally are committed to their investments for years. When liquidity is highly prized (such as during a credit crisis), listed private equity vehicles will trade at a discount to net asset value, as sellers pay for the ability to exit their investment. This may represent a buying opportunity for long-term investors who have convinced themselves of the quality and sustainability of the underlying portfolio.

Private equity portfolios

An old adage in private banking says that you should concentrate investments to get wealthy (at the risk of losing your shirt), but that having become wealthy, you should diversify to maintain the wealth that you have already accumulated. This has parallels with the safety-first and aspirational portfolios described by behavioural finance (see Chapter 2). Private equity is about exploiting information advantages by identifying entrepreneurial skill. It is not about being financially conservative. It may form a component of an efficient diversified approach to investing, but within that it clearly forms part of an aspirational strategy to accumulate wealth.

This leads to several conclusions:

■ Well-diversified fund of funds arrangements are likely to diversify away precious elements of information advantage, which will be further eroded by the burden of high fees.

■ If high leverage persists across the funds, intrinsic volatility may still be surprisingly high even with a well-diversified fund of funds.

■ It can be entirely appropriate to have a modest allocation to a small number of funds (even from just one team), so long as the combined allocation to private and quoted equity is reasonably balanced.

■ A common danger in private equity investing is to fail to diversify private equity over time. Once a preferred arrangement has been selected, it makes sense to maintain a commitment to the market over time, most probably staying with the same team (or teams). Otherwise, risks that were particularly prevalent in the market at a particular point in time (for example, high leverage or exposure to particular themes in venture capital investing) will unduly characterise the investor's experience of investing in private equity.

Private equity returns

Before making an investment in private equity, investors need to be confident that it is likely to be worthwhile. It is not sufficient that private equity firms should improve the financial performance of the companies they hold in their funds (research suggests that on average they do). Private equity funds need to raise performance to a degree that rewards investors adequately for the additional risks they encounter including illiquidity and leverage. A major self-imposed hurdle private equity funds have to overcome is the high level of direct and indirect fees charged by the private equity firms that manage buy-out and venture capital funds. Another, which is related, is the asymmetry of information that always confronts investors in their dealings with investment managers in private equity.

Private equity performance data suffer (as do those for private equity risk) from the absence of market indications of the value of private businesses. They need to rely on appraisal estimates which smooth the reported performance included in published calendar-year performance results. Appraisal valuations are still useful as they provide important management information for investors on what is "work in progress". However, the only private equity performance data that really matters is the internal rate of return (IRR) earned on investments. This combines the amount invested, the amount received back and the interval of time in between. In substance, these are the only financial magnitudes that the investor eventually knows for certain when investing in private equity (or any private investment). The IRR is the standard rate of return reported for funds and individual investments, but it is important to note that unrealised investments will be included at an appraisal value in reports of fund IRRs.

Industry data often report IRRs for funds started in a particular "vintage" year. This information does not reveal the volatility of those returns or enable like-for-like comparison with stockmarket performance. Such information is often broken down in marketing material to show the attractive performance of better-performing managers (for example, the top 25%), with the message that it is important to select a manager who will be in the top quartile in the future. It is always desirable to select winners, but the issue is whether the historical performance data of private equity managers provides any guide to future performance.

In mutual fund investing it is agreed that past performance in league tables is a poor predictor of future league table performance. But in private equity there have long been suggestions that success is repeatable, and there is now increasing evidence from academic research that this may be the case.

One of the challenges in assessing private equity managers is the difficulty of comparing the performance of a manager, or a private equity fund, with that of the stockmarket. One way to do this is to compare the IRR that a fund achieved on its private equity investments with the IRR that it would have achieved if the cash had instead been invested, on the same dates, in the stockmarket index, and if the correspondingly equivalent distributions had then been made to investors (this is sometimes called the public market equivalent or PME). Academic research published in 2005 has done this for funds on the Thomson Venture Economics database of US venture capital and buy-out funds. Examining data from 1980 to 2000, researchers found that the average performance of such funds, after fees, was approximately in line with the S&P 500 index (though such comparisons make no allowance for comparisons of illiquidity and other investment risks). Other more recent research confirms the impression that the average investor in private equity funds does not outperform the broad stockmarket. There is a wide dispersion of results among funds as well as evidence that good and poor performance persisted in successive launches of funds by particular private equity teams. However, the usefulness of this finding is less clear than it seems, as money is typically committed to a new fund before the results of its predecessor fund are known. In other words, such marketing claims may rely on out-of-date information.

This research highlights the importance of a number of themes emphasised earlier in this chapter. First, the hurdle of fees is high, particularly when a investor can gain exposure to global stockmarkets through low-cost passive funds. Ludovic Phalippou of Oxford University's Saïd Business School, in a 2011 report for the Norwegian Ministry of Finance, said:

> A buy-out fund with a return after fees equal to the historical average return of the US stockmarket (over the last 30 years, ie, 11% per annum) would charge 6% fee per year.

This is after taking into account headline fees (typically 2% per year plus 2% of total return in excess of the hurdle rate, often 8%) and any consulting and advisory fees that may be charged by the buy-out fund to the companies in its portfolio. It probably should not be a surprise that investors in private equity have not, after fees, on average earned a premium reward to compensate them for the extra financial gearing or illiquidity involved in private equity.

A second theme is that investors need to convince themselves that they can identify better-than-average managers. Skill is essential. Investors cannot profit from market returns in private equity through a passive, market-matching strategy, so they should not expect to do even averagely well unless they can gain access to skilled managers, which requires more than reliance on a possibly out-of-date track record. Without skilled managers, investors will be condemned to underperform unless, for a period, they happen to get lucky. The problem is that it is most likely that a private equity manager who presents to an investor will be able to claim upper quartile performance. In the same report, Phalippou included an appendix, "Is there any fund that is not top quartile?" He starts by saying that "the oft-repeated private equity quip that '75% of funds claim to be in the top quartile' may indeed be true". The good news, he goes on to say, is that no evidence has been found of managers systematically mis-stating their own performance. Instead, the flexibility was found in their choice of benchmark, and the ambiguity that exists about when a fund properly opens for business.

Private investments, successful transactions and biases in appraisal valuations

Everyone likes to get a good price in any transaction. One way to increase the likelihood of a successful transaction is to ensure that the criterion by which success is judged is credible but undemanding. In private investments, the immediate benchmark against which a transaction is judged is the most recent appraisal valuation for that investment.

However successful or disappointing an investment might have been, private equity and real estate managers always like to be able to demonstrate the successful terms on which they achieved a sale (such ready benchmarks do not exist when a manager makes a purchase). Evidence to support these assertions relies mostly on anecdotal comments over the years from private equity and real estate managers, as well as an indication that real estate turnover declines in down markets when it becomes much harder to achieve a "successful" price (because the level of the market is more likely to be below the most recent appraisal valuation).

The art market, whose pre-auction brochures give appraisal valuations, provides an opportunity to study the existence of such a bias. Auction houses claim a proven track record in "meeting or exceeding" pre-sale estimates of value. Some years ago the author and a colleague found that of 1,700 works of art sold at auction, largely over the decade before 1991, 28% failed to reach the auctioneer's low estimate of value, 25% fell between the low and high estimates, and 47% exceeded the high estimates. Successful results were so much more common than disappointments (as indicated by the frequency with which the high and low estimates were overshot or undershot) that there is little likelihood of there being no downward bias in these pre-auction estimates. More recent evidence for such a bias in pre-auction appraisal valuations comes from the market for rare stamps. Apex Philatelic Auctions, a British stamp auctioneer, reported in its November 2005 catalogue that its preceding £8m of stamp sales "fetched 104.21% of estimate on average", confirming the pattern of realised prices tending to exceed pre-auction estimates.

11 Real estate

THE EXPERIENCE OF INVESTORS in real estate is determined by three things: the performance of the market; the skill of their advisers; and the degree of leverage involved in the vehicle they use to access the market. This, in turn, is influenced by the level of interest rates and whether the rent generated by the properties can cover the debt interest payments. It is a routine weakness in appraising real estate managers to fail to account properly for the impact of leverage on performance and risk.

Developments in the US public market for real estate investment trusts (REITs), a US innovation dating from the early 1970s, and parallel developments elsewhere in the world, have made the public market for real estate comparable to the rest of the quoted equity market. Investors can obtain, at low cost, exposure to the real estate market. The REIT market is a leveraged market and in the years before 2007 many new investors were introduced to the power of leverage. This was when debt interest costs were lower than the income received from real estate rents, the underlying market conditions appeared benign and performance was strong. During the real estate crisis of 2007–09 and the credit crunch investors were reminded that an income yield higher than the debt service cost is a necessary but not sufficient condition for financial success with a levered property portfolio.

Property investments can be either private or public. Private investment involves the direct ownership of properties. The public market involves ownership through a public commingled fund, or through stock exchange listed vehicles, most commonly REITs. REITs grew substantially in the years before the global financial crisis and in the United States their aggregate market capitalisation reached $438 billion at the end of 2006, declining to $192 billion at the end of 2008, and then rebounding to $603 billion by the end of 2012. Similar entities have been introduced in a range of jurisdictions including Australia, Brazil, Canada, France, Hong Kong, Japan, the Netherlands, Singapore and the UK. In the United States, individual REITs specialise by sector of the market, with a minority investing primarily in mortgages.

The principal difference between a REIT and a conventional company, whose business is investing in and managing properties, lies in their tax treatment. Generally, REITs are exempt from profit or corporation tax and, in the United States, have a guideline that at least 90% of their income must be distributed to investors as a taxable dividend. Guidelines vary between countries. The equivalent in Australia is the large, long-established listed property trust market.

The main differences between listed real estate vehicles, such as REITs, and direct investments in property are that the former are securitised, have daily prices and are typically leveraged to some degree through borrowing. They are ideally suited to giving diversified exposure to real estate for modest levels of investment. Since they have daily prices, appraisal valuations of underlying properties help analysts construct estimates for the net asset value of REITs, but they do not set the terms on which investors transact.

What is real estate investing?

It is common to divide the real estate market into segments such as those shown in Figure 11.1. In a number of international markets, private equity funds have become important participants in the real estate market. Private equity real estate funds brought a more aggressive attitude to leverage, with the introduction of high-risk, potentially high-return "mezzanine" debt into real estate transactions. These developments mean that investors now have more ways of gaining access to real estate returns than was previously the case.

The underlying real estate market is divided into the main types of property: retail, office, industrial and residential. (Other categories include hotels and resorts and mixed category properties.) The REIT market provides access to each segment of the market. Two principal databases for institutional real estate are the National Council for

FIG 11.1 **The four quadrants of real estate investing**

	Private investments	Public or quoted investments
Real estate equity	Direct properties Real estate commingled funds	Real estate investment trusts (REITs) Real estate operating companies (REOCs) Real estate mutual funds Listed property trusts Other listed property companies
Real estate debt	Individual mortgages "Mezzanine" debt	Commercial mortgage-backed securities (CMBS)

Source: Author

Real Estate Investment Fiduciaries (NCREIF) in the United States and IPD (formerly known as the Investment Property Databank), which is based in the UK. The US National Association of Real Estate Investment Trusts (NAREIT) is the source for information about US

TABLE 11.1 **Direct real estate investment by type of property**
%

	NCREIF Dec 2012	REIT[a] Jul 2013	UK IPD Dec 2012	Euro zone IPD Dec 2012
Retail	22.8	26.8	48.8	29.5
Office	35.2	10.4	26.5	44.4
Industrial	14.2	12.2[b]	15.3	6.1
Apartments/residential	25.2	14.3[c]	3.5	15.3
Health care	0.0	12.1	–	–
Other	2.6	24.2[d]	5.9	4.7
Value, $bn	320.0	571.8	228.1	359.9

a Equity REITs only.
b Including mixed use and self-storage.
c Including manufactured homes.
d Including diversified, lodging/resorts, health care, speciality.
Sources: IPD; National Association of Real Estate Investment Trusts; National Council of Real Estate Investment Fiduciaries

REITs. Table 11.1 gives a breakdown of the types of properties owned by investors in the United States and Europe.

What are the attractions of investing in real estate?

The traditional reasons for making investments in real estate equity include portfolio diversification; accessing premium and relatively secure income yields; and the potential for attractive total returns that should offer some protection from inflation.

Diversification

Appraisal valuations of properties unavoidably smooth changes in the level of property prices. This complicates an assessment of the diversification qualities of real estate. Smoothing performance often gives short-term comfort to private investors and pension fund trustees who do not need to be confronted with the reality of market prices except when they transact. This paucity of reliable price information does not provide a substantive reason for favouring real estate investment. The market for REITs gives a market valuation and a time series of transaction prices, which permits a market-based assessment of the contribution of real estate in an investment portfolio, although allowance has to be made for the value of the debt held in a REIT.

Modern real estate indices and assessing the diversifying role of real estate

In recent years the illiquid real estate market has seen the benefits of more reliable market indices, which make use of transaction prices as well as appraisal valuations. (See Chapter 12 for a discussion of corresponding developments in the art market.) One of the features of transaction-based indices is that they enable more accurate measurement of the volatility of prices in illiquid markets, which is normally smoothed by appraisal values. The repeat sales regression (RSR) methodology, which was originally proposed in 1963, builds on the purchase and sale information of individual properties to generate a market index that is based on transaction prices rather than estimates of value. The Case-Shiller US house price index series, which grew out of research undertaken in the 1980s, provides the quality benchmark for these transaction-based indices in illiquid markets. The UK's Land Registry index follows the same principles for measuring house price developments in England and Wales.

For institutional investors in real estate, a related development in recent years was the development of a transaction-based index by the Massachusetts Institute of Technology Center for Real Estate (CRE). This has been taken forward by the NCREIF's National Transaction Based Index (NTBI), which uses the transaction data underlying its National Property Index (NPI). It is a simplified version of the CRE's index. The NTBI is not a repeat-sales index. It uses transactions data to assess the extent to which transaction prices, across the NCREIF universe of US tax-exempt institutions' direct investments in real estate, deviate from the appraisal prices for those properties which applied before the start of sales negotiations. It then applies the average of such differences to the NPI index to calculate the NCREIF transaction-based index, NTBI. To avoid the NTBI being unduly influenced by a small number of large transactions it is equally weighted; the NPI is a value weighted index.

Figure 11.2 compares the cumulative total return performance of these two series. It shows that the NPI is obviously smoother than the NTBI (the cumulative difference between the two series may largely reflect the different index weighting methodologies). In Europe, a corresponding development has been the publication of transaction-linked indices (TLI) by IPD, a property performance measurement consultancy (see Figures 11.3 and 11.4). Like the NTBI, it makes use of the relationship between transaction values and the recent appraisal valuations of those transacted properties to adjust appraisal-based valuation indices. IPD's valuation-based and transaction-linked indices are value weighted price indices, that is excluding the accumulation of income receipts.

In the United States and the UK there were indications that appraisal values of institutional real estate responded more rapidly to the decline in transaction prices in 2008–09 than was the case in earlier years.

The greater use of transaction-based or transaction-linked indices for the real estate market has highlighted a number of characteristics of these measures, which also apply to the art market. The first is that the new indices require transactions data, and when market liquidity dries up because of a shortage of willing buyers or sellers, interpretation of the data becomes troublesome. For example, in the first three months of 2009, just 19 transactions were recorded in the NCREIF database of US institutional real estate, one-tenth of the previous average volume. This inevitably increases

FIG 11.2 **Valuation-based and transaction-based measures of total return from real estate investments in the US**

Cumulative total return index, $, Dec 1993 = 1.00

- Transaction-based index NTBI
- Valuation-based index NPI

Source: National Council of Real Estate Investment Fiduciaries

FIG 11.3 **Valuation-based and transaction-linked measures of commercial real estate prices in the UK**

Cumulative price index, £, 2001 Q4 = 100

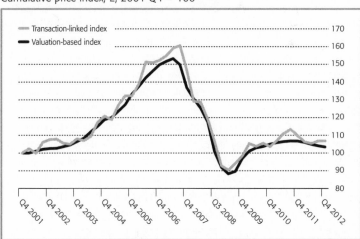

- Transaction-linked index
- Valuation-based index

Source: IPD

FIG 11.4 **Valuation-based and transaction-linked measures of commercial real estate prices in the euro zone**
Cumulative price index, €, 2001 Q4 = 100

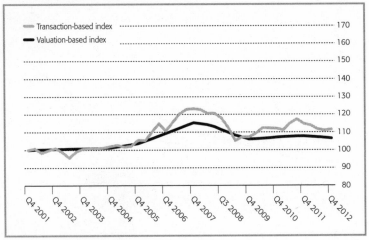

Source: IPD

uncertainty about the interpretation of market indices when few transactions occur.

Over time, the appraisal and transaction-based or linked indices for US and also for European institutional direct real estate investment appear to give similar results, and it is the short-term pattern of returns that can differ. For long-term investors, it may be thought that the difference is of little importance. This is not correct. Transaction-based indices allow more accurate measures of the volatility of the direct real estate market and of how real estate correlates with the stock and bond markets. These should enable more reliable assessment of the diversification role of real estate in an investment strategy. Research published in 2006 by Martha S. Peyton and Fabiana Lotito of TIAA-CREF, a US retirement fund for university staff, "Real estate: the classic diversifying asset", and separately a 2007 article in *Journal of Portfolio Management* by Shaun Bond, Soosung Hwang, Paul Mitchell and Stephen Satchell, "Will private equity and hedge funds replace real estate in mixed asset portfolios?", point the way to how illiquid investments are increasingly being modelled in asset allocation exercises. The key is to correct for the smoothing impact of appraisal values in illiquid investments, such as real estate, hedge funds and private equity (and

FIG 11.5 **Cumulative performance of US equities and REITs**
1984–2013, Dec 1984 = 1.0

Sources: FTSE NAREIT; MSCI

to allow for the costs of illiquidity). Both studies are strongly supportive of the
diversifying role of real estate, and the second article answers its title's question
with its pithy subtitle: "Not likely".

Private investors access real estate through direct ownership of individual
properties (which is difficult to diversify) and through the public market for
REITs. The potential diversification role of REITs in overall investment strategy
was demonstrated during the equity bear market of March 2000–March 2003.

Figures 11.5 and 11.6 compare the performance and volatility of the US
equity market and US equity REITs. The performance chart shows that REITs
can behave very differently from the rest of the stockmarket, and so provide
valuable diversification. This happened in the late 1990s and early 2000s,
when REITs first missed out on the technology boom and then avoided the
subsequent market downturn. However, REITs can at other times act as if they
are a levered play on the stockmarket. In the years leading up to 2007, REITs
experienced a strong bull market, fuelled by credit and the housing boom,
and amplified the subsequent downturn and then recovery after 2008. These
differences are also shown in Figure 11.6: for many years REITs, despite their
sector focus and degree of leverage, had a volatility no more than the equity
market, and often less. After 2007 their volatility was considerably more than

FIG 11.6 **Volatility of US equity REITs and US stockmarket, rolling 36-month standard deviations of return**
% per year, 1987–2013

Sources: FTSE NAREIT; MSCI

the market as a whole. This emphasises an important lesson: be cautious about relying on counter-intuitive statistics that may well not persist in the future.

Equity REITs are typically leveraged, around 40–60%, whereas the NPI and TBI series exclude the impact of any borrowing. (About 10% of US REITs are mortgage REITs, which have a much higher level of leverage than equity REITs. The business of equity REITs is to invest in properties; the business of mortgage REITs is to invest in mortgages. Mortgage REITs are normally more volatile than equity REITs.)

Table 11.2 gives statistics for three real estate market measures for the United States, UK and the euro zone. It shows the annualised volatility (standard deviation) of the indices for the period 2002 to 2012, the extent to which performance in one period is correlated with the previous period (serial correlation, which can be an indicator of price smoothing) and the correlation of each series with the stockmarket. Not surprisingly, in each region the performance of REITs is more volatile than the measures of institutional property values and is more highly correlated with the stockmarket than is the performance of direct institutional investments in real estate. In each case the valuation-based measures of institutional property performance show high

TABLE 11.2 **US, UK and euro zone real estate market indices: volatility, and correlations with stocks and bonds**
March 2002–December 2012

US	FTSE NAREIT Equity REITs	NCREIF Transaction Based Index (NTBI)	NCREIF property index (NPI)
Standard deviation, % per year	28.60	12.30	6.40
Serial correlation	0.16	−0.13	0.85
Correlation with MSCI USA	0.58	0.11	0.21
Correlation with Barclays US Aggregate bond index	−0.04	−0.11	−0.17

UK	FTSE EPRA UK REITs	IPD UK Transaction-linked property valuation index	IPD UK Valuation-based property valuation index
Standard deviation, % per year	29.80	7.90	9.80
Serial correlation	0.17	0.47	0.76
Correlation with MSCI UK	0.70	0.35	0.38
Correlation with Barclays UK Aggregate bond index	−0.03	0.06	−0.12

Euro zone	FTSE EPRA Eurozone REITs	IPD Eurozone Transaction-linked property valuation index	IPD Eurozone Valuation-based property valuation index
Standard deviation, % per year	26.00	4.90	1.50
Serial correlation	0.19	0.17	0.88
Correlation with MSCI Eurozone	0.72	0.00	0.17
Correlation with Barclays Eurozone Aggregate bond index	0.10	−0.10	−0.34

Source: Author's calculations based on Barclays, FTSE NAREIT, IPD, MSCI and NCREIF index data for calendar quarters.

levels of serial correlation, demonstrating smoothing prices. This is absent from the NCREIF transaction-based index, but apparently not, for example, from IPD's transaction-linked index.

The relatively high serial correlation in the UK transaction-linked series (and the comparatively high volatility of IPD's UK valuation-based index) during this period echoes the finding of 2012 research into the behaviour of UK property prices by Colin Lizieri, Steve Satchell and Warapong Wongwachara. This found that appraisal valuations and transaction prices seem to respond vigorously to stockmarket moves when those moves are strongly negative, a process which seems to reinforce serial correlation in property prices. In turn, this is one aspect of the rise in correlations between risk assets at times of great risk aversion.

Income yield

A recurring argument in favour of real estate investing is the provision of a dependable income that can be expected to increase in line with inflation. The ability to gain access to seemingly reliable income becomes particularly attractive to investors at times of low nominal interest rates.

Table 11.3 compares the income return offered by different investment markets. Over the period, the income return for REITs has been comparable to that on investment grade bonds, which have, in aggregate, been subject to much less price risk. The income stream from REITs may appear stable, on average, but the price volatility

TABLE 11.3 **Income yield from REITs, quoted equities and bonds**
Jan 1990–Dec 2012, % annual average income yield

	North America REIT	MSCI US index	MSCI EAFE ® index	Barclays Credit index[a]	Barclays government bond index[a]	Barclays Municipal bond index[a]
1990–94	8.6	3.4	2.0	7.9	6.6	5.9
1995–99	7.4	2.4	1.9	6.7	5.8	5.0
2000–04	8.2	1.5	2.1	5.5	4.0	4.0
2005–09	4.9	2.1	3.1	5.6	3.5	4.0
2010–12	4.4	2.3	3.5	3.3	1.2	2.9

a Redemption yields.
Sources: Barclays; FTSE NAREIT Global Real Estate Index; MSCI

has been comparable to equities. This means that REITs cannot be regarded as "low-risk" substitutes for a high-quality bond portfolio.

Inflation hedge

Real estate investments always have one clear advantage over investments in conventional bonds: while bonds are eroded by any unexpected inflation, rents from real estate should be expected to respond over time to inflation. This does not mean that rents will always keep up with inflation. A market with excess or obsolete capacity should expect to see rents fall. Nevertheless, it is reasonable to assume that rents will increase faster the higher is the rate of inflation. This in turn will be reflected in the value put on buildings, which should also respond to inflation. In this way long-term investments in real estate provide an element of insurance against the biggest danger facing long-term investors in conventional bonds: erosion of wealth by inflation. (But see the discussion of rental income below.)

Styles of real estate investing and opportunities for active management

Entrepreneurial real estate managers have always liked real estate for the same reason that money managers of any asset class do: they see it as an opportunity to use their skills to make money for themselves and their clients. Since the real estate market is such a heterogeneous, lumpy and immobile market, it provides a natural habitat for well-informed, skilled managers to add value (and for other market participants to underperform). This, together with its other advantages such as long-term inflation hedging, helps explain why some investors have focused on developing an expertise and portfolio concentration in real estate investing.

Equity managers are often characterised by their style of investing, and this also happens with real estate managers. It has the advantage of helping investors understand better what to expect from a particular manager. Broadly, there are two approaches to real estate investing: a core approach, with an emphasis on the generation of steadily growing income from a balanced portfolio of well-let prime properties; and an opportunistic approach, which is more concerned with the prospects for price appreciation through redevelopment and exploiting changes in market trends and fashions. The first should deliver a less volatile, less exciting performance than the second. Real estate managers point to a third category, a distinctive "core-plus" approach for the more entrepreneurial commingled or institutional portfolios. The more aggressive, opportunistic approach is likely to be reflected in the real estate activities of, for example, private equity or hedge funds. These have become, and are likely to remain, major players in parts of the international real estate market.

What is a property worth and how much return should you expect?

One of the attractions of real estate investing is that it is often easy to analyse individual investments in direct property quantitatively. Although this is no guarantee of investment success, it helps to identify any opportunities that rely on unusually strong assumptions.

The financial appraisal of real estate requires assessment of a number of variables:

- today's government bond yield;
- market supply and demand forecasts as influences on prospects for rental incomes;
- tenant creditworthiness;
- property depreciation or obsolescence.

No real estate investment should be undertaken unless it is expected to perform better than the guaranteed return from high-quality government bonds. And any real estate investment should be sold if it is expected to underperform government bonds over some relevant time horizon.

Rental income

The return to be expected from a property is the discounted value of the expected rental income, net of expenses, plus the proceeds from selling the property at some date in the future. The key variables in this evaluation are the future rate of change in rents and the appropriate rate at which to discount that rental stream back to a present value or fair price for the property.

Just as forecasts of corporate earnings growth drive an analyst's valuation of a company, so in real estate investing the principal driver of valuation is the forecast change in a property's rental income. Detailed projections for local or regional real estate markets can provide the raw material for these calculations. When appraising these forecasts, it is often helpful to gauge how the rent forecast relates to a forecast for economy-wide inflation. This is because rents need to be forecast, either implicitly or explicitly, for long periods, if only to provide a basis for estimating the price at which the building might be sold in the future (which will itself be a function of expected rents).

This focus on rental income is important to avoid two common mistakes. First, the value of a property often has little to do with the cost of rebuilding it. It is the value of future rent that determines its value. Given the value of the property, this can be broken down into the cost of rebuilding, proxied by the insurance value put on the property, and a residual, which is the value of the land underneath the building. Second, a property is never expensive because the land underneath it is expensive. It is always the other way round. Land is expensive because rents are high, and because rents are high property is expensive. A third important feature for real estate investing follows from this: the price of land, the residual in property valuation, can be extremely volatile. A simple illustration is given in Table 11.4.

TABLE 11.4 **Direct real estate investment by type of property**
$m

	Initial value	Subsequent value
Property value	10	11
Cost of rebuild	9	9
Land value	1	2

Source: Author

In this example, if the value of the property increases by 10%, and if rebuilding costs stay the same, the value of the land will double to $2m. This is important both as an explanation for the speculative nature of development land and as a useful cross-check on valuations. Equally, the importance of the price of land will depend upon the scarcity of land. Where land is abundant and planning restrictions do not impede new construction, rents will tend towards reimbursing with a "normal" profit the marginal cost of new building, which may or may not keep pace with the general level of inflation.

So long as this situation persists, land will always be cheap. With technological progress in building, commercial properties risk becoming a commodity that individuals or corporations who need to use real estate (for homes, offices, industrial or retail space) must decide whether to own, rent or lease on the same basis as other financial decisions. So although rents, and the cost of land, will move with changes in supply of and demand for properties, there is no inexorable tendency for them to increase faster than inflation. Rents can lag behind inflation for a long time. For example, at the height of a boom in City of London property in 1973, rents were reported to have been in the region of £20 per square foot. Allowing for inflation since then, rents should now be in excess of £200 per square foot. But in early 2013 prime rents in the City of London were only around £55 per square foot (partly because of competition from the new financial district of Canary Wharf). There is no assurance that rents will keep pace with inflation, and little reason to expect them to increase in line with the rate of growth of the economy.

However, it may be reasonable to assume that the growth of equity dividends is ultimately related to the growth of the economy. It follows that real estate investors rely on rental income, rather than capital appreciation, as the principal source of investment performance. This also explains why the income yield from real estate investing is normally much higher than the income yield from mainstream equity investing.

It is not clear how much premium return over government bonds should be expected by financial investors in real estate in the long term. This required premium is reduced by the diversification benefits that real estate brings to a balanced investment strategy. It can be influenced by the degree of confidence that investors have in the quality of the investment process that they are able to deploy in investing in real estate markets. Most importantly, as with private equity, direct investors in real estate should not assume that they will earn the market return. The prerequisite is to put in place a demonstrably skilful investment process. However, the more skill that is assumed, the easier it will be to justify a large allocation to real estate. In this case, great caution needs to be exercised in assessing the basis for a belief that the investor can access unusual skill. Particular care is needed in interpreting past performance, in isolating the effects on performance of leverage during a rising market and in differentiating between skill and luck. As was emphasised in Chapter 4, in the presence of uncertainty, the prudent approach is to err on the side of caution.

Government bond yields as the benchmark for real estate investing

Using government bond yields as the benchmark for assessing real estate investments is helpful in several respects. It focuses on the only legitimate reason to move away from safe-haven investing: to achieve a superior return that more than compensates for the risk of a disappointing result. In real estate, the prospects for superior returns will be influenced by the state of the market and also by the quality of the contractual rental income. For this, the creditworthiness of the tenants, as well as other factors such as building depreciation, will be critical.

Tenant credit risk

A property with a government agency as a long-term tenant will be directly comparable with government bonds, although allowance should be made for the illiquidity of the real estate investment, as well as the likely existence of options to break the contract. Organisational issues may inhibit the ability of institutional investors to exploit fully the comparison between long-term holdings of government bonds and a long-term rental income from a government agency. Other investors such as hedge funds have no such inhibition, so long as they can access the liquidity needed to exploit the opportunity. Nevertheless, all real estate investors should make the effort to analyse opportunities in this way.

The spread over government bond yields paid by private-sector tenants needs to allow for the credit risk associated with those tenants, as well as the illiquidity of the contract. The credit risk is the risk that the tenant will fail to meet the terms of the lease; that there will be an interruption to rental payments; that there will be costs associated with attracting new tenants; and that a new tenant might be attracted at less favourable terms than the existing one. These potential costs will be influenced by the state of the market – in a buoyant market replacement tenants can be found more quickly and at less expense than in a depressed market. Corporate credit ratings can provide a guide to the credit risk spread that investors should demand from tenants. When a tenant fails, a replacement can normally be found in due course and so it is unclear whether the credit spread should apply to the entire rental stream expected from the client.

Property obsolescence

The required yield also needs to allow for the expected depreciation of the property, which may be a very different cost from the actual outlay on property maintenance. This rate of obsolescence will be a major determinant of the rents that will be earned on the property in the future. Obsolescence is partly a matter of physical deterioration, but it is also accelerated by changes in the pattern of demand for particular types of building or location. Standard depreciation schedules rarely reflect actual experience, which is what matters for market investment values. Obsolescence is always subject to uncertainty, but it is uncertainty of a kind that can affect whole parts of a diversified real estate portfolio. As Green Street Advisors, a real estate consultancy, has said: "One of the real estate industry's dirtiest little secrets is the degree to which depreciation is a very real expense." This is why it is appropriate to allow a material risk premium for obsolescence.

Private and public markets for real estate

The parallel private and public markets for real estate invite comparisons of where it is cheaper to buy exposure to real estate: by buying REITs or by directly buying properties. This is the old

FIG 11.7 **Is it cheaper to buy real estate on Wall Street or Main Street? US REITs' share price compared with Green Street estimates of property net asset value**
% premium or discount to Green Street estimate of NAV, Jan 1990–Jul 2013

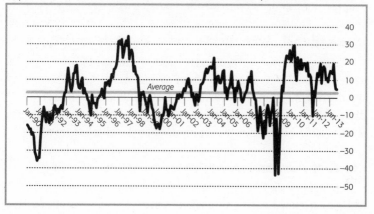

Source: Green Street Advisors

stockmarket valuation question: are corporate assets valued below or above their replacement value? The ratio of the market value of a company to the replacement cost of its net assets is called Tobin's Q. In theory this ratio, if the underlying data are free from measurement biases, should tend towards 1 (see Chapter 4). The greater liquidity of REITs might normally cause them to trade at a premium to net asset values, and on average they have done. In Figure 11.7 evidence from the United States is shown for the movement in this ratio for the real estate market in recent years and its average value. Substantial real estate investors in countries with a thriving REIT market have a clear choice between investing in direct property or through REITs, although for most private investors it is not realistic to seek to achieve a diversified portfolio in direct real estate.

The relationship between the two real estate markets in the United States shown in Figure 11.7 illustrates that over almost 25 years to 2013 the prices of REITs have (when taken together) ranged from a premium to net asset value of the underlying properties of 32.6% in 1997 to a discount of 43.6% in November 2008. Green Street Advisors, whose research is shown in Figure 11.7 (and whose UK and continental European research on REIT valuations shows a similar pattern though for a shorter time period), says that after the early 1990s bond and equity markets had a much more direct influence on property market developments than previously.

International diversification of real estate investment

With the spread of REIT markets around the world, international diversification of real estate investing has never been easier. The word diversification implies risk reduction. But does international diversification of real estate reduce risk? It turns out that currency risk is a particularly knotty issue for international real estate investing.

Currency risk and international real estate investing

The guidelines on foreign currency exposure and the desirability of foreign currency hedging suggested in this book can be summarised as follows:

- Lower volatility international investments need to be hedged for foreign exchange risk otherwise currency fluctuations will transform the risk and return of the underlying investments by markedly increasing their volatility.

- Higher volatility international investments (such as equities) do not need to be hedged for currency risk because currency hedging will simply alter the pattern of returns, not materially increase or decrease the magnitude of volatility (but see Chapter 7 for a discussion of exceptions to this rule of thumb).

- It is easy to put in place foreign currency hedges between the major liquid currencies and to hedge liquid investments. It can be expensive or impractical to hedge the foreign exchange risks which involve one or more less liquid currencies.

- Foreign currency hedging involves frequent accounting for cash gains or losses on the hedged investment. These gains and losses are much easier to accommodate in an investment arrangement if the hedged investment is itself highly liquid. In these circumstances, for example, currency gains on an investment can be offset by investment sales to fund offsetting currency losses on the currency hedge. With an illiquid investment this is much more difficult to achieve. Accumulated cash flow losses from a persistent home currency depreciation can require additional injections of cash, which may be substantial. Investors should therefore not hedge illiquid and lumpy international investments, such as whole properties, unless they are sure that they can fund the potential liquidity drain from the hedge. (Note that an alternative is to raise a mortgage abroad to fund the foreign investment, and if need be to offset this with a cash deposit at home so as to reduce the scale of leverage. This would reduce the scope for liquidity pressures in managing the investment, and would hedge the greater part of the foreign exchange risk.)

The implications of this for international real estate diversification are as follows:

- Private market international real estate investments should not be hedged because the investments are illiquid and the holdings are generally indivisible.

- This means that the unhedged investments will be volatile and so should only be made for their opportunistic performance potential and not, for example, for the potential income yield. An exception to this arises if investors genuinely have an exceptionally long time horizon (and do not simply wish that they had). In this case, an investor may be justified in putting faith in an expectation that eventually currency movements will keep track with the relative purchasing power of different countries.

- Investments in public market real estate securities (such as REITs) in international markets can easily be hedged. This will be necessary if investors intend to rely on the income from the overseas REIT. However, they should check whether the level of leverage in the REIT causes it to have a volatility that will swamp any cushioning effect from hedging. Nevertheless, hedged or unhedged, investors should expect the price of a REIT that invests in direct real estate equity to be volatile.

12 Art and investments of passion

"I WOULD RATHER MY FAMILY'S WEALTH was tied up in a Titian than in a bank share," one art consultant told the author. Many people have collections of paintings, other works of art or items such as stamps, rare books, classic cars or fine wines on which they have expended significant amounts of money. Such collections are sometimes called investments of passion, but they are primarily treasured collections. Consistent anecdotes from a range of markets indicate that few acquire fine art or collectibles solely to earn a financial return. The prospect of earning an emotional, not financial, dividend from owning a beautiful work or a prized possession is almost always the catalyst for a decision to buy.

In the years following the darkest days of the financial crisis at the end of 2008 and the extraordinary easing of monetary conditions that followed, interest rates were close to zero and the prices of a wide range of risk assets recovered strongly. Investments of passion from classic cars to fine wines and also fine art shared in this and in many cases had never been so strong. Although it is difficult to verify, market participants and analysts agree that the monetary environment encouraged more spending and higher prices in these niche areas. With no interest being paid on cash, the opportunity cost of indulging in a passion for collecting has not been lower in living memory. As an article in the *New York Times* put it in April 2013, "Whether he intended it or not, or even realises it, Ben S. Bernanke has become a patron of the arts."

How monetary easing probably inflated the prices of fine art and collectibles

Any purchase involves choices. By purchasing a painting a collector decides to forgo the interest that could be earned on a bank deposit or from a government bond of roughly the maturity in years that the collector might own the painting. Collectors buy paintings because they prefer the prospect of enjoying the art at least as much as they would benefit from the income that could be earned from cash or government bonds. Chapter 4 reported evidence from the Capgemini and RBC Wealth Management "World Wealth Report" 2013 that the world's high net worth families may hold over one-quarter of their financial wealth as cash or deposits. The income of these families will have been reduced by around $100 billion per year for each 1% cut in interest rates. When interest rates fall to almost zero, it is much easier to justify spending money on art (or on almost anything) rather than leaving the money in the bank. Easy money almost certainly increased the demand for and prices of fine art and collectibles.

This increase in demand for collectibles has occurred against the background of the internet having facilitated price discovery and, almost certainly, the liquidity of auction markets for collectibles. Websites such as eBay are much more accessible than traditional "bricks and mortar" auction houses, though investors may fear that counterparty risk is a bigger issue with online auction houses. Even the humblest auction house can now put its catalogues for forthcoming auctions online, and there are well-developed internet services which enable almost any local auction house to accept online bids. It is easy to forget how difficult it was before the internet to access information that is routinely of interest and importance to a collector. Furthermore, online auction websites (which traditionalists argue are not suitable for many treasured possessions) are a powerful force for reducing transaction costs. This, together with easier price discovery and the enormously reduced "shoe-leather" costs of attending auctions should provide an enduring lift to demand for collectibles, well after the impact of ultra-low interest rates has passed.

Psychic returns from art and collectibles

Collectors collect and art lovers buy art because they expect to enjoy their collections. This aesthetic or "psychic" reward is a dividend to be valued over and above any monetary return that they might hope to get when (or if) they eventually sell their collection.

A number of economists have attempted to estimate the psychic return from art. Some have used data on the cost of renting art (for example, by corporations) and produced high implied psychic returns, in the order of 10–30% per year. These high figures have been criticised for combining the cost of a valuable consultancy service, which is advising individuals on which art they ought to rent, with the enjoyment that flows from a treasured possession. In a 2013 research paper, Rachel Pownall, associate professor of finance at Maastricht University, together with Steve Satchell and Nandini Srivastava, both members of the economics faculty at Cambridge University, have evaluated alternative approaches for measuring psychic returns to cultural assets. After taking into account the substantial transaction costs, apparent long holding periods for works of art and likely proportions of investable wealth invested in art, they estimate that psychic returns from fine art are probably in the region of a bit less than 1% to 2% per year of the cost of a painting. Among their other findings is that in France and the UK fine art may account for around 4–5% of investable wealth (data issues prevented the authors from considering a global approach). They find that the long periods for which works of art are generally held mean that the impact of high transaction costs in the art market (for example, commission rates at auction – see below) is less of a burden in comparison with stockmarket investing (where holding periods are much shorter) than the headline numbers suggest. Their conclusion is that an annual expense advantage to investing in equities over buying a painting of between 0.5% and 1% per year seems plausible, if both the painting and the investment in the stockmarket are held for 20–30 years.

Recent trends in prices for fine art and collectibles can be seen more clearly thanks to the publication by academics of annual price indices which trace the evolution of the prices of fine art, stamps and violins over the past 100 years. For shorter time periods there exists a multiplicity of indices for different segments of the art market (and even for individual artists) as well as for a surprisingly wide range of collectibles.

Two of the academics, Elroy Dimson, emeritus professor of finance at London Business School, and Christophe Spaenjers, associate professor of finance at HEC, a business school in Paris, have calculated that the average price increase of art, stamps and violins over the period from 1900 to 2012 beat the investment return on cash and government bonds but noticeably underperformed the stockmarket. The three types of "emotional" assets, when measured in sterling (most of the data were originally expressed in sterling), produced average returns of between 2.4% and 2.9% per year, after inflation, compared with 1.5% per year from bonds, and 0.9% per year from cash compared with 5.2% per year from equities. Other studies have also placed the price performance of fine art over differing long time periods as being somewhere below that of equities but better than cash.

In practice, the average collector of fine art will not have done so well, because the data take no account of the costs of buying and selling items from their collections. Transaction costs are generally higher in illiquid markets such as those for collectibles, and can easily be 25% of the price of an object offered for sale (see below). Average index returns from illiquid markets are earned by no one and they also hide fluctuations over time and of fashions within it.

An important source of detailed historical information on the prices of fine art is Gerald Reitlinger's 1960 study, *The Economics of Taste*, which, in his words, traced "the rise and fall of picture prices" after 1760. One illustration he gave was of a pair of paintings by Claude Lorrain, a 17th-century landscape artist, which were sold in 1808 for £12,600, making them, according to Reitlinger, then the most expensive paintings ever sold, the price being equivalent to roughly £900,000 in 2013 prices. The same paintings were sold together 140 years later for £5,355, equivalent to £170,000 in today's prices. Great paintings, which are bought at a high price, can represent an appalling return on money, even if held for a great length of time. If properly maintained, and if attribution is not in doubt, they are, however, not going to decline in value to zero, which is the fate of a shareholding in a company which becomes bankrupt.

FIG 12.1 **Returns from fine art, stamps, violins, gold and financial assets**
1900–2013, 1900 = 1

Note: Figure 12.1 shows the deflated index values for different emotional and financial asset classes over 1900–2012. Data exclude transaction and other costs, including insurance. Each index is set equal to 1 at the beginning of 1900. The data for equities, bonds and bills come from Dimson, Marsh, and Staunton (2013). The data for art were sourced from Goetzmann, Renneboog and Spaenjers (2011) and Artprice.com; for stamps from Dimson and Spaenjers (2011); for violins from Dimson and Spaenjers (2014); for gold from the World Gold Council.
Source: Dimson, E. and Spaenjers, C., 2014

Research by Michael Moses, formerly a professor at New York's Stern School of Business, and Jiangping Mei, an associate professor of finance at Stern School of Business, indicates that underperformance of the broader market by a masterpiece is not unusual. They found that indicators suggesting high quality for a work of fine art (such as the purchase price of the painting or the number of scholarly citations or the number of exhibitions featuring the work) provide no assurance that it is going to outperform the rest of the art market in the future, and it may perform considerably worse.

Most art is not a masterpiece. William Grampp, emeritus professor of economics at the University of Chicago, in his 1989 book *Pricing the priceless: art, artists and economics* sought to reconcile the aesthetic and the monetary value of art. He argues that there is a correlation between price and assessments of aesthetic value in fine art (presumably, he argues, the prices paid by leading art galleries reflect their judgments of artistic quality). He also asks what became of the 20,000 paintings produced each year in late 19th-century France. He points out that most art declines in value to zero when it is no longer enjoyed, and then gets discarded. Art that suffers this fate might be described as "local" art. Some fine art maintains critical appreciation from generation to generation (see below) and so keeps a significant monetary as well as aesthetic value. This is not the fate of pictures that most picture buyers buy.

Reitlinger's book has proved to be a treasure trove for researchers. It was a prime source for the art price series in Figure 12.1, and three of the five studies of the evolution of art prices over time that were reviewed by Grampp in 1989 used Reitlinger's data. Grampp concludes: "All except [one] give the same answer to the question: Is buying art simply to resell at a higher price likely to be profitable? The answer is no."

One of the five studies was a 1986 article, "Unnatural value or art as a floating crap game", by William Baumol, emeritus professor of economics at Princeton University. He was one of the sceptics and argued that art prices "float more or less aimlessly and their unpredictable oscillations are apt to be exacerbated by the activities of those who treat such art objects as 'investments'". Baumol's calculations showed an average return, after inflation, of close to zero, though the other studies have given somewhat higher estimates.

This does not mean that the paintings were not worth owning, rather that a collector of paintings (or of stamps, classic cars or vintage wine) will judge a good investment differently from an institution which is only concerned with financial return. For collectors, the combination of the price change and the dividend of being able to enjoy the treasured possession provides the criteria to assess success.

Wealth, inequality and the price of art

Recent research has explored the relationship between art prices and the economy. William Goetzmann, Edwin J. Beinecke professor of finance at Yale School of Management, Luc Renneboog, professor of corporate finance at Tilburg University, and Christophe Spaenjers have shown, using UK data, that the art market has followed the fortunes of the stockmarket and is also influenced by changes in income inequality. When high-end incomes increase much faster than average incomes, art prices tend to respond strongly. This has been seen in the patterns of art market booms and stagnations over the past century. Art prices did not reach their 1914 levels, after inflation, until a strong recovery in the 1960s. The intervening long period of stagnation occurred despite personal income rising almost fourfold. It was, however, a period when income inequality declined sharply, eroding the relative buying power of the wealthiest.

The past 100 years show that a disappointing environment for the art market can persist for decades. After the 1970s, inequality (measured by the authors as the share of the top 0.1% of UK income earners in total income) increased strongly, having declined during the preceding 70 years. Since the 1960s, fine art prices have easily outpaced inflation, supported by much higher top incomes, and have climbed to levels not seen before, even though there have been significant setbacks in the overall market and marked changes of fashion within it. Figure 12.1 shows a similar pattern in the indicators for prices of stamps and violins over the past century, although their periods of weakness do not always coincide with those in the art market.

This pattern in prices for art and collectibles over 100 years is reflected in prices for luxury goods. Although millions of people reportedly collect assorted treasured items, the top end of each category of luxury goods, be it fine wine, fine art, rare stamps, classic cars or even violins, will be influenced by the incomes, wealth and perceptions of competing investment opportunities of the most affluent. The spending power of hedge fund managers, Russian oligarchs and Chinese billionaires helped to propel art prices in the years up to 2008, and the continuing demand from the wealthy in China helped the market to recover after 2009 much faster than after the bear market in the early 1990s. Investment managers as collectors of stamps, moguls from the entertainment and fashion world as collectors of classic cars, and Chinese multimillionaires as buyers of fine wine each point to similar influences on the top end of markets for collectibles as have been found in the art market.

The rise of China as a major player in the fine art market has been remarkable. London and especially New York had dominated the art

FIG 12.2 **Worldwide fine art auction house sales**
$bn

Source: www.artprice.com

auction market, at least from the early 1960s to 2008. However, in each year from 2009 to 2012 fine art auction sales in China for the first time exceeded by revenue those in the United States. In earlier years, Hong Kong was the principal marketplace for art in China, but according to Arts Economics, a consultancy, Hong Kong's share of Chinese art auction revenues in 2009-12 was less than 20%, with Beijing taking the lion's share. The change in the art auction market has also led to Chinese works of fine art overwhelmingly, by value, being sold in China. Nevertheless, according to Arts Economics, Chinese buyers have also represented a growing share of purchases in Western art markets.

Economics may help explain overall market trends, but it is less clear which criteria explain the financial value of the work of individual artists. The valuation of any painting ought to be an assessment of what someone else would be willing to pay for it, which will be strongly influenced by assessments of its quality. Maintenance of value is likely to be supported where critical acclaim for an artist survives from one generation to another. Several studies have looked for this. Victor Ginsburgh and Sheila Weyers of the University of

Louvain examined the critical recognition of Italian Renaissance artists over the past 450 years. They used as their benchmark the prominence given to artists in authoritative art history textbooks at different dates over this period. The measures used were the number of citations and the length of written reviews of each artist.

Ginsburgh and Weyers's analysis starts with the assessment published in 1550 by Giorgio Vasari, a notable artist and also a pioneering art historian. They compare this with six other sources spread over the years since then, ending with *The Grove Dictionary of Art*, which was published as 34 volumes in 1996 and has now been superseded by an online edition. This is widely available through public library subscriptions (particularly in the UK) and includes around 21,000 biographies, written by art experts from around the world. Ginsburgh and Weyers highlight an impressive persistence in the art establishment's apparent rating of the leading figures of Italian Renaissance painting. They show that each of the seven selected art authorities from the past 450 years appear to have chosen Giotto, Michelangelo and Raphael as among the top ten Italian Renaissance artists, with six also including Titian and five Leonardo da Vinci.

This pattern of persistent recognition of quality over five centuries of the top-ranking Italian old master painters demonstrates that some assessments of art quality can be relied on to endure. This helps to underpin the financial value of acclaimed artists from one generation to the next. It seems to be a safe bet that in 200 years a painting by Raphael will be prized and highly valued. An art gallery is unlikely to be embarrassed by owning it, but it does not mean, if it ever came to market, that it would perform well as a financial investment.

In the market for contemporary art there is no history of critical acclaim, and whether a contemporary artist's work is judged by art experts to be "strong" or "weak" is largely a matter of subjective opinion. The support of influential opinion formers and patrons has always been important in securing recognition and commercial success for artists, and this can take time even for those later acknowledged as masters. The celebrated example, which gives hope to countless yet-to-be-discovered artists, is Vincent Van Gogh, who died penniless and apparently sold only one painting during his brief lifetime despite his brother's being an art dealer.

Don Thompson, the author of *The $12 million Stuffed Shark: the Curious Economics of Contemporary Art and Auction Houses*, comments on the importance of brand in the market for contemporary art. Branding or, as art market people call it, "validation" can be provided by an artist being supported by a leading art dealer, or by work being offered for sale by either Sotheby's or Christie's, still the world's two dominant art auction houses, or by being exhibited at or bought by a leading modern art gallery, or by having works bought by a celebrated collector. These are the gatekeepers, the most important arbiters of perceived quality in the market for contemporary art. When a contemporary artist has been validated by several of these, he or she becomes a branded artist whose work will henceforth command a higher price. If a collector had the ability to anticipate this process by buying pre-branded, yet-to-be-discovered artists, the road to financial success in collecting contemporary art would be secured. In practice, there may be many good contemporary artists, but only a few secure financial success by becoming branded.

Over the ages there have been countless wealthy patrons, collectors and sponsors of art. Among these are some whose collections have subsequently become extremely valuable. There is little indication that a desire to accumulate wealth rather than a love of art motivated their collections, even though history might judge them to have been canny collectors. An outstanding example of this is the collection of 20th century art, including some by Pablo Picasso and Jasper Johns, amassed over the lifetimes of Victor and Sally Ganz of New York. The Ganz estate sold 114 paintings at auction in 1997, raising a total of $207m compared with an original outlay of $764,000. William Landes, the Clifton R. Musser professor of law and economics at the University of Chicago, found that the performance of the Ganz collection easily beat investing in the US stockmarket over the same period; and although data comparisons are difficult, it seems clear that the Ganz collection outperformed the wider art market. Landes found that the financial performance of the Ganz collection was not simply attributable to the extraordinary results from one or two paintings, but showed a degree of persistence from one artist to another and across time periods of investing. He also found that paintings and prints from the Ganz collection appeared to attract a premium price because they came from the Ganz collection.

Art market indices

Art collectors wish (if only for insurance purposes) to have an estimate of the value of their most treasured works. The section at the end of Chapter 10 discusses biases that seem to affect appraisal valuations of private investment, including fine art and collectibles. In recent years there has been the development of a number of competing providers of art market indices and online art valuation services. The role of the auction houses has facilitated the development of these services by providing a degree of transparency to pricing that would not be available if all transactions occurred through dealers' galleries or at art fairs. However, each of the art indices suffers from weaknesses. Some are common to the measurement of performance in any illiquid market; some are more specific to the art market; and others reflect differences in methodological approach and coverage.

Each of the leading art indices reflects transactions that occur at public auction but not those, by their nature confidential, that occur through dealers' galleries or at art fairs. It is estimated by Clare McAndrew, founder of Arts Economics, that public auctions account for around 50% of the value of the turnover of the fine art market. However, the ready availability of price information makes auctions a goldmine for statisticians and analysts. Unlike some illiquid markets where all transactions are private and where indices of market performance need to rely on expert valuations, in the art market the index providers are able to use auction prices. As in other markets, the indices exclude the impact on financial performance of commission costs, and typically the index providers also exclude items that fail to reach their reserve price and so remain unsold (or "bought-in"). In its annual review of the global fine art market, Artprice, an art market information provider, says that 37% of items submitted for auction in 2012 outside China were bought-in, a figure broadly in line with previous experience, whereas in China, the largest marketplace for fine art in recent years, the comparable figure was 54%, much higher than indicated by recent experience.

There are three main approaches to measuring art market performance:

■ The first is simply to measure the change in the average price paid for paintings at auction. Refinement is added by breaking the indices down into the average price paid for different categories (for example, impressionist paintings) or for individual artists and by removing outliers. This is sometimes called a "naive" index, but it has some significant strengths. The weaknesses of this approach are clear – one work, even by the same artist, is qualitatively different from another and may be expected to command a very different price. However, the attractions of this approach include transparency, ease of understanding and of computation, an expectation that errors in measurement will reduce as large numbers of works are included, and importantly, that it includes all the available price information from the auction houses. Other approaches, see below, may cover a minority of the transactions at art auctions, and will be particularly weak in their coverage of paintings which have not previously sold at auction – contemporary art in particular. In practice, this approach makes use of moving averages and so will react with a lag to any market changes and can exclude the highest and lowest 10% by value of auction prices to reduce the possible distorting effect of outlying transactions.

■ The second approach attempts to take account of physical characteristics of a work of art that experience suggests influence its price. These include the name of the artist, the category of the art, the size of the painting and the name of the auction house. This is the "hedonic" approach and aims to remove non-standard influences from the movement in the art market index. The advantage of the hedonic approach over the simple average price method is that it makes use of supplementary information that appears to have been important in past auctions. It can also make use of all the price data from the auction houses.

■ The third, much loved by purists, is the "repeat sales regression" approach. This makes use of pairs of data for individual works of art, comparing a purchase price with the subsequent sales price for the same work at a later date. The strength of this method is that it uses realised returns from individual works of art and combines them into a representative series for the market as a whole. The methodology is comparable to that of the authoritative Case-Shiller series for the US housing market, where transaction information is made publicly available. There are some difficulties with applying the methodology to the art market that do not apply in the housing market to the same degree:

  – The first is that the need to rely on repeat sales substantially restricts the amount of auction price data that is being used in the index.
  – The second is that the auction market does not cover the whole market as it fails to capture transactions by dealers. This would not

matter if price trends in the two market segments were believed to be comparable. However, there may be a survivor bias which inflates the repeat-sales indices if works by artists who were formerly fashionable are no longer accepted for sale at the leading auction houses, and instead are sold by dealers at reduced prices which are not reflected in the indices.

–   The third is that the need for a pair of auction transactions (a purchase and a later sale) for an individual work before it joins the database means that it will always lag in its coverage of contemporary art.

–   The fourth, the importance of which will diminish as the number of transactions measured by an index increases, is that the purity of repeat-sales analysis assumes that a painting is the same painting when it is resold. However, changes in expert opinion about a painting's authenticity or attribution will influence the price subsequently achieved at auction. This does not affect the value of other works by that artist or of the market as a whole, but it may distort the index between those transaction dates. Corresponding issues arise with real estate and the possibility of physical improvements or deterioration in a property between purchase and sale. The influence of such distortions will be diluted as the number of repeat transactions recorded by an index increases.

Price indices for other investments of passion or "collectibles"

In any market, attempts to construct price indices are constrained by the available data. A major source of price indices for a large range of collectibles is Art Market Research, a consultancy based in London, which computes prices for different categories of collectibles and then removes outlying observations. Its impressive range of items includes Colt revolvers, wrist watches, Chinese ceramics and German toy trains. Other approaches which only compare directly the prices of identical items (such as the same painting when bought and then when sold) use only a subset of the available data and will miss out on new market trends (until a record is established of purchases and later sales of particular items within the new trend).

In some markets (for example, classic cars) auctions play an important role in providing one ready source for index compilers. In other markets, auctions may have a smaller role and index compilers prefer to rely on a consistent source that is available for long periods of time. In the market for British stamps, for example, although there is an active auction market, the available long-run price information is contained in the catalogues published by Stanley Gibbons, a stamp dealer, which has been the main source of reference for collectors of British stamps. This is the source of price data used by Dimson and Spaenjers in their 2011 study "Ex Post: the investment performance of collectible stamps". These have been available around most year-ends since the late 19th century and they represent estimated selling prices of Stanley Gibbons at the time of publication for new or used stamps in "fine condition".

The attraction of this data series is that it is available, on a reasonably consistent basis, for almost all years and that the dealer provides an assurance of attribution. The weakness of the data is primarily that they reflect a dealer's valuation estimates rather than transaction prices and so are likely to lag behind market developments and be less volatile than actual prices, and that the catalogue prices are likely to be difficult to reconcile with advertised online or public auction prices. There may also be changes over time in the spread between the price at which Stanley Gibbons offers to sell and the price at which it is willing to buy. Furthermore, a catalogue encourages the unwary to interpret the dealer's offer prices for a particular item as an indication of value for a broad category of collectibles. Philatelists know that thousands, perhaps hundreds of thousands, of examples of the Penny Black, the first prepaid adhesive postage stamp in the world, have survived in some form out of the 55 million (some sources say 68 million) that were printed in the UK between 1840 and 1841. They also know that one unused Penny Black in fine condition can have a very different value from another unused Penny Black in fine condition.

Stamps, coins and probably most collectibles are extremely heterogeneous, and gaining and growing an understanding of their distinctive differences is central to a collector's expertise. However, making use of a wide cross-section (50 in the case of the Dimson and Spaenjers study) of catalogue prices for representative items for almost every year for over a century will greatly reduce the uncertainty that derives from the comparability of items from one period to another. A market index is not attempting to reflect the idiosyncrasies of individual items, but rather to reflect broad movements in the overall level of the market.

Assessing changes in the level of prices in the market for classic cars introduces new challenges. In this market, a particular car which is bought and subsequently resold is only the same car in terms of its chassis number: collectors will always be working on their cars, and without maintenance they always deteriorate. Maintenance might cost 2.5–5% of the value of a car each year, which can be seen as a negative dividend attached to this investment of passion. So whereas an art index or a house price index may seek data on repeat sales of the same painting or house, in the market for classic cars such information, even where it is available, is not seen as useful for constructing an index of market prices. The price level for classic cars is measured by the Historic Automobile Group International (HAGI) index, which has been constructed since 2008 by a group of finance industry car enthusiasts, with expertise in compiling stockmarket indices. The index, which includes 50 valuable car models, was estimated in mid-2013 to have a capitalisation of around $15 billion, which represents the estimated number of surviving cars multiplied by the price for the type and assumed condition of the car. The HAGI indices are based only on transactions for cars in "very good" or "highly original" condition and exclude prices strongly influenced by extraneous factors, such as celebrity former owners. The United States dominates the classic car auction market, with the UK and continental Europe in subsidiary roles. Unlike in the art market, mainland China has not emerged as a major centre for classic cars.

The prices for the HAGI indices are sourced from auctioneers (which account for around one-third of the market) and from the confidential transaction records of dealers and collectors. If there are no trades for a category of classic car during a month, the index for that category will show no change that month (which, in common with a number of other methodologies for constructing indices of collectibles, could slow the index's response to a market downturn). Although they will not collect every transaction, the index compilers are confident that they are able to capture the majority of relevant

FIG 12.3 **Calendar year performance of global equities and classic cars**
1980–2008, Dec 1980 = 100

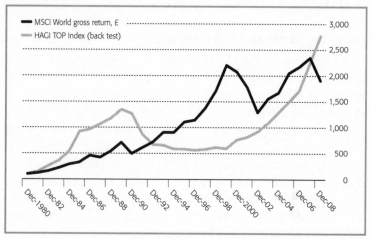

Sources: Historic Automobile Group International; MSCI

FIG 12.4 **Monthly performance of world equities and classic cars**
Dec 2008–Sep 2013, Dec 2008 = 100

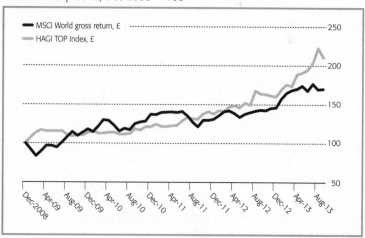

Sources: Historic Automobile Group International; MSCI

transactions globally. The HAGI has supplemented the monthly series since 2008 with back-filled annual data back to 1980 (see Figures 12.3 and 12.4).

Investing in art and collectibles

There has been a great deal of talk about investing in art, but apparently little purely financial investment. Art consultants are asked from time to time to give presentations on the potential role of a portfolio of works of art in an investment strategy. But as often as not it seems that investing in art is looked upon as an interesting and imaginative idea for investors to have considered rather than an idea that they wish to implement. The one exception to this is the market for art funds, though even these are more talked about than purchased. There have been numerous attempts to launch art funds. Michael Findlay, an art dealer and the author of *The Value of Art*, says that "there is an adage among old hands in the art world that the emergence of art investment funds signals that a boom is over". He cites an early example from 1904 when a French financier and 12 friends formed a fund called, "with intentional irony", La Peau de l'Ours ("the skin of the bear") after a fable in which hunters sell the skin of a bear which they are then unable to catch. This fund was a great success, having acquired works by emerging artists including Gauguin and Monet and two then "unknowns", Matisse and Picasso. And it was a financial success, thanks to shrewd selection of works of art and extraordinary good luck in winding up after ten years, just before the start of the first world war. The new long-run price index for the art market shows that this was also a peak level for art market prices, which was not reached again, after allowing for inflation, for over 50 years.

Immediately before the 2008 financial crisis, there was a flurry of ambitious plans to launch funds, especially in China, to invest in differing parts of the art market. In the West, proposals included proposed funds to invest in art from emerging economies, to invest in emerging artists (irrespective of home country), to support promotions so as to "brand" new artists, and to focus on relatively high turnover and also on relatively low turnover.

In 2013, there were relatively few funds operating, although the combined assets under management have been estimated at around $1 billion (which is difficult to verify). Art funds offer the prospect of making a financial investment in a diversified portfolio of works of art. In practice, the transaction charges levied by dealers and auction houses impose a difficult hurdle on relatively short-life funds to buy, hold, then sell art and give a competitive return to investors. Art funds need to get round this hurdle, and one avenue is to deal directly with buyers and sellers (who for contemporary works might be the artists). The management of funds has sought to overcome the hurdle of transaction costs by providing liquidity to art collectors who wish to sell art quickly or anonymously (or both). To this extent, investors in an art fund have been investing in and providing valuable liquidity to a business that can be compared with an art dealership. However, an attractive feature of an art fund for investors is that they may be able to borrow works of art from the fund for display in their own homes or offices.

Overall, though, the development of art funds has been disappointing, with a few successes. A few private banks have flirted with the idea of launching them, but the banks' more common role is advising their wealthiest clients on the management of their art collections and, in particular, the arrangement of credit facilities secured against their art. Works of art may represent a significant part of the wealth of such investors, but they are normally better described as collections, rather than as investment portfolios.

A rare example from the past of an institutional foray into the art market was the investment portfolio created by the British Rail Pension Fund in the years following 1974. The decision to make this unusual alternative investment was a response to the financial crises of the time (especially in the UK) and led to the purchase of a portfolio comprising 2,505 individual works of art. (This total was inflated by the acquisition of several portfolios comprising modest value items.) The purchases occurred between 1974 and 1980 and the final item was sold in 2003. The fund had spent £41.1m acquiring the works and the proceeds from the sales (net of commissions, fees and taxes, but not allowing for intervening storage and insurance costs) was £170.4m. This represented an internal rate of return of

FIG 12.5 **British Rail Pension Fund realised rates of return for 2,505 individual works of art acquired between 1974 and 1980**
Internal rates of return, % per year, after inflation

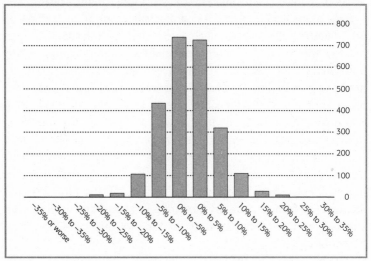

11.3%, or 3.7% per year after allowing for the impact of UK inflation. Set against the benchmarks that would have been established at the outset, the experience was a success. Nevertheless, it did not persuade the pension fund to continue with its experiment. This example is more relevant for potential investors than that of the Ganz collection because it does not suffer from the hindsight bias that affects that highly successful private collection. The Ganz collection is interesting because it happened to be financially successful; the British Rail portfolio is interesting because it is a single example of a well-diversified financial investment in art.

The British Rail example sheds light on the financial risk of collecting art. Figure 12.5 plots the distribution of rates of return, after allowing for UK inflation, for each of the individual items, which were originally chosen for their contribution to a diversified portfolio of works of art. The similarity between this figure and the corresponding one drawn by Baumol in his 1986 article (based on 640 purchases and then sales of paintings) is striking. Figure 12.5 shows that the performance of individual works was widely dispersed around that of the median, or middle ranking, holding, which was just -0.39% per year. Despite this, the performance of the portfolio as a whole was 3.7% per year, helped by the exceptional performance of the pension fund's holdings of impressionist paintings.

The British Rail experiment was perhaps too short term. Great collections hold works of art from generation to generation; the average holding period in the British Rail works of art collection was just 12.9 years.

Shared characteristics of fine art and other investments of passion

Investments of passion, or hobby collections, share a number of characteristics:

■ The importance of "provenance", that is authentication and ownership history of any item. Even the grandest art collections and galleries run the risk of having major works reassessed by experts. The implications on valuation of having an important work reassessed as "from the school of" rather than by a particular old master painter would be severe; to have a treasured work of art exposed as a forgery would be much worse. Corresponding threats confront a collection of stamps or coins: differences in qualitative assessment can seem arcane to an outsider but can make an important difference to judgments of the quality of a collection. The expertise and passion of the collector, whether of fine art or collectibles, are directed at minimising such risk.

■ The asymmetry of information that exists between market insiders and most investors is a feature that is shared with all illiquid markets. Those wishing to build a collection need to appreciate that an informational advantage almost always lies with the market professional.

■ The prevalence of high transaction costs, which are normally much higher than in more liquid securities markets. At art auctions, transaction costs are dominated by the buyer and seller "premia", or commissions. For example, at one of the major auction houses, where the buyer's commission is calculated on a sliding scale, the commission payable for a purchase with a hammer price of $1.5m could be 17.5%, with 25% payable on the first $50,000. Commissions payable by the seller (or consignor) of a work are also significant, but since a price-fixing scandal in 2002, they may now be more susceptible to economic pressures. Nevertheless, it is safe to assume that the auction houses may extract 25% of the price of a high-value painting and more for smaller value items. Such transaction costs are likely to cripple most approaches to investments of passion that do not involve a patient buy-and-hold strategy.

The financial resources that could in principle be allocated to acquisitions of art are enormous relative to the size of the global art market. Deep pockets in the Middle East are funding new national galleries. More importantly, there is a traditional imbalance between the tiny size of the art market compared with total private financial wealth. Art auctions had a record turnover in 2012 according to Artprice of $12.3 billion in 2012, but investable financial wealth was estimated by the Capgemini and RBC 2013 "World Wealth Report" to have been $46.2 trillion (that is, $46.2 thousand billion), with perhaps $12 trillion available as cash or deposits.

The insignificant size of the art market, in relation to disposable wealth, means that a move by any substantial investor or group of investors to establish or extend a major art collection is likely to provide considerable support to prices. The easiest way to justify a purely financial investment in sought-after parts of the fine art market would be a belief that prices would increasingly be supported by at least some such investors for decades ahead. As Baumol implied, economics is unable to suggest any upper limit for the prices of highly prized art.

Appendix 1
Glossary

THIS GLOSSARY DOES NOT REPEAT definitions and explanations of concepts that are provided in the main text, for example in Chapter 2 (terms relating to behavioural finance) and chapters in Part 2 (for terms relating to equity markets, credit markets, hedge funds, private equity and real estate). For references to these, please consult the index.

Active management	Investment strategies of active investment managers who are appointed in the expectation or hope that they will perform better than the market as a whole, after allowing for the extra fees paid for active management. These strategies always involve avoidable turnover (compared with a passive or market matching strategy) and the avoidable risk of underperforming the market. See also **passive strategies**.
Annualised returns	See **geometric average returns**.
Arithmetic average returns	The simple average over time of investment returns. This is higher than the compounded or geometric average of returns. The difference is easy to illustrate. Suppose a portfolio performance in one period is −50% and in the next is +100%. The arithmetic average performance is +25% [(−50 + 100) ÷ 2]. The geometric average or compound return, however, is 100 × (0.5 × 2.0) − 100 or 0%. Standard risk measures such as the standard deviation should be used in conjunction with the arithmetic average. However, the geometric or compound return describes the evolution of wealth over time.

Asset allocation	Allocation of investments among different markets. Contrast with stock selection, which is the allocation of investments within a particular market.
Base currency	Investors' home currency in which their investment objectives are expressed. Their base currency is normally, but not always, unambiguous. See Chapter 1.
Basis point (BP)	One hundredth of one percent, or 0.01%.
Beta	A measure of the extent to which a stock might provide diluted exposure (if the measure of beta is less than 1.0) or leveraged exposure (if the measure of beta is greater than 1.0) to equity market risk. See Chapter 7 for discussion of the fundamental insights, strengths and weaknesses of the capital asset pricing model, in which the concept of "beta" plays a central role.
Bond ladder	A portfolio of high-quality bonds of successive maturities designed to provide a steady stream of investment income. See Chapter 5.
Break-even rate of inflation	This is (approximately) the difference between the redemption yield on conventional government bonds and that on inflation-linked government bonds of the same maturity. If inflation happens to equal the break-even rate, the total return on inflation-linked and conventional government bonds will be approximately identical. See Chapter 3.
Business angel	An entrepreneur who contributes finance and often business expertise to support a venture capital investment in return for a significant shareholding.
Call option	A contract that gives the right to buy a specified investment at a given time in the future for a predetermined price. See also **option** and **put option**.
Capital Asset Pricing Model (CAPM)	See **beta** and Chapter 7.

Coefficient of loss aversion	A concept from behavioural finance. The ratio of the sensitivity to losses compared with the sensitivity to gains. A commonly cited result is that the coefficient is around 2, in other words, that investors weigh losses twice as highly as they weigh gains.
Contrarian	An investor, or a strategy, that deliberately seeks to be unfashionable and to go against recent market trends. Typically, this is an adjective that is used to describe value investors; see Chapter 7.
Conventional bond	A fixed-income bond (which has a predetermined schedule of fixed-interest coupons and a fixed redemption value). The word "conventional" is used to distinguish the bond from inflation-linked or floating-rate bonds. Inflation-linked bonds have coupons and/or redemption values that are adjusted in line with inflation. Floating-rate bonds have coupons that are reset in line with a specified short-term reference rate of interest, such as the London Interbank Offered Rate (LIBOR).
Convertible bond	Usually a corporate bond that gives investors the option to convert it at some stage in the future into a given number of ordinary shares of the issuing company. Convertible bonds generally pay lower coupons than bonds issued by the same company which do not offer the option to convert into equity.
Convexity	A measure of the change in a bond's duration that is a result of a change in interest rates. Allowance for a bond's convexity enables a more accurate assessment of how its price will respond to interest rate changes than can be provided by considering only its duration. This is because the relationship between a change in interest rates and the consequent change in bond prices is generally not linear. Positive convexity is a desirable characteristic and is an attribute of conventional bonds whose duration increases as interest rates fall and decreases as interest rates rise. This is because the present value of future payments increases with lower interest rates and vice versa. Thus these bonds perform better than calculations based only on the bond's duration

would suggest when interest rates change. Negative convexity is the opposite, and bonds which display this characteristic tend to underperform when interest rates fall and/or rise. Bonds which are exposed to certain types of embedded options, such as mortgage bonds, can display negative convexity. See Chapter 8.

Correlation
The degree of linear association between two variables. In other words, it is a measure of the extent to which the prices of two investments move together (but not necessarily by the same amount). The correlation coefficient, R, can vary between –1 and +1. A correlation coefficient of 0 suggests no relationship between the movements in the prices of the two investments. A positive correlation suggests that the prices of the two investments tend to rise or fall at the same time. A negative correlation suggests that the prices of the two investments tend to move in opposite directions at any particular time. Negative correlations are highly desirable in constructing portfolios of risky assets, because they reduce risk. However, negatively correlated attractive investments are rare.

Credit spread
The extra yield offered by a risky bond over that offered by the Treasury for a bond of the same maturity to compensate an investor for the risk that the issue might default. Extra yield may also be paid to compensate for the illiquidity of an issue.

Derivatives
Derived investment contracts, which are designed to replicate certain aspects of risk that can be obtained from direct investment in markets such as equity or fixed income.

Directional funds
A common categorisation of hedge fund strategies is to divide them between directional and non-directional strategies. Directional strategies are those whose performance is expected to be highly correlated with equity or other market risk.

Disinflation	The process of reducing the rate of inflation – that is, the rate at which prices are increasing. Disinflation should not be confused with deflation, which refers to actual declines in prices.
Duration	The average life of a bond and also a measure of a bond's sensitivity to movements in interest rates. (Slight differences in calculation are reflected in these definitions.) Duration is the weighted average time to the total of scheduled payments, where the weights are determined by the present value of each payment. Duration is shorter than the maturity of a bond, because it takes account of the earlier dates on which interest coupons are paid. The exception is a zero coupon bond, the duration of which is the same as its maturity. There are two common but similar technical definitions of duration: Macaulay duration, which is most useful in precisely matching a future stream of payments; and modified duration, which provides a measure of the sensitivity of a bond portfolio to small changes in interest rates.
Efficient frontier	On a graph which plots for different investments (and for portfolios of different investments) the expected return (y-axis) and expected volatility (x-axis) of those investments, the efficient frontier shows the most efficient combinations of risk and return. At any point on the frontier curve for a given level of volatility, expected return is maximised, and for a given level of expected return, expected volatility is minimised. See **fuzzy frontier** and Chapter 5.
ETF	Short for exchange traded fund, an investment product that gives exposure to a particular market. The ETF itself is listed on the stockmarket, and so is highly liquid and generally accessible at modest transaction prices.
Family office	The private office of a wealthy family which is entrusted with the management of the family's financial affairs.
Fat tails	See **kurtosis**.

Forward contract — Similar to a futures contract, except that it may not be standardised (though most probably it will be) and does not benefit from the transparent pricing and support of a formal exchange. As a result forwards may not be marked to market each day. This gives rise to larger issues of counterparty risk than exist with futures contracts, which are transacted on a formal exchange.

Futures contract — A standardised contract entered into on a futures exchange to buy or sell a particular investment or basket of investments at a given date in the future. The exchange guarantees payments between members of the exchange (but not their clients). In practice, profit and loss on a futures contract is calculated on a daily basis and reflected in payments of variation margin to and from the exchange's clearing house by both parties to a contract.

Fuzzy frontier — An adaptation of the concept of the efficient frontier which acknowledges that, because investment relationships and investment classifications are to a degree uncertain, there is rarely one most efficient strategy that a particular investor should follow. Instead there is always a range of broadly efficient appropriate strategies. See Chapter 2.

Geometric average returns — Another term for compound or annualised investment returns. For the difference between geometric or compound and arithmetic investment returns, see **arithmetic average returns**.

Hedged — An indication that market risk, for example from the stockmarket or a foreign exchange market, has been neutralised using derivatives or other instruments. But see Chapter 9 for a discussion of the loose use of the term "hedging" by hedge funds.

Heuristic — A simple procedure that helps find adequate though often imperfect answers to difficult questions. A shortcut.

High watermark — This concept is important for the calculation of hedge fund performance fees. It refers to the preceding highest cumulative total return. Hedge fund performance fees are normally payable only if cumulative performance exceeds the preceding "high watermark". See Chapter 9.

High-yield bond	A debt issue which is judged by credit-rating agencies to be at best speculative or not well secured. See also **sub-investment grade**, **investment grade** and Chapter 8.
Inflation risk premium	An amount by which the break-even rate of inflation may exceed the expected rate of inflation to allow for the risk that inflation may be higher than expected. See Chapter 3.
In-the-money	A call option is said to be "in-the-money" when the market price of the underlying investment is above the "strike" price at which the option to buy that investment can be exercised. A put option is in-the-money when the market price is below the strike price at which the option can be exercised. An option can be exercised profitably only if it is in-the-money.
Investment grade	The group of credit ratings given by the principal rating agencies to debt securities whose credit rating is assessed as being at least moderate to good quality. This differentiates investment grade debt from issues which are judged to be at best speculative or not well secured. See **sub-investment grade** and Chapter 8.
Kurtosis	Also called excess kurtosis. A measure of whether a series of investment returns has more extreme results than would be suggested by the normal distribution. A distribution with more than expected extreme results is called leptokurtic. This phenomenon is more commonly referred to as "fat tails". A number of hedge fund strategies, and some stockmarket returns, demonstrate pronounced fat tails or excess kurtosis. See Chapter 9.
Large cap	One of the largest companies by stockmarket capitalisation. In the United States a common definition is that a quoted company is large cap if its market capitalisation exceeds $10 billion. See Chapter 7.
Leverage	An indication of the extent to which an investment, and thus its performance, is geared through the level of debt embedded in it.

Liquidity	An indication of the ease with which investments can be bought or sold at close to their advertised price. In illiquid markets it can be difficult to buy and sell investments.
Listed investment	An investment, typically a stock or bond, which is listed on a recognised exchange and provides regular quotations for its price. Contrast with an unlisted or private investment (such as a venture capital investment or a property investment), the price of which, except when it is bought and sold, represents appraisal valuations.
Lognormal distribution	See **normal distribution**.
Long-only strategy	A traditional investment strategy or portfolio consisting only of investments which are owned, not investments which are borrowed or sold short. See also **short position**.
Long position	An investment which is owned, as distinct from an investment which is borrowed. See also **short position**.
Mark-to-market	The process of accounting for the value of investments, and so profits and losses, at their market prices, rather than their book or historical cost.
Market risk premium	The premium return expected for investing outside the secure safe haven and incurring the risks associated with investing in volatile markets that offer systematic investment returns to investors.
Mean reversion	The belief, fundamental to the outlook of value investors, that prices in financial markets tend to overreact, oscillating between overvaluation and undervaluation. Mean reversion refers to an expectation that expensive markets can be relied upon to become cheaper and inexpensive markets can be relied upon to become priced closer to "fair value". See Chapters 3, 5 and 7.
Mental accounting	A concept from behavioural finance. The set of cognitive operations used by individuals and households to organise, evaluate and keep track of financial activities.

Mezzanine debt	Often the most junior – that is, the most risky – category of debt in a borrower's balance sheet. Typically it will be accompanied by options to convert into equity. It is best considered as sharing the risk characteristics of equity rather than debt.
Natural habitat	The natural investment home for a particular investor, such as long-dated Treasury bonds for a pension fund.
Negative convexity	See **convexity**.
Noise	Meaningless apparent market signals which make it more difficult to interpret market developments. Noise is both a cause and a reflection of uncertainty. One cause of noise is the impact on markets of the transactions of investors who lack insight or who transact for reasons other than in response to market signals (for example, investors who have an impact on markets because, for whatever reason, they need to sell). See Chapter 6.
Normal distribution	The normal and lognormal distributions are the two most commonly used statistical models in finance. A normal distribution is symmetrical, with a bell-shaped curve and one peak; a lognormal distribution is skewed to the right. Return series that are lognormally distributed lead to geometric, or logarithmic, returns that are themselves normally distributed. The popularity of the normal and lognormal distributions reflects their comparative ease of use in analysis and the evidence that they provide a plausible approximation to many market performance data series. Much effort has been invested in examining when the normal, or lognormal, distribution fails to describe how markets behave. See, for example, Chapters 3, 5 and 7.
Option	A contract that gives the purchaser the right, but not the obligation, to buy (call option) or sell (put option) a particular investment at a given price on (if a European option) or before (if an American option) the given expiry date for the contract.

Passive strategies	Market-matching investment strategies which involve minimal turnover and expense. Turnover typically occurs only to accommodate inflows or outflows of investor funds and to improve the market-matching features of the investment portfolio.
Ponzi scheme	A type of scam named after the fraudster Charles Ponzi who in the 1920s defrauded thousands of New England residents with the promise of superlative returns on their savings by exploiting anomalies in the rates of exchange offered on international mail coupons. A Ponzi scheme is an investment fraud that offers the promise of enticing performance by diverting cash from new investors to provide the promised returns to exiting old investors. Such a scheme is doomed to fail and works only as long as new inflows at least match the demand for cash from leavers.
Prepayment risk	The risk that a bond, particularly a mortgage bond, will experience faster than scheduled repayments of principal because residential mortgage holders, particularly in the United States, can exercise the right to repay mortgages earlier than specified in a repayment schedule. This reduces the term of a mortgage bond and is most likely to happen when interest rates fall (or when mortgage providers compete aggressively for new business), giving profitable opportunities for borrowers to remortgage property at more attractive interest rates. See Chapter 8.
Price/earnings ratio	The ratio of the share price of a company to its earnings divided by the number of shares it has issued. A high price/earnings (P/E) ratio indicates that the stockmarket expects the company's earnings to grow fast, and vice versa.
Price performance	The performance of an investment that makes no allowance for its income or dividend yield. Contrast with total return, which includes the price performance and the income return.
Prime broker	A department of an investment bank which provides banking services to hedge funds.

Private investment	An unlisted or unquoted investment for which price quotations are generally not readily available.
Prospect theory	A key part of behavioural finance. It is based on experiments that indicate that people are more motivated by losses than by gains (see **coefficient of loss aversion**) and so will try hard to avoid realising losses. See Chapter 2.
Public investment	A listed or quoted investment for which prices are regularly quoted on a formal exchange at which, or close to which, transactions can be effected.
Pure discount bond	See **zero coupon bond**.
Put option	A contract that gives the right to sell a specified investment at a given time in the future for a predetermined price. See also **option** and **call option**.
Quoted investment	A public investment.
R^2	The square of the correlation coefficient. This measures the percentage of variation (that is, variance) in the price of one investment that is "explained" by a change in the price of another.
Real interest rate	The rate of interest after allowing for inflation.
Redemption yield	See **yield to maturity**.
Relative risk	Typically, the risk of an actively managed portfolio relative to that of the market or the investor's benchmark or neutral investment policy.
Risk premium	See Chapter 3.
Safe haven	An investor's minimum risk strategy. See Chapter 3.
Sharpe ratio	A measure of risk-adjusted performance. For an investment portfolio or strategy, the Sharpe ratio is the ratio of performance in excess of the risk-free investment (generally Treasury bills) to the volatility of performance relative to the risk-free rate. Performance and volatility are generally calculated as annualised rates. Investors should be aware that illiquid investment strategies

distort measurement of Sharpe ratios since the apparent volatility of those strategies will be artificially reduced by markets that rely on appraisal valuations of underlying investments. Furthermore, Sharpe ratios are only meaningful if the distribution of performance of the underlying investments approximately resembles a normal distribution. It follows that Sharpe ratios should not be used for investment strategies which resemble insurance programmes and which incorporate a marked degree of optionality. For both these reasons, Sharpe ratios shown for many hedge fund strategies are more likely to misinform investors than to inform them. See Chapter 9.

Short position
Arises when investors sell an investment that they do not own. Unless the short position is established on a futures exchange, investors will need to borrow the investment to deliver it to the counterparty who bought it from them. The short seller will need to provide collateral to the stock lender when borrowing the stock (or other investment).

Skewness
A measure of the symmetry between investment returns from a market. If the returns are tilted towards the left (more negative) side of the distribution, a distribution is said to exhibit negative skewness. If returns are tilted towards the right (more positive) side of the distribution, the results are said to exhibit positive skewness.

Small cap
A smaller company by stockmarket capitalisation. In the United States a common definition is that a quoted company is small cap if its market capitalisation is less than $2 billion. See Chapter 7.

SMID
Short for small or mid cap companies, a group of companies that is reckoned to be either small or mid cap by value of market capitalisation. In the United States a common definition is that a quoted company is SMID if its market capitalisation is less than $6 billion. See Chapter 7.

Sovereign wealth fund (SWF)	A government-owned investment fund, typically arising from persistent balance-of-payments surpluses. See box, What is a sovereign wealth fund?, in Chapter 4.
Speculative grade	A debt issue judged by credit-rating agencies to be at best speculative or not well secured. See also **high-yield bond**, **investment grade** and Chapter 8.
Standard deviation	The standard measure of the volatility of the price or performance of an investment. Common interpretations of the standard deviation derive from the normal distribution. For example, if an equity portfolio has an expected return of 7% a year and an expected volatility of 15% a year, it would be expected, approximately, to have returns of between –8% and 22% in two years out of three.
Stock selection	The allocation of investments in a portfolio within a particular market. Contrast with the allocation of investments among different markets, which is known as asset allocation.
Strategic asset allocation	Decisions, typically intended to be quite long term in nature, to manage risks and opportunities relative to an investor's ultimate payment obligations or objectives. Strategic asset allocation involves the allocation of investments between an investor's safe-haven investment and an efficient diversity of other market risks. See Chapter 4.
Structured product	An investment or investment strategy that is typically sold with some element of principal protection and/or of leverage to give accelerated exposure to the underlying market. Structured products are sold by investment banks and typically involve either some combination of zero coupon bonds, which mature with the structured product, together with call options on the relevant underlying market; or a dynamic strategy that adjusts exposure to the underlying investment and government bonds to ensure that the issuing bank will be able profitably to honour the promised capital repayment at maturity.

Sub-investment grade	A debt issue judged by credit-rating agencies to be at best speculative or not well secured. See also **high-yield bond**, **investment grade** and Chapter 8.
Systematic return	The market return that is expected to be provided for bearing well-diversified systematic risk. Often thought of in terms of equity market return, systematic return also refers to the return that should be expected for bearing any type of market risk for which market participants are willing to pay. This includes, in addition to equity market risk, credit market risk, as well as various types of insurance and other risk transfer services. Such alternative sources of systematic return are now understood to be an important potential source of hedge fund returns.
Systematic risk	The market risk that remains after diversification. Most commonly this refers to equity market risk, but it can also refer to the risk associated with a range of different sources of systematic return.
Tactical asset allocation	Decisions, typically short or medium term, to allocate more or less of an investment strategy to different markets in the hope of profiting from expected differential performance between markets.
Tobin's Q	Named after James Tobin, a Nobel Prize-winning economist from Yale University, this is the ratio of the stockmarket value of a firm to its replacement cost. If Q is less than 1 it would be cheaper to buy the firm's shares than to expand to replicate that firm. See Chapter 4 for its application to the US equity market and Chapter 11 for its application to the US real estate market.
Total return	The total performance of an investment, combining income yield as well as price performance.
Tracking error	See **relative risk**.
Tranche	A slice, specifically of a collateralised debt obligation (CDO), that has different risk characteristics from other tranches of the same CDO. See Chapter 8.
Treasury bill	Government debt with less than one year's original maturity (typically 1–6 months).

Treasury bond	Government debt with more than one year's original maturity. In designing broad investment strategies, it is conventional to treat a government bond with a remaining maturity of less than 12 months as if it were a Treasury bill. In the United States, Treasury debts with between one and ten years' original maturity are called "notes". In this book, the expression "Treasury bond" refers to any Treasury security of more than one year's maturity.
Unhedged	An indication that market risk, for example from the stockmarket or a foreign exchange market, has not been neutralised using derivatives or other instruments.
Utility	An indication of satisfaction, often proxied by money.
Volatility	Fluctuations in the price or performance of an investment, typically measured by the annualised standard deviation of returns.
Warrant	An option to a buy a security at a particular price and subject to particular time constraints.
Yield curve	See Chapter 3.
Yield to maturity	The standard measure of the return an investor will receive from a Treasury bond if the bond is held to maturity. Yield to maturity (YTM) takes account of the interest income and any capital gain or loss on the bond over that time.
Zero coupon bond	Zero coupon bonds, also known as zeros, ZCBs, or pure discount bonds, pay no interest, only the repayment of principal at maturity. Their maturity is equal to their duration, and for long maturities they represent the most volatile of high-quality bonds. Prior to maturity, zero coupon bonds trade at a discount to face value.

Appendix 2

Essential management information for investors

SIMPLE MANAGEMENT INFORMATION is a prerequisite for taking control of investments, and it should be easy to obtain. Investment management firms routinely provide easy-to-comprehend portfolio summaries, although the format will differ from one firm to another and some will be more useful than others. However, investors who employ more than one manager need to have reliable overall snapshots that they can drill down into to see individual positions if they wish.

Some illustrative portfolio summaries are shown in Tables 1–4 below. They need to be adapted to particular situations, but they provide a general impression. Investors need to decide whether the information is best presented in an aggregated form, adding together all their investments from different accounts. This will often be the best way to proceed. However, if investments are held in different accounts tied to different investment objectives with different risk tolerances, aggregating the holdings may encourage inappropriate conclusions, which take insufficient account of the objectives of the various accounts, to be drawn. Conversely, a failure to aggregate holdings could cause concentrated, inappropriate or inefficient risk exposures to be overlooked. This is discussed in Chapter 2 and needs careful consideration, preferably with the assistance of a professional adviser.

Performance measurement and comparing with the performance of the lowest risk strategy

As well as transparent holdings information, investors should pay attention to how performance information is presented to them. It will normally be appropriate to aggregate all their listed, or at least frequently valued, investments to review the performance of the overall strategy. For unquoted investments, review of management information on the investments needs to take the place of review of accurate performance information. Where different accounts have been established to meet different objectives with different risk tolerances, performance against those objectives should be monitored. Even when it has not been an option to fully hedge a particular objective (because it is too expensive), it is still useful to show performance relative to the notional performance of the fully hedged strategy.

A similar way of achieving the same objective is to measure how the purchasing power of an investment portfolio evolves in terms of its ability to support continuing flows of expenditure. The easy way to do this for a (very) long-term investor is to take the inflation-linked yield on the longest dated TIPS in the domestic market – assuming it is positive – to generate a hypothetical recurring income from the investments. For example, for each $1,000 of investments, if the yield on TIPS moved from 1% to 2% a year, the supportable income would increase from $10 to $20 a year. Doing the same exercise with nominal government (or municipal) bond yields will provide an apparently more reassuring level of income, but this is subject to erosion by inflation over time. How this level of supportable income changes as markets move will reflect the degree of investment risk in the investment strategy. This is a simple measure that could be useful, particularly for cautious long-term investors.

Performance measurement is a substantial subject. One of the principal features is that the performance that matters is an investment fund's total return, which comprises price changes and net interest and dividend receipts. This should preferably be after payment of fees and taxes. When the performance of a fund is being compared with a market index, it is important that a like-for-like comparison is made. For example, if the purpose is to evaluate the skill of a money manager, the comparison should be with the total return index that best represents the market and strategy of that manager. Comparing an equity manager's performance with that of a bond index is inappropriate if the intention is to shed light on manager skill. However, comparing the performance of an equity fund with a government bond index may be useful in monitoring the ability of that fund to meet particular objectives in the future.

There are two principal measures of total return:

- money weighted rate of return (MWR), which is also known as the internal rate of return (IRR);
- time weighted rate of return (TWR).

The difference between them concerns the treatment of cash flows. The TWR enables a fair comparison between a fund that receives cash flows and the performance of a market index that does not. This is by far the most common basis for the formal measurement of investment performance of stocks and bonds and frequently valued funds. However, the MWR or IRR takes account of the timing of cash flows and is the usual way to measure the performance of funds (such as private equity funds) for which market valuations are not usually available, and where the key measure is a comparison of the amount invested, the amount returned to investors and the time taken. An IRR should not be compared with the time weighted return on a market index (though frequently it is).

Summary risk information

All investors should try to get simplified risk information on their portfolios. Since 2008 some easily accessed online quantitative services have been withdrawn. The easiest way for investors to obtain informative risk information is to track the volatility of the monthly performance of an investment fund. This can then be used to gauge comfort levels. For example, if a fund has been performing well, how would the investor respond, and would objectives be threatened, if the pattern of volatility was translated into a corresponding, unsurprising pattern of disappointing performance? But the pattern of recent monthly performance should not be relied upon as a sufficient measure of risk-taking.

TABLE 1 **Summary asset allocation**

Percentages of total investment holdings	Most recent data			End previous quarter			Year ago		
	Holdings	Policy	Difference	Holdings	Policy	Difference	Holdings	Policy	Difference
Quoted equities									
Private equity									
Real estate									
Hedge funds									
of which foreign currency									
Other alternatives[a]									
Fixed income									
of which foreign currency									
TIPS									
of which foreign currency									
Cash									
of which foreign currency									
Total									

a Including structured products.
Note: References to foreign currency are intended to highlight unhedged foreign exposures which would be safe haven or low to modest volatility investments in their base currency, but whose risk is magnified by foreign currency risk.

TABLE 2 **Equity investment allocation**

Percentages of quoted equity holdings	Most recent data			End previous quarter			Year ago		
	Holdings	Policy/ market	Difference	Holdings	Policy/ market	Difference	Holdings	Policy/ market	Difference
Quoted equities by region									
North America									
Developed Europe									
Japan									
Pacific excl Japan (developed markets)									
Emerging markets									
Total	100%	100%	0%	100%	100%	0%	100%	100%	0%
Total (cash values)									
Quoted equities by GICS sector[a]									
Energy									
Materials									
Industrials									
Consumer discretionary									
Consumer staples									
Health care									
Financials									
of which: REITs									
Information technology									
Telecommunica- tions services									
Utilities									
Total	100%	100%	0%	100%	100%	0%	100%	100%	0%
Breakdown by market capitalisation									
% of equity holdings with market cap:									
>$10bn									
<$10bn >$2bn									
<$2bn									
Quoted equities, further information:									

Percentages of quoted equity holdings	Most recent data			End previous quarter			Year ago		
	Holdings	Policy/ market	Difference	Holdings	Policy/ market	Difference	Holdings	Policy/ market	Difference
Largest holding									
2nd largest holding									
3rd largest holding									
Summary style information, by region or sector compared with market, to include at least:									
Average price/ earnings ratio									
Average dividend yield									

a Global Industry Classification Standard.

TABLE 3 **Alternative investment allocation**

	Most recent data			End previous quarter			Year ago		
Market values	Holdings	Policy	Difference	Holdings	Policy	Difference	Holdings	Policy	Difference
Private equity									
Breakdown by type of fund, stage of development and geography									
Direct holdings of real estate properties or funds (excl REITs)									
Breakdown by type, and location									
Hedge funds									
Breakdown by strategy, and fund base currency									
Equity risk substitute hedge funds[a]									
Alternative beta hedge funds[a]									
Structured products									
List individually with concise summary of risk return characteristics									

a See Chapter 9.

TABLE 4 **Fixed income and cash allocation**

	Most recent data			End previous quarter			Year ago		
	Holdings	Policy	Difference	Holdings	Policy	Difference	Holdings	Policy	Difference
Cash[a]									
Average remaining maturity (days)									
Currency exposure:									
Credit quality by short- or long-term rating									
Largest non-gov holding									
Next largest non-gov holding									
Fixed income (total)									
Domestic fixed income[b]									
Breakdown by maturity band (% of domestic bond holdings):[c]									
Short dated									
Medium dated									
Long dated									
Average maturity of cash and bonds									
Average duration of cash and bonds									
% floating rate debt									
Maturity of floating rate debt									
Breakdown by issuer type (% of domestic bond holdings):									
Government bonds									
Agencies									
Pass thru mortgages									
Corporate debt									
Credit quality (S&P) (% of domestic bond holdings)									
AAA									
AA									
A									
BBB									
BB and below									
Largest exposures (% of domestic bond holdings)[d]									
Largest non-gov bond holding									
2nd largest non-gov bond holding									
3rd largest non-gov bond holding									
Foreign currency fixed income (unhedged)									
Structured debt products									
List by holding and credit rating									
TIPS holdings									
Average maturity of TIPS holdings									

a That is, liquid investments which are realisable at face value within a short period of time.   b Including foreign bonds hedged into local currency.   c Conventions on maturity bands differ between markets.   d Aggregating all holdings of an individual issuer.

Appendix 3

Trusting and aligning with your adviser

CHOOSING AN ADVISER is the most important investment decision that investors make. Good investment advice is extremely valuable, so investors must be willing to pay for it. Giving good advice will involve teasing out from investors their objectives and their motivations as well as their aversion to incurring losses or failing to meet objectives. Such discussions can be intensely personal, and for the relationship to be successful, the investor needs to be frank with an adviser. For this, there needs to be respect between the investor and the adviser. A successful advisory relationship is rarely restricted to investment advice. If self-advised investors or investors who are advised by pure investment advisers fail to account for the full range of financial planning issues (including, for example, tax and generational planning), they may not know if they are meeting their objectives, or if they are doing so efficiently.

Two features of investment advice are particularly important for the relationship between advisers and their clients. One concerns the scope for potential conflicts of interests. The other, which is less obvious but also important, is the investment style of the adviser; in other words, how does the adviser think that investments should best be managed, or what are the adviser's "investment beliefs" (see below)? Over periods of time, both these aspects of investment advice are important for success in managing wealth, and the investment beliefs of the adviser need to be well-aligned and suitable for meeting the objectives of the investor.

Investment beliefs

Different advisers embrace different approaches to investment which often reflect deeply held beliefs about how best to invest. For example, some advisers will look at the roller-coaster path taken by equity markets in the ten years after 2000 and conclude that investors have to try to time markets, to avoid the "bad times" and to pay quite high fees to invest in funds which try to do this. Others will be more sceptical, and suggest that net of fees, this is unlikely to be rewarding, and will more naturally stick to a pre-agreed strategy, perhaps anchored on the security of government bonds. A third group will from time to time suggest revisions to strategy if they are convinced that one or other market is markedly overpriced or underpriced. These three options represent important differences of approach, which will be reflected in different levels of activity in a portfolio, and potentially quite different investment outcomes. As discussed in Chapters 4 and 5, these are areas of debate on which advisers may have strong views, which would be reflected in their investment advice. Another major area of difference is whether an adviser expects to identify skilled managers who can, net of fees, with some consistency outperform in particular markets. Related to both of these is the issue of whether to invest in high-cost investment vehicles, such as private equity or hedge funds.

These differences of opinion are reflected in debates about how the largest and also the most modest investors should invest, and institutional investors often describe their views on these debates as their "investment beliefs". Many institutional investors take time to record their beliefs, and publish them, as a form of public accountability. These are tailored to their understanding of the opportunities presented by markets and their own particular circumstances, and they reflect (or should reflect) the way they invest.

Investment beliefs are implicit in how an investor invests. The same applies to the different recommendations that different advisers make to investors. These will reflect differences of opinion – for example, on the costs and benefits of paying high or low fees, or accepting illiquidity, and on the ability to time markets – and, more generally, differences in style of investing. An important part of building trust in a relationship with an adviser is for investors to have an understanding of their adviser's investment beliefs, and to find them both credible and appropriate for their particular circumstances.

One risk for self-advised investors is that they may not have properly thought through their attitudes to investment markets. This can be particularly dangerous if they fail to account sufficiently for the likelihood of "bad times" in how they design their strategy. Furthermore, in bad times, having a trusted adviser to consult, and to remind them why the strategy is designed as it is, can be of great value. A poorly self-designed strategy that, for example, generates income in good times only by incurring risks of loss of capital and income in bad times can easily prove to be an irreversible mistake. The recent history of tumultuous markets gives scope to ask advisers for references from clients who should be able to testify to the skills shown by those advisers in helping investors through bad times.

Conflicts of interest

Regulation in a number of countries is pushing advice towards explicit advisory fees and away from transaction commissions. This is helpful for encouraging an advice-driven rather than a sales-driven culture in the management of wealth. However, both good and poor advice can come from either approach to remunerating advisers.

The potential for conflicts of interest between investors and their advisers is often known as the principal–agent problem, or more loosely as "agency issues". These arise because the principal (the investor) has inferior access to information than the agent (the investment adviser) does. This can encourage advisers to use superior information in a way that serves their own interest rather than the best interest of the investor. Although institutional investors typically have structures that can mitigate this, such conflicts are common. One way investors can reduce their exposure to these conflicts is to distance themselves from much of the detailed investment decision-making, and employ discretionary investment managers whose remuneration is transparent and who are (depending upon the jurisdiction) under an obligation to provide best execution to their clients. However, this can easily lead to advice which is less well tailored to the circumstances of an investor, and some investments, which best suit particular investors, may be available only on an advisory basis.

Many private clients prefer an advisory relationship where they retain control over each investment decision. The danger is that this can also lead to the accumulation of a portfolio of ad hoc investments, each of which "seemed a good idea at the time". However, with good advice this can be avoided, and effective management of overall risk and balance in a strategy maintained.

The danger, though, is that investors will be sold what an adviser wishes to sell rather than deciding to buy what they need for their investment strategy. The best safeguard is for investors to satisfy themselves that their interests and those of their advisers are appropriately aligned, and that conflicts of interest are in the open. In practice, reassurance on this will depend more on the characters of the individuals concerned than the institutional arrangements within which they work.

Ultimately, no advisory business model will be successful if it fails to put the establishment and nurturing of trust between clients and their advisers first. However, investors must always be aware that conflicts of interest are endemic in the financial services industry. The key to unlocking the problem of these conflicts is to have transparency of fee arrangements and then to decide on a case-by-case basis how to proceed. The general message is "buyer, beware". For some categories of investor (or investor account) in some jurisdictions, regulators insist on disclosure of all sources of investment management or private bank remuneration from a client account. Clients should request information on the adviser's (or the bank's) financial interest in a proposed transaction.

Lastly, remember that good advice is valuable, and when the going gets tough, simple handholding by an adviser which prevents short-term mistakes may be the most valuable service that the adviser provides. Superficially it will come for free – but there is a relationship that provides fee income for the adviser and access to advice for the investor. The self-advised investor misses out on this. Know what you are paying, and review but don't quibble over each item. Make sure that you are comfortable with the overall level of fees, and do, from time to time, ask your advisers whether they would make a recommended investment on their own account. Low fees do not ensure that good advice is being offered, or that an investment strategy is sensible or that risk-taking is appropriate, but over periods of years, differences in fee levels can make a significant difference to wealth accumulation.

Appendix 4

Sources and recommended reading

Part 1: The essentials

1 Setting the scene

There are a number of investment classics which provide a general background to the first part of this chapter (and other parts of the book). *Manias, Panics and Crashes* (6th edition, Wiley, 2011) by the late Charles Kindleberger and Robert Z. Aiber is always worth re-reading, never more so than in the light of the 2007–09 credit crunch and the scandals which it helped to uncover. The discussion in Chapter 1 on the Madoff scandal draws on extensive discussions with wealth management professionals.

Other classics that should adorn any investor's bookshelf include:

Bernstein, P.L., *Against the Gods: The Remarkable Story of Risk*, John Wiley & Sons, 1998

Carswell, J., *The South Sea Bubble*, 3rd edition, Sutton Publishing, 2001

Galbraith, J.K., *The Great Crash*, Penguin Books, 1992

Mackay, C., *Extraordinary Popular Delusions and the Madness of Crowds*, Wordsworth Editions, 1995

The introduction to risk draws on:

Kritzman, M.P., *The Portable Financial Analyst: What Practitioners Need to Know*, 2nd edition, John Wiley & Sons, 2003

Kritzman, M. and Rich, D., "The Mismeasurement of Risk", *Financial Analysts Journal*, May/June 2002

The discussion of risk tolerance and its relation to risk aversion and loss aversion draws on a number of different sources, including conversations with financial planners and academics. Some particularly useful sources are:

Guillemette, M.A., Finke, M. and Gilliam, J., "Risk Tolerance Questions to Best Determine Client Portfolio Allocation Preferences", *Journal of Financial Planning*, July 2012

Kahneman, D., "The Myth of Risk Attitudes", *Journal of Portfolio Management*, Fall 2009

Roszkowski, M.J. and Davey, G., "Risk Perception and Risk Tolerance: Changes Attributable to the 2008 Economic Crisis", *Journal of Financial Service Professionals*, July 2010

2 Understand your behaviour

This chapter draws heavily on Daniel Kahneman's magisterial *Thinking Fast and Slow* (Farrar, Straus and Giroux, 2011), which provides a retrospective assessment of the progress made in recent decades (often led by Kahneman and his colleague, the late Amos Tversky) in understanding the strengths and weaknesses of how we take decisions.

Other useful sources include:

Barberis, N. and Thaler, R., "A Survey of Behavioral Finance", in Constantinides, G.M. *et al.* (eds), *Handbook of the Economics of Finance: Financial Markets and Asset Pricing*, Elsevier/North-Holland, 2003

Lo, A., "The Adaptive Markets Hypothesis", *Journal of Portfolio Management*, 30th anniversary issue, 2004

Statman, M., *What Investors Really Want: Know What Drives Investor Behavior and Make Smarter Financial Decisions*, McGraw-Hill, 2010

Thaler, R.H. and Sunstein, C.R., *Nudge: Improving Decisions About Health, Wealth and Happiness*, Penguin Books, 2009

3 Market investment returns

The section titled "Are government bonds risk free?" draws on Carmen Reinhart and Kenneth Rogoff's *This Time is Different: Eight Centuries of Financial Folly* (Princeton University Press, 2009). Some of the historical examples of default they cite appear to have been misclassified. In the UK, instances of the government exercising its option to refinance marketable debts (gilts) to take advantage of low market interest rates in 1932 and also in the 19th century are listed as "*de jure*" defaults. The prospectus for the 1932 debt conversion indicates that this was voluntary, with an option to redeem at par. The prospectus can be found at: www.dmo.gov.uk/docs/gilts/public/prospectus/announcement300632.pdf. The steps that the UK government took in the late 19th century to refinance debt were described by A.C. Miller in his 1890 article "The Conversion of English Debt", which is available from: http://qje.oxfordjournals.org.

The title for the box "A country called Europe" comes from a series of broadcasts and speeches on the prospects for European monetary union which were given in the late 1990s by Peter Jay, then the BBC's economics editor.

Other important sources include the following:

The term structure of real and nominal interest rates

Buraschi, A. and Jiltsov, A., "Inflation Risk Premia and the Expectations Hypothesis", *Journal of Financial Economics*, Vol. 75, Issue 2, February 2005

Campbell, J.Y., Shiller, R.J. and Viceira, L.M., "Understanding inflation-indexed bond markets", Brookings Papers on Economic Activity, Spring 2009

Ilmanen, A., *Expected Returns: An Investor's Guide to Harvesting Market Rewards*, John Wiley & Sons, 2011

Ilmanen, A., *Expected Returns on Major Asset Classes*, CFA Institute 2012

Pflueger, C.E. and Viceira, L.M., "Inflation-Indexed Bonds and the Expectations Hypothesis", Harvard Business School Working Paper H-11–095, 2011

The equity risk premium

Brett, H.P., Leibowitz, M.L. and Siegel, L.B. (eds), *Rethinking the Equity Risk Premium*, CFA Institute, 2011

"Credit Suisse Global Investment Returns Sourcebook", 2013

"Credit Suisse Global Investment Returns Yearbook", 2013

Dimson, E., Marsh, P. and Staunton, M., *Triumph of the Optimists: 101 Years of Global Investment Returns*, Princeton University Press, 2002

Dimson, E., Marsh, P. and Staunton, M., "Irrational Optimism", *Financial Analysts Journal*, January/February 2004

Siegel, J., *Stocks for the Long Run*, 5th edition, McGraw-Hill, 2014

4 How should and how do investor strategies evolve?

The provocative article underlying this chapter is the late Peter L. Bernstein's 2003 article "Are Policy Portfolios Obsolete?" in the *Economics and Portfolio Strategy* newsletter. In recent years, whether market returns predictably vary from one period to another has been the subject of extensive published research. A good summary is provided by Antti Ilmanen's *Expected Returns* (2011).

The second part of this chapter looks at how investors have altered portfolios since 2007. This is an area that is fraught with statistical difficulties, from which it is easy to draw spurious conclusions. The chapter draws on the IMF's 2011 report, *Long-Term Investors and Their Asset Allocation: Where*

Are They Now? as well as the data sources listed in Table 4.1, the Money Management Institute and industry sources.

5 The time horizon and the shape of strategy: keep it simple

The chapter opens with the suggestion, which arises from James Tobin's "separation theorem", that investment strategy for any investor can be reduced to an appropriate balance between just two investments: an allocation to risk-free assets and an allocation to the market portfolio of risk assets. (The market portfolio is often, as in the first part of this book, proxied by the global equity market.) Tobin set out his theorem in a 1958 article, "Liquidity preference as behaviour towards risk", in the *Review of Economic Studies* which explained how investors, with different attitudes to risk, choose to allocate monetary assets between cash and volatile assets. The separation theorem, which is also known as the "two fund money separation theorem" or the "mutual fund separation theorem", relies on strong assumptions. Thus if the global market for risky investments is fully represented by listed equities (which it is not) and if the prices of risky investments are determined efficiently (which they are not) and if expected returns in excess of the risk-free rate are constant (which they are not), then using an investor's degree of risk aversion to select appropriate proportions of risk-free and risk assets will provide a suitable strategy for any investor.

In practice, to address the shortcomings of the highly simplified approach requires high-fee actively managed investment strategies, whereas Tobin's two-investment approach can be proxied by low-cost global equities and cash (or government bonds). The costs of the more complicated versions, which seek to address the criticisms of Tobin's simplified model, place them at a significant disadvantage to the simplicity of the low-cost two-portfolio approach. The simplified allocation between diversified equities and cash or government bonds remains a useful reference strategy for investors, and, in effect, reflects practice for many financial advisers. The discussion in the chapter (and here) reflects discussions with Stephen Satchell and Mark Ralphs of the Financial Planning Corporation.

John Campbell and Tuomo Vuolteenaho's "Bad Beta, Good Beta" (*American Economic Review*, Vol. 94, No. 5, December 2004) is one of those occasional articles that develops a simple investment idea that then has powerful policy (as well as investor education) implications. It is the inspiration for this chapter's discussion of good and bad price declines as well as Chapter 7's discussion of apparent stockmarket anomalies. In a similar vein is Zvi Bodie's "Thoughts for the Future: Life-Cycle Investing in Theory and Practice" (*Financial Analysts Journal*, January/February 2003), where the different strands of traditional and behavioural finance are synthesised into designing suitable strategies for loss averse investors.

Other important sources for this chapter include:

Campbell, J.Y. and Viceira, L.M., *Strategic Asset Allocation: Portfolio Choice for Long-Term Investors*, Oxford University Press, 2002

Swensen, D., *Pioneering Portfolio Management: An Unconventional Approach to Institutional Investment*, 2nd edition, Free Press, 2009

The analysis of bond ladders in managing retirement income forms a core part of this book and builds on discussions about bond ladders and the US municipal bond market with Jeffrey Bryan of Merrill Lynch's Private Banking and Investment Group and Norman Deitrich of High Tower Advisors. Hildy Richelson and Stan Richelson's *Bonds: The Unbeaten Path to Secure Investment Growth* (2nd edition, Bloomberg Press, 2007) gives a guide to the practical aspects of managing and establishing bond ladders.

The title of the box "Models behaving badly" is taken from Emanuel Derman's 2011 book of the same title.

Part 2 Implementing more complicated strategies

6 Setting the scene

The discussion of the costs of liquidity draws heavily on the work of Andrew Ang, for example, "Illiquid Assets" (*CFA Institute Conference Proceedings Quarterly*, Vol. 28, No. 4, 2011). During the credit crisis, it was immediately evident that illiquidity was imposing heavy costs on investors; see, for example, Laurence B. Siegel's article "Alternatives and Liquidity: Will Spending and Capital Calls Eat Your 'Modern' Portfolio?" (*Journal of Portfolio Management*, Fall 2008). There is nothing new about the dangers of illiquidity, which were amply highlighted in, for example, Dan Borge's *The Book of Risk*, published in 2001 (John Wiley & Sons).

The major changes in the costs of liquidity from before 2007 to the period of the crisis and the maintenance of historically high transaction costs after 2008 have been highlighted by investment managers – see, for example, Blackrock Investment Institute's 2012 report *Got liquidity?* and comments in Chapter 5 on changes in investment patterns in the US municipal bond market.

Analysis of arbitrage opportunities in this chapter relies heavily on Nicholas Barberis and Richard Thaler's survey of behavioural finance (see Chapter 2 sources above).

The discussion of taxation makes use of:

Evensky, H. and Katz, D. (eds), *The Investment Think Tank: Theory, Strategy, and Practice for Advisers*, Bloomberg Press, 2004

Poterba, J.M. and Samwick, A.A., "Taxation and Household Portfolio Composition: US Evidence from the 1980s and 1990s", *Journal of Public Economics*, Vol. 87, No. 1, January 2003

7 Equities

The treatment of the capital asset pricing model (CAPM) and the stockmarket anomalies draws on Eugene Fama and Kenneth R. French's article "The Capital Asset Pricing Model: Theory and Evidence" (*Journal of Economic Perspectives*, 2004), helpful suggestions from Stephen Satchell, and John Campbell and Tuomo Vuolteenaho's article "Bad Beta, Good Beta" (see Chapter 5 sources).

The discussion of equity investing draws on papers presented and debated at seminars sponsored by Norway's Ministry of Finance and Norges Bank Investment Management, in particular papers by Campbell Harvey (2011), Andrew Ang (2011), Elroy Dimson (2011 and 2013), and Jacquelyn Humphrey and David Tan (2013).

The discussion of whether to hedge international equity investments for investors whose base currencies might have "safe-haven" status during times of crisis draws on John Campbell, Karine Serfaty-de Medeiros and Luis Viceira's article "Global Currency Hedging" (*Journal of Finance*, February 2010).

8 Credit

Kay Giesecke, Francis A. Longstaff, Stephen Schaefer and Ilya Strebulaev's article "Corporate Bond Default Risk: A 150-year Perspective" (*Journal of Financial Economics*, 2011) provides the historical context for the discussion of corporate credit risk and reward in this chapter. By contrast, Kwok-Yuen Ng and Bruce Phelps, "Capturing the Credit Spread Premium" (*Financial Analysts Journal*, May/June 2011), and Antii Ilmanen (*Expected Returns*, 2011, especially Chapter 10, The credit risk premium) explain why many investors do not manage to turn the yield premium over government bonds on offer when they buy investment grade corporate bonds into corresponding superior performance.

The discussion of debt markets and instruments draws on market contacts and on Frank Fabozzi and Steven Mann (eds), *The Handbook of Fixed Income Securities* (8th edition, McGraw-Hill, 2011).

9 Hedge funds

This chapter draws on market contacts as well as industry reviews and academic analyses. A number of articles over the past decade have highlighted weaknesses in the reporting of hedge fund risk and return, and these seem as relevant in 2014 as when the articles were first written.

Useful sources include:

Asness, C., "An Alternative Future", *Journal of Portfolio Management*, 30th Anniversary Issue, 2004

Asness, C., "An Alternative Future II", *Journal of Portfolio Management*, Vol. 31, No. 1, Fall 2004

Getmansky, M., Lo, A.W. and Makarov, I., "An Econometric Model of Serial Correlation and Illiquidity in Hedge Fund Returns", *Journal of Financial Economics*, Vol. 74, No. 3, 2004

Goltz, F. and Schroeder, D., "Hedge fund reporting survey", EDHEC Risk and Asset Management Research Centre, November 2008

Gregoriou, G. and Lhabitant, F-S., "Madoff: A Riot of Red Flags", EDHEC Risk and Asset Management Research Centre, January 2009

Hasanhodzica, J. and Lo, A.W., "Can hedge fund returns be replicated?: The linear case", *Journal of Investment Management*, Vol. 5, No. 2, 2007

Kat, H. and Palaro, H., "Hedge Fund Returns: You Can Make Them Yourself!", *Journal of Wealth Management*, No. 8, 2005

Prequin, *Global Hedge Fund Report 2013*, provided an invaluable resource on industry trends

10 Private equity: information-based investment returns

A number of articles in recent years have sought to assess the costs of illiquidity, leverage, fees and agency issues that need to be addressed before making investments in private equity funds. These include Andrew Ang and Morten Sorensen, "Risks, Returns, and Optimal Holdings of Private Equity" (*Quarterly Journal of Finance*, Vol. 2, No. 3, 2012) and Ludovic Phalippou and Oliver Gottschalg, "The Performance of Private Equity Funds" (*Review of Financial Studies*, No. 22, 2009). Phalippou's 2011 report for the Norwegian Government Pension Fund (Global) provides an update to earlier evidence of persistence of outperformance by some private equity managers.

Steven Kaplan and Per Stromberg's article "Leveraged Buyouts and Private Equity" (*Journal of Economic Perspectives*, American Economic Association, Vol. 23, No. 1, Winter 2009) provides a review of how private equity firms seek to improve the performance of their investee companies. Issues in measuring risk of private equity funds are discussed in Susan Woodward, "Measuring

Risk for Venture Capital and Buyout Portfolios", *Journal of Performance Measurement*, Vol. 17, No. 1, 2012.

11 Real estate

This chapter draws on market contacts and published resources including the *Journal of Portfolio Management*'s special real estate issues of 2011 and 2007. Particularly relevant is an article by Shaun Bond, Soosung Hwang, Paul Mitchell and Stephen Satchell, "Will Private Equity and Hedge Funds Replace Real Estate in Mixed Asset Portfolios?" (*Journal of Portfolio Management*, special real estate issue, 2007) and Jim Clayton and others, "The Changing Face of Real Estate Investment Management" (*Journal of Portfolio Management*, special real estate issue, 2011). Ralph Block's *Investing in REITs: Real Estate Investment Trusts* (4th edition, Bloomberg Press, 2011) is an invaluable source on investing in REITs.

12 Art and collectibles

This chapter draws on discussions with a range of market and academic contacts. Recommended published sources include:

Baumol, W.J., "Unnatural value or art as a floating crap game", *American Economic Review*, Vol. 76, 1986

Dimson, E. and Spaenjers, C., "Ex Post: The Investment Performance of Collectible Stamps", *Journal of Financial Economics*, Vol. 100, No. 2, 2011

Dimson, E. and Spaenjers, C., "The investment performance of emotional assets", in Dempster, A. (ed.), *Risk and Uncertainty in the Art World*, Bloomsbury Press, 2014

Findlay, M., *The Value of Art*, Prestel, 2012

Goetzman, W., Renneboog, L. and Spaenjers, C., "Art and Money", *American Economic Review*, Vol. 101, No. 3, 2011, pp. 222–6

Grampp, W.D., *Pricing the Priceless: Art, Artists, and Economics*, Basic Books, 1989

Plattner, S., "A Most Ingenious Paradox: The Market for Contemporary Fine Art", *American Anthropologist*, Vol. 100, No. 2, 1998

Pownall, R., Satchell, S. and Srivastava, N., "The Estimation of Psychic Returns from Cultural Assets", mimeo, 2013

Reitlinger, G., *The Economics of Taste: The Rise and Fall of Picture Prices, 1760–1960*, Barrie and Rockliff, 1961

Renneboog, L. and Spaenjers, C., "Buying Beauty: On Prices and Returns in the Art Market", *Management Science*, October 2012

Satchell, S. (ed.), *Collectible Investments for the High Net Worth Investor*,
  Elsevier, 2009
Thompson, D., *The $12 Million Stuffed Shark: The Curious Economics of
  Contemporary Art*, Aurum Press, 2008

Other useful sources

Acharya, S. and Dimson, E., *Endowment Asset Management*, Oxford
  University Press, 2007
Ang, A., *Asset Management: A Systematic Approach to Factor Investing*, Oxford
  University Press, forthcoming
Arnott, R.D., Berkin, A.L. and Ye, J., "Loss Harvesting: What is it Worth to a
  Taxable Investor?", *Journal of Wealth Management*, Spring 2001
Asness, C., Krail, R. and Liew, J., "Do Hedge Funds Hedge?", *Journal of
  Portfolio Management*, Fall 2001.
Athayde, G. and Flores, R., "A CAPM with Higher Moments: Theory and
  Econometrics", *Ensaios Economicos*, No. 317, Rio de Janeiro, 1997
Athayde, G. and Flores, R., "Incorporating skewness and kurtosis in
  portfolio optimisation: a multi-dimensional efficient set", in Satchell,
  S. and Scowcroft, A. (eds), *Advances in Portfolio Construction and
  Implementation*, Butterworth-Heinemann, 2003
Athayde, G. and Flores, R., "Do Higher Moments Really Matter in Portfolio
  Optimisation?", Fundação Getúlio Vargas, No. 574, 2004
Baltussen, G., "Behavioral Finance: an introduction", 2009, available at:
  SSRN, http://ssrn.com/abstract=1488110 or http://dx.doi.org/10.2139/
  ssrn.1488110
Banz, R., "The Relationship between Return and Market Value of Common
  Stocks", *Journal of Financial Economics*, March 1981
Bateman, H., Eckert, C., Geweke, J., Louvière, J.J., Satchell, S.E. and Thorp,
  S., "Investment Risk Framing and Individual Preference Consistency",
  UNSW Australian School of Business Research Paper No. 2010ACTL08,
  April 10th 2011
Benartzi, S., "Excessive extrapolation and the allocation of 401(k) accounts to
  company stock", *Journal of Finance*, October 2001
Benartzi, S. and Thaler, R., "Naive diversification strategies in defined
  contribution savings plans", *American Economic Review*, March 2001
Bilo, S., Christophers, H., Degosciu, M. and Zimmermann, H., "Risk, returns,
  and biases of listed private equity portfolios", WWZ Working Paper No.
  1/05, 2005
Black, F., "Noise", *Journal of Finance*, July 1986

Bloomfield, R., "Traditional vs Behavioral Finance", Cornell University, Johnson School Research Paper Series #22, 2010

Bodie, Z., Kane, A. and Marcus, A.J., *Investments*, 6th international edition, McGraw-Hill, 2005

Bodie, Z., Merton, R. and Samuelson, W., "Labor Supply Flexibility and Portfolio Choice in a Life Cycle Model", NBER Working Paper 3954, 1992

Bodie, Z. and Taqqu, R., *Risk Less and Prosper: Your Guide to Safer Investing*, John Wiley & Sons, 2012

Bohnet, I., Greig, F., Herrmann, B. and Zeckhauser, R., "Betrayal Aversion: Evidence from Brazil, China, Oman, Switzerland, Turkey, and the United States", *American Economic Review*, Vol. 98, No. 1, 2008

Boyle, P.S., Loewy, D., Riess, J.A. and Weiss, R.A., "The Enviable Dilemma: Hold, Sell, or Hedge Highly Concentrated Stock?", *Journal of Wealth Management*, Fall 2004

Brealey, R.A., Myers, S.C. and Allen, F., *Principles of Corporate Finance*, 11th edition, McGraw-Hill, 2013

Brown, J.R., Mitchell, O.S., Poterba, J.M. and Warshawsky, M.J., *The Role of Annuity Markets in Financing Retirement*, MIT Press, 2001

Brunel, J.L.P., *Integrated Wealth Management: The New Direction for Portfolio Managers*, Institutional Investor Books, 2002

Brunnermeier, M. and Nagel, S., "Hedge funds and the technology bubble", *Journal of Finance*, Vol. 59, No. 5, 2004

Buiter, W.H., "James Tobin: An Appreciation of his Contribution to Economics", NBER Working Paper, 2003

Burnham, T., *Mean Markets and Lizard Brains*, John Wiley & Sons, 2005

Cai, F. and Warnock, F.E., "International Diversification at Home and Abroad", International Finance Discussion Paper 2004-793, Board of Governors of the Federal Reserve System, December 2004 (www.federalreserve.gov/pubs/ifdp/2004/793/default.htm)

Calverley, J., *When Bubbles Burst: Surviving the Financial Fallout*, Nicholas Brealey, 2010

Campbell, J.Y., Giglio S. and Polk C., "Hard Times", *Review of Asset Pricing Studies*, Vol. 3, No. 1, 2013

Campbell, J.Y. and Rathjens, P., *The Case for International Diversification*, Arrowstreet Capital, May 2003

Chambers, D. and Dimson, E., "IPO underpricing over the very long run", *Journal of Finance*, Vol. 64, No. 3, 2009

Chan, N., Getmansky, M., Haas, S. and Lo, A., "Systemic Risk and Hedge Funds", in Carey, M. and Stulz, R. (eds), *The Risks of Financial Institutions*, University of Chicago Press, 2007

Cole, R., *The Unwritten Laws of Finance and Investment*, Profile Books, 2011

Cole, S.E. and Cole, R.A., "How accurate are commercial real estate appraisals? Evidence from 25 years of NCREIF sales data", *Journal of Portfolio Management*, real estate issue, 2011

Constantinides, G., "Rational Asset Prices", *Journal of Finance*, August 2002

Cumming, Douglas, *The Oxford Handbook of Private Equity*, Oxford University Press, 2012

Damodaran, A., *Investment Fables*, Financial Times–Prentice Hall, 2004

Darst, D.M., *The Art of Asset Allocation*, 2nd edition, McGraw-Hill, 2008

Deacon, M., Derry, A. and Mirfendereski, D., *Inflation Indexed Securities: Bonds, Swaps and Other Derivatives*, 2nd edition, John Wiley & Sons, 2004

diBartolomeo, D., "Equity Risk, Credit Risk, Default Correlation, and Corporate Sustainability", *The Journal of Investing*, Vol. 19, No. 4, Winter 2010

diBartolomeo, D., "The Volatility of Financial Assets Behaving Badly: the example of the high yield bond market", *Northfield News*, March 2013

Dimson, E. and Jackson, A., "High Frequency Performance Monitoring", *Journal of Portfolio Management*, Fall 2001

Dimson, E., Karakas, O. and Li, X., "Active Ownership", presented at the JAE/ Harvard Corporate Accountability conference, 2013

Dimson, E. and Marsh, P., *Numis Smaller Companies Index: 2013 Annual Review*, Numis Corporation, January 2013

Dreyfuss, B., *Hedge Hogs: The Cowboy Traders Behind Wall Street's Largest Hedge Fund Disaster*, Random House, 2013

Drobney, S., *The Invisible Hands: Top Hedge Fund Traders on Bubbles, Crashes, and Real Money*, John Wiley and Sons, 2011

Dunbar, N., *Inventing Money: The Story of Long-Term Capital Management and the Legends Behind It*, John Wiley & Sons, 2000

Eichengreen, B., Hausmann, R. and Panizza, U., "The Mystery of Original Sin", in Eichengreen and Hausmann (eds), *Other People's Money: Debt Denomination and Financial Instability in Emerging Market Economies*, University of Chicago Press, 2005

Ellis, C.D., *Winning the Loser's Game*, 4th edition, McGraw-Hill, 2002

Evensky, H., Horan, S. and Robinson, T., *The New Wealth Management: The Financial Advisors Guide to Managing and Investing Client Assets* (CFA Institute Investment Series), 2011

Faff, R., Mulino, D. and Chai, D., "On the linkage between financial risk tolerance and risk aversion", *Journal of Financial Research*, Spring 2008

Fama, E. and French, K., "The Equity Premium", *Journal of Finance*, April 2002

Fawley, B.W. and Neely, C.J., "Four Stories of Quantitative Easing", *Federal Reserve Bank of St Louis Review*, January/February 2013

Fraser-Sampson, G., *Private Equity as an Asset Class*, John Wiley & Sons, 2008

Fung, W. and Hsieh, D., "Hedge Fund Benchmarks: A Risk Based Approach", *Financial Analysts Journal*, September/October 2004

Géhin, W. and Vaissié, M., *The Right Place for Alternative Betas in Hedge Fund Performance*, EDHEC, 2005

Gibson, R.C., *Asset Allocation: Balancing Financial Risk*, 2nd edition, Irwin, 1996

Ginsburgh, V., Mei, H. and Moses, M., "The Computation of Prices Indices", in Ginsburgh and Throsby, D. (eds), *Handbook of the Economics of Art and Culture*, Vol. 1, Elsevier, 2006

Ginsburgh, V. and Weyers, S., "Persistence and Fashion in Art: Italian Renaissance from Vasari to Berenson and Beyond", *Poetics*, Vol. 34, Issue 1, February 2006

Graham, B., *The Intelligent Investor*, updated by Zweig, J., Harper, 2003

Gregoriou, G., Karavas, V., Lhabitant, F.-S. and Rouah, F., *Commodity Trading Advisors, Risk, Performance Analysis and Selection*, Wiley Finance, 2004

Gregory, David, "Private Equity and Financial Stability", *Bank of England Quarterly Bulletin*, Q1, 2013

Halstead, J.M., Hedge, S. and Schmid Klein, L., "Orange County Bankruptcy: Financial Contagion in the Municipal Bond and Bank Equity Markets", *Eastern Finance Association: The Financial Review*, 39, 2004

Hammond, P.B., Leibowitz, M.L. and Siegel, L.B., *Rethinking the Equity Risk Premium*, CFA Institute, 2011

Harvey, C.R., "Allocation to Emerging Markets in a Globally Diversified Portfolio", advice to Norwegian Ministry of Finance, March 2012, sourced from http://www.regjeringen.no/pages/1934920/Harvey.pdf

Harvey, C.R., Liechty, J.C. and Liechty, M.W., "Parameter Uncertainty in Asset Allocation", December 17th 2009, available at SSRN: http://ssrn.com/abstract=1525121 or http://dx.doi.org/10.2139/ssrn.1525121

Harvey, C.R., Liechty, J.C., Liechty, M.W. and Müller, P., "Portfolio Selection With Higher Moments", in Sury, S.M. (ed.), *Essential Readings in Applied Financial Economics*, San Diego: University Readers, 2013

Hatlapa, D., *Better Than Gold: Investing in Historic Cars*, HAGI Publishing, April 2011

Holton, G.A., "Defining Risk", *Financial Analysts Journal*, November/December 2004

Humphrey, J. and Tan, D., "Does it Really Hurt to be Responsible?", *Journal of Business Ethics*, May 2013

Ilmanen, A. and Kizer, J., "The Death of Diversification has been Greatly Exaggerated", *Journal of Portfolio Management*, Spring 2012

Kahneman, D., "Maps of Bounded Rationality", Nobel Lecture 2002, available at http://nobelprize.org/economics/laureates/2002/kahnemann-lecture.pdf

Kahneman, D. and Tversky, A., "The Psychology of Preferences", *Scientific American*, Vol. 246, 1982

Kahneman, D. and Tversky, A., "Prospect Theory: An Analysis of Decision Under Risk", *Econometrica*, 47, 1979

Kajuth, F. and Watzka, S., "Inflation expectations from index-linked bonds: Correcting for liquidity and inflation risk premia", *Quarterly Review of Economics and Finance*, Vol. 51, No. 3, June 2011

Kaplan, P.D., *Frontiers of Modern Asset Allocation*, John Wiley & Sons, 2012

Kaplan, S. and Schoar, A., "Private Equity Performance: Returns, Persistence and Capital Flows", *Journal of Finance*, August 2005

Kaplan, S.N. and Strömberg, P., "Characteristics, Contracts, and Actions: Evidence from Venture Capitalist Analyses," *Journal of Finance*, American Finance Association, Vol. 59, No. 5, October 2004

Kay, J., *The Long and the Short of it: A Guide to Finance and Investment for Normally Intelligent People Who Aren't in the Industry*, The Erasmus Press, 2009

Kay, J., *The Truth About Markets*, Penguin Books, 2004

Keynes, J.M., *Collected Writings, Vol XII, Investment and Editorial*, Macmillan, 1983

Kritzman, M.P., *Puzzles of Finance*, John Wiley & Sons, 2000

Kritzman, M.P., "The Graceful Aging of Mean Variance Optimisation", *Journal of Portfolio Management*, Winter 2011

Lack, S., *The Hedge Fund Mirage*, John Wiley & Sons, 2012

Landes, W., "The Test of Time: Does 20th Century American Art Survive?" in Ginsburgh, V. (ed.), *Contributions to Economic Analysis: The Economics of Art and Culture*, Elsevier Science, 2004

Leibowitz, M.L., Bova, A. and Brett Hammond, P., *The Endowment Model of Investing*, Wiley Finance, 2010

Lhabitant, F.-S., *Hedge Funds: Myths and Limits*, Wiley Finance, 2002

Lintner, J., "The Valuation of Risk Assets and the Selection of Risky Investments in Stock Portfolios and Capital Budgets", *Review of Economics and Statistics*, Vol. 47, No. 1, 1965

Lizieri, C., Satchell, S. and Wongwachara, W., "Unsmoothing Real Estate Returns: A Regime-Switching Approach", *Real Estate Economics*, Vol. 40, No. 2, 2012 (DOI: 10.1111/j.1540-6229.2012.00331.x)

Lo, A., *Hedge Funds: An Analytical Perspective*, Princeton University Press, 2008

Löffler, G., "Avoiding the rating bounce: why rating agencies are slow to react to new information", *Journal of Economic Behavior and Organization*, Vol. 56, No. 3, 2005

Longstaff, F., Mithal, S. and Neis, E., "Corporate Yield Spreads: Default Risk or Liquidity? New Evidence from the Credit Default Swap Market", *Journal of Finance*, October 2005

Lopes, L., "Between Hope and Fear: the Psychology of Risk", *Advances in Experimental Social Psychology*, 20, 1987

Lowenstein, R., *When Genius Failed: The Rise and Fall of Long-Term Capital Management*, Fourth Estate, 2001

Lustig, Y., *Multi-Asset Investing: A Practical Guide to Modern Portfolio Management*, Harriman House, 2013

McAndrew, C., *The Art Economy*, The Liffey Press, 2007

Malkiel, B.G., *A Random Walk Down Wall Street*, Norton, 2003

Malkiel, B.G. and Saha, A., "Hedge Funds: Risk and Return", *Financial Analysts Journal*, November/December 2005

Mandelbrot, B.B. and Hudson, R., *The (Mis)Behaviour of Markets: A Fractal View of Risk, Reward and Ruin*, Profile Books, 2004

Mehra, R. and Prescott, E., "The Equity Premium: A Puzzle", *Journal of Monetary Economics*, Vol. 15, 1985

Merton, R.C., "Thoughts on the Future: Theory and Practice in Investment Management", *Financial Analysts Journal*, January/February 2003

Merton, R.C. and Bodie, Z., "Design of Financial Systems: Towards a Synthesis of Design and Structure", *Journal of Investment Management*, Vol. 3, No. 1, 2005

Oldfield, R., *Simple But Not Easy: An Autobiographical and Biased Book About Investing*, Doddington Publishing, 2007

Perold, A., "Risk is a choice not a fate", *Journal of Portfolio Management*, Fall 2009

Peyton, M. and Lotito, F., "Real Estate: The Classic Diversifying Asset", TIAA-CREF White Paper, 2006

Phalippou, L., "An evaluation of the potential for GPFG to achieve above average returns from investments in private equity and recommendations regarding benchmarking", February 2011, sourced from: http://www.regjeringen.no/upload/fin/statens%20 pensjonsfond/2011/phalippou.pdf

Poterba, J.M., "Portfolio Risk and Self-Directed Retirement Saving Programmes", *Economic Journal*, Vol. 114, No. 494, March 2004

Rabin, M., "Inference by Believers in the Law of Small Numbers", *Quarterly Journal of Economics*, Vol. 117, 2002

Ratner, R.K. and Herbst, K.C., "When good decisions have bad outcomes: The impact of affect on switching behavior", *Organizational Behavior and Human Decision Processes*, 96, 2005

Reb, J. and Connolly, T., "Decision Justifiability and Regret", manuscript, 2004

Reich, R., "Who is Us?", *Harvard Business Review*, January/February 1990

Roll, R., "Empirical TIPS", *Financial Analysts Journal*, January/February 2004

Ross, S.A., "Forensic Finance: Enron and Others", *Rivista di Politica Economica*, November/December 2002

Ryland, P., *Investment: an A–Z Guide*, Profile Books, 2009

Scholes, M., "The Future of Hedge Funds", *Journal of Financial Transformation*, Vol. 10, Capco, April 2004

Scholtes, C., "On Market-Based Measures of Inflation Expectations", *Bank of England Quarterly Bulletin*, Spring 2002

Securities and Exchange Commission, *Report on the Municipal Securities Market*, July 2012

Sharpe, W.F., "Capital Asset Prices: A Theory of Market Equilibrium under Conditions of Risk", *Journal of Finance*, September 1964

Shefrin, H., *Beyond Fear and Greed: Understanding Behavioural Finance and the Psychology of Investing*, Oxford University Press, 2002

Shefrin, H. and Statman, M., "Behavioral Portfolio Theory", *Journal of Financial and Quantitative Analysis*, June 2000

Shiller, R., "Do Stock Prices Move too Much to be Justified by Subsequent Changes in Dividends?", *American Economic Review*, June 1981

Shiller, R., "Stock Prices and Social Dynamics", Brookings Papers on Economic Activity, 2, 1984, pp. 457–98

Shiller, R., *Irrational Exuberance*, Princeton University Press, 2000

Shiller, R., "Bubbles, Human Judgement and Expert Opinion", *Financial Analysts Journal*, May/June 2002

Shiller, R., *The New Financial Order: Risk in the 21st Century*, Princeton University Press, 2003

Siegel, J., *The Future for Investors*, Crown Business, 2005

Sortino, F. and Satchell, S., *Managing Downside Risk in Financial Markets*, Butterworth Heinemann, 2001

Stanyer, P. and Long, K., "Unquoted Risk: The Art of Measurement", *Professional Investor*, March 1993

Statman, M., "Behavioral Portfolios: Hope for Riches and Protection from Poverty", Pension Research Council Working Paper, 2003-9

Statman, M., "Normal Investors, Then and Now", *Financial Analysts Journal*, March/April 2005

Statman, M., "The cultures of risk tolerance", 2010, available at SSRN: http://ssrn.com/abstract=1647086 or http://dx.doi.org/10.2139/ssrn.1647086

Statman, M. and Wood, V., "Investment Temperament", manuscript, June 2004

Staub, R. and Diermeier, J., "Segmentation, Illiquidity and Returns", *Journal of Investment Management*, Vol. 1, No. 1, 2003

Stein, D.M. and Siegel, A.F., "The Diversification of Employee Stock Options", AIMR Conference Proceedings, Investment Counselling for Private Clients IV, 2002

Taleb, N.N., *Fooled by Randomness: The Hidden Role of Chance in Life and in the Markets*, Thomson Texere, 2004

Taleb, N.N., *The Black Swan: The Impact of the Highly Improbable*, Penguin Books, 2007

Temin, P. and Voth, H-J., "Riding the South Sea Bubble", *American Economic Review*, December 2004

Thaler, R.H., "Mental Accounting Matters", *Journal of Behavioral Decision Making*, Vol. 12, 1999

Thaler, R.H., "The End of Behavioral Finance", *Financial Analysts Journal*, November/December 1999

Turner, J. (ed.), *The Grove Dictionary of Art*, illustrated edition, Oxford University Press, 2003

Wilcox, J., Horvitz, J.E. and diBartolomeo, D., "Investment Management for Taxable Private Investors", CFA Institute, 2006

Zadeh, L.A., "Fuzzy Sets", *Information and Control*, Vol. 8, 1965

Zhang, L.A. and Petkova, R., "Is Value Riskier than Growth?", *Journal of Financial Economics*, Vol. 78, No. 1, 2005

Notes on sources

THE PUBLISHER AND AUTHOR wish to thank the following sources for the use of their website information and other copyright material:

Artprice, www.artprice.com (Figure 12.2)
Bank of England (Figures 3.2, 3.5, 3.9–10)
Barclays plc https://indices.barcap.com/index (Figures 1.1, 4.4, 5.2–3, 8.2–6; Tables 5.2–3, 5.5, 5.7, 8.1, 8.4–8, 9.1, 9.3, 9.5–7, 9.9–10, 11.2–3)
BarclayHedge, www.barclayhedge.com (Figures 9.1, 9.3; Table 9.2)
Bloomberg Finance LP (Figures 10.1–2)
Capgemini and Merrill Lynch Wealth Management "World Wealth Report" 2003 for 2002 numbers and Capgemini and RBC Wealth Management "World Wealth Report" 2013 for 2007 and 2012 numbers (Tables 4.1–2)
Chicago Board Options Exchange, www.cboe.com (Figure 4.1)
Citigroup Index LLC. Copyright © 2013, Citigroup Index LLC ("Citi Index"). All rights reserved. "Citigroup" is a registered trademark and service mark of Citigroup Inc. or its affiliates, is used and registered throughout the world. Citi Index data and information is the property of Citi Index or its licensors, and reproduction in any form is prohibited except with the prior written permission of Citi Index. Because of the possibility of human or mechanical error, Citi Index does not guarantee the accuracy, adequacy, timeliness, completeness or availability of any data and information and is not responsible for any errors or omissions or for the results obtained from the use of such data and information. CITI INDEX GIVES NO EXPRESS OR IMPLIED WARRANTIES, INCLUDING, BUT NOT LIMITED TO, ANY WARRANTIES OF MERCHANTABILITY OR FITNESS FOR A PARTICULAR PURPOSE OR USE. In no event shall Citi Index be liable for damages of any kind in connection with any use of the Citi Index data and information. (Figures 8.7–9)
Center for Research in Security Prices (CRSP®), The University of Chicago Booth School of Business (2013). All rights reserved. Calculated (or Derived) based

Index

"*Successfully translates sophisticated academic thinking into simple, intuitive principles that can be used by both individual and institutional investors. These principles are all the more valuable as Stanyer applies them to the full range of asset classes and investment strategies available today.*"

John Campbell, Morton L. and Carole S. Olshan Professor of Economics, Harvard University

"*Over the years I've had the privilege of reviewing many investment books, but this is unquestionably one of the best. I could go on at length explaining why I am so impressed but suffice it to say, it will be a well read and prominent book in my personal library. Every financial planner, wealth manager, broker, investment adviser and serious individual investor owes it to themselves to carefully read this extraordinary book.*"

Harold Evensky, President, Evensky & Katz, LLC

"*Peter Stanyer has a rare gift for making advanced and seemingly esoteric ideas such as betrayal aversion or psychic returns not just accessible but highly relevant. In addition to the help this guide will provide individual investors on what to make of all the arcana flooding from business schools and fund managers, it is a book that provides welcome light and insight in a world in which the global financial crisis has highlighted the importance of financial education and literacy.*"

Stephen Satchell, Fellow, Trinity College, Cambridge

"*If you want to understand the key factors in constructing a successful investment strategy that suits you, this book will enable you to make better informed choices.*"

Mark Ralphs, Partner, Financial Planning Corporation LLC

"*Broad in its overview, filled with recent data and research, and clearly written, this useful guide should appeal to both experienced and new investors. The author delivers relevant, practical advice by deftly discussing both the big picture at the overall portfolio level and the nuances and institutional details at the asset class level.*"

Andrew Ang, Ann F. Kaplan Professor of Business, Columbia Business School, New York

"*Peter Stanyer stands out as an extraordinarily clear thinker and he carries that clarity through to his writing in this book on, for example, hedge funds. In addition he is tremendously good at explaining what works best in establishing and adapting an investment strategy. This is a book every chief investment officer should read.*"

Roger Urwin, Global Head of Investment Content, Towers Watson

PublicAffairs is a publishing house founded in 1997. It is a tribute to the standards, values, and flair of three persons who have served as mentors to countless reporters, writers, editors, and book people of all kinds, including me.

I. F. STONE, proprietor of *I. F. Stone's Weekly*, combined a commitment to the First Amendment with entrepreneurial zeal and reporting skill and became one of the great independent journalists in American history. At the age of eighty, Izzy published *The Trial of Socrates*, which was a national bestseller. He wrote the book after he taught himself ancient Greek.

BENJAMIN C. BRADLEE was for nearly thirty years the charismatic editorial leader of *The Washington Post*. It was Ben who gave the *Post* the range and courage to pursue such historic issues as Watergate. He supported his reporters with a tenacity that made them fearless and it is no accident that so many became authors of influential, best-selling books.

ROBERT L. BERNSTEIN, the chief executive of Random House for more than a quarter century, guided one of the nation's premier publishing houses. Bob was personally responsible for many books of political dissent and argument that challenged tyranny around the globe. He is also the founder and longtime chair of Human Rights Watch, one of the most respected human rights organizations in the world.

•   •   •

For fifty years, the banner of Public Affairs Press was carried by its owner Morris B. Schnapper, who published Gandhi, Nasser, Toynbee, Truman, and about 1,500 other authors. In 1983, Schnapper was described by *The Washington Post* as "a redoubtable gadfly." His legacy will endure in the books to come.

Peter Osnos, *Founder and Editor-at-Large*